ORDNAN

Cycle TOURS

24 one-day routes in

East Anglia South

Compiled by
Nick Cotton

HAMLYN

Contents

Acknowledgements
AA Photo Library 25 *background*, 37, 49, 61, 73, 107, 119, 123 *top*, 123 *bottom*, 127, 137 • Nick Cotton *back cover*, 43, 85, 97, 103, 115 • B & S Thomlinson 79 • Judy Todd 67, 91, 139

Off-road routes

Back cover photograph: Rape fields near Belchamp St Paul

First published 1995 by

Ordnance Survey and Hamlyn, an imprint of
Romsey Road — Reed Consumer Books Ltd
Maybush — Michelin House
Southampton — 81 Fulham Road
SO16 4GU — London SW3 6RB

First edition 1995

A catalogue record for this atlas is available from the British Library

ISBN 0 600 58125 X
(Ordnance Survey ISBN 0 319 00485 6)

Made, printed and published in Great Britain

Newark-on-Trent
NOTTINGHAMSHIRE
LINCOLNSHIRE
Nottingham
Sleaford
Boston
Hunstanton
THE WASH
Grantham
Loughborough
Melton Mowbray
Spalding
Bourne
King's Lynn
LEICESTERSHIRE
Leicester
Stamford
Oakham
Wisbech
R Nene
March
Downham Market
Wigston
Market Harborough
R Welland
Corby
Peterborough
Oundle
Chatteris
CAMBRIDGESHIRE
Kettering
Thrapston
Ely
Rugby
Huntingdon
Wellingborough
Rushden
Cambridge
Newmarket
Daventry
Northampton
St Neots
R Gt Ouse
NORTHAMPTONSHIRE
Bedford
Towcester
BEDFORDSHIRE
Royston
Haverhill
R Stour
Sudbury
Brackley
Milton Keynes
Saffron Walden
Buckingham
Halstead
BUCKINGHAMSHIRE
Stevenage
Bishop's Stortford
Great Dunmow
Bicester
Leighton Buzzard
Luton
Braintree
Luton Airport
Stansted Airport
Dunstable
Aylesbury
HERTFORDSHIRE
Oxford
Hemel Hempstead
St Albans
Harlow
Hertford
ESSEX
Thame
The Chilterns
Hatfield
Chelmsford
Amersham
Abingdon
High Wycombe
Brentwood
Watford
LONDON
GREATER LONDON
Wallingford
Ilford
Basildon
Beaconsfield
Dagenham
Maidenhead
Slough
Henley-on-Thames
Tilbury
Grain
Reading
Heathrow Airport
Richmond
Dartford
Gravesend
Rochester
Bracknell
Staines
Orpington
Chatham
Sutton
Esher
Croydon
Woking
Leatherhead
Surrey Hills
Basingstoke
Guildford
SURREY
Sevenoaks
Maidstone

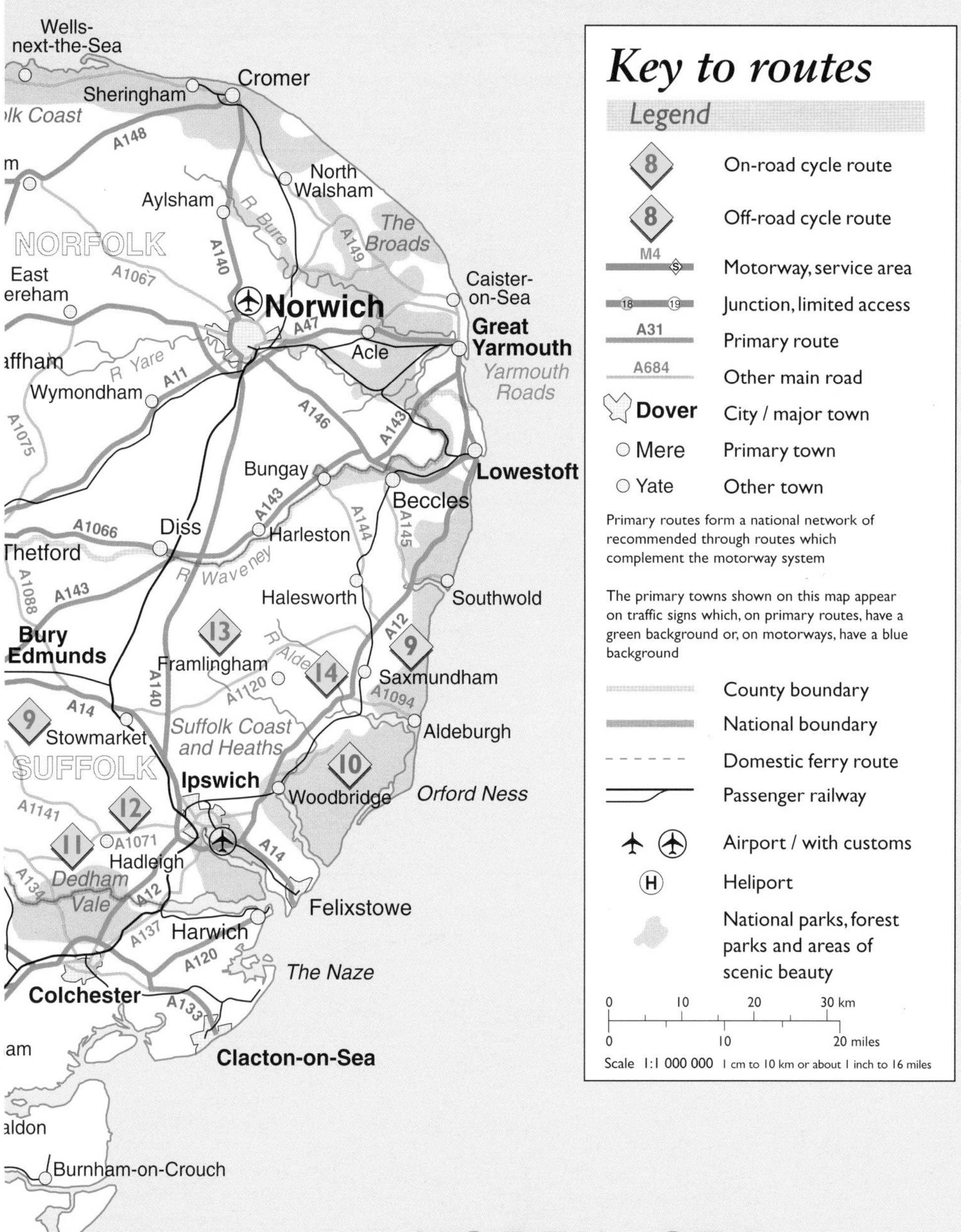
Key to routes
Legend
On-road cycle route
Off-road cycle route
M4
Motorway, service area
Junction, limited access
A31
Primary route
A684
Other main road
Dover
City / major town
Mere
Primary town
Yate
Other town
Primary routes form a national network of recommended through routes which complement the motorway system
The primary towns shown on this map appear on traffic signs which, on primary routes, have a green background or, on motorways, have a blue background
County boundary
National boundary
Domestic ferry route
Passenger railway
Airport / with customs
Heliport
National parks, forest parks and areas of scenic beauty
0 10 20 30 km
0 10 20 miles
Scale 1:1 000 000 1 cm to 10 km or about 1 inch to 16 miles
Wells-next-the-Sea
Cromer
Sheringham
North Walsham
Aylsham
NORFOLK
The Broads
East Dereham
Caister-on-Sea
Norwich
Great Yarmouth
Yarmouth Roads
Acle
Wymondham
Lowestoft
Bungay
Beccles
Diss
Harleston
Thetford
Southwold
Halesworth
Bury Edmunds
Framlingham
Saxmundham
Aldeburgh
Stowmarket
Suffolk Coast and Heaths
SUFFOLK
Ipswich
Woodbridge
Orford Ness
Hadleigh
Dedham Vale
Felixstowe
Harwich
The Naze
Colchester
Clacton-on-Sea
Burnham-on-Crouch
NORTH SEA
Sheerness
Isle of Sheppey
Herne Bay
Margate
North Foreland
Whitstable
Sittingbourne
Ramsgate
Sandwich
Canterbury
Deal

Quick reference chart

	Route	Page	Distance (miles)	Grade (easy/moderate/strenuous)	Links with other routes[1]	Tourist information centres[2]
	On-road routes					
1	*From St Neots to Grafham Water and south to Thurleigh*	18	37		2	Huntingdon 01480-425831
2	*East from St Neots through open farmland to Great Gransden and Conington*	24	33		1	Bedford 01234-215226
3	*Quiet Hertfordshire lanes through woods and farmland around Stevenage*	30	37			Hertford 01992-584322
4	*Northwest from Saffron Walden along the valley of the Cam to Barrington*	36	33		5,6	Saffron Walden 01799-510444
5	*Southwest from Saffron Walden through pretty Essex villages of Arkesden, the Pelhams and Manuden*	42	34		4,6	Saffron Walden 01799-510444
6	*East from Saffron Walden through Thaxted, Finchingfield and the Bumpsteads*	48	32		4,5, 7,10	Saffron Walden 01799-510444
7	*South from Thaxted through the heart of Essex*	54	33		6	Braintree 01376-550066
8	*Southeast from Newmarket past the gallops and the studs in the heart of horseracing country*	60	36		9	Newmarket 01638-667200
9	*North from Lavenham towards Bury St Edmunds and east to the village of Rattlesden*	66	33		8,11,12	Lavenham 01787-248207
10	*Southwest from Sudbury to Castle Hedingham and the Belchamps*	72	33		6	Sudbury 01787-881320
11	*South from Lavenham to Boxford, Stoke-by-Nayland and Hadleigh*	78	32		9,12	Lavenham 01787-248207
12	*A ring around Hadleigh returning via the attractive villages of Bildeston and Chelsworth*	84	33		9,11	Hadleigh 01473-822922

	Route	Page	Distance (miles)	Grade (easy/moderate/strenuous)	Links with other routes[1]	Tourist information centres[2]
13	*West from Framlingham via quiet Suffolk lanes to the attractive village of Debenham*	90	29		14	Stowmarket 01449-676800
14	*East from Framlingham to the Maltings at Snape and the Minsmere Levels*	96	37		13	Ipswich 01473-258070
	Off-road routes					
1	*From Aldbury, along the Icknield Way and back through the woodland of Berkhamsted Common*	102	20		2	Wendover 01296-696759
2	*Between Tring and Berkhamsted through woods and hills*	106	17		1,3	Wendover 01296-696759
3	*Woodland tracks and the Grand Union Canal in southwest Hertfordshire*	110	22		2	Hemel Hempstead 01442-60161
4	*From Great Offley the Icknield Way Path*	114	20,10	or		Luton 01582-401579
5	*Woods, lanes, streams and fords southeast of Stevenage*	118	24			Hertford 01992-584322
6	*Woodland tracks and a dismantled railway path southwest from Hertford*	122	14			Hertford 01992-584322
7	*Tracks, lanes and the Icknield Way through undulating countryside southeast of Royston*	126	22			Saffron Walden 01799-510444
8	*Byways and Roman Roads east from Fulbourn near Cambridge*	130	23			Cambridge 01223-322640
9	*A figure of eight loop on the Suffolk Coast heathland east of Westleton*	134	18			Ipswich 01473-258070
10	*South from the Maltings at Snape along a section of the Three Forest Trail*	138	18			Ipswich 01473-258070

[1] ***Links with other routes*** Use this information to create a more strenuous ride or if you are planning to do more than one ride in a day or on a weekend or over a few days. The rides do not necessarily join: there may be a distance of up to three miles between the closest points. Several rides are in pairs, sharing the same starting point, which may be a good place to base yourself for a weekend.

[2] ***Tourist Information Centres*** You can contact them for details about accommodation. If they cannot help, there are many books that recommend places to stay. If nothing is listed for the place where you want to stay, try phoning the post office or the pub in the village to see if they can suggest somewhere.

East Anglia – South

The area covered by this book runs from the steep wooded hills of the Chilterns in the west across through the chalk and flint of Suffolk and Essex to the sandy heathland of the Suffolk Coast. It dips into five counties – Bedfordshire, Hertfordshire, Essex, Suffolk and the southern half of Cambridgeshire. Instinctively one thinks of the area north from London into East Anglia as being flat; in broad terms this is true – the land east of the Chilterns rises to barely above 400 feet. However, unlike the Fenland further north, the landscape of the area covered tends to be undulating rather than dead flat, providing the very best country for leisure cycling – sufficient height is gained to offer fine views but no hill lasts for more than 300 feet.

The area has a high density of population, but with the exception of some off-road woodland rides in the west of the area near to Berkhamsted, the rides stay clear of the bigger towns and stay on the quiet lanes that offer the most relaxing cycling.

Two on-road rides start from St Neots and explore the delights of Grafham Water and the surrounding countryside, four are based near the attractive old town of Saffron Walden and make forays into the rolling farmland and pretty villages of thatched cottages and flint churches nearby; a further four are centred upon Lavenham, surely one of the most beautiful places in the whole country, and two strike out from Framlingham with its imposing 12th-century castle.

The off-road routes are more concentrated in the western half of the area covered simply because the terrain offers a greater concentration of good bridleways and woodland trails. It cannot be stressed often enough that some of these rides are only worth doing in the summer as the conditions from late autumn to late spring or after heavy rain can be hard-going in the extreme, with mud that either stops your chain or wheels from turning.

Should you wish to cycle off-road on easier trails which are passable all year round you have several options: the Grand Union Canal and the Lee and Stort Navigation both have good quality towpaths. Hertfordshire has four dismantled railways converted to recreational use: one starts from St Albans, one from Hertford (used in off-road ride 6), one from Wheathampstead and the last from Harpenden. Essex has the Flitch Way from Braintree and Bedfordshire has the Willington Countryway from near Bedford.

Abbreviations and instructions

Instructions are given as concisely as possible to make them easy to follow while you are cycling. Remember to read one or two instructions ahead so that you do not miss a turning. This is most likely to occur when you have to turn off a road on which you have been riding for a fairly long distance and these junctions are marked ***Easy to miss*** to warn you.

If there appears to be a contradiction between the instructions and what you actually see, always refer to the map. There are many reasons why over the course of a few years instructions will need updating as new roads are built and priorities and signposts change.

If giving instructions for road routes is at times difficult, doing so for off-road routes can often be almost impossible, particularly when the route passes through woodland. With few signposts and buildings by which to orientate yourself, more attention is paid to other features, such as gradient and surface. Most of these routes have been explored between late spring and early autumn and the countryside changes its appearance very dramatically in winter. If in doubt, consult your map and check your compass to see that you are heading in the right direction.

Where I have encountered mud I have mentioned it, but this may change not only from summer to winter but also from dry to wet weather at any time during the year. At times you may have to retrace your steps and find a road alternative.

Some routes have small sections that follow footpaths. The instructions will highlight these sections where you must get off and push your bike. You may only ride on bridleways and by-ways so be careful if you stray from the given routes.

Directions

L	left
LH	left-hand
RH	right-hand
SA	straight ahead or straight across
bear L or R	make less than a 90-degree (right-angle) turn at a fork in the road or track or at a sharp bend so that your course appears to be straight ahead; this is often written as *in effect SA*
sharp L or R turn	is more acute than 90 degrees
sharp R/L back on yourself	an almost U-turn
sharp LH/RH bend	a 90-degree bend
R then L or R	the second turning is visible then immediately L from the first
R then 1st L	the second turning may be some distance from the first; the distance may also be indicated: *R, then after 1 mile L*

Junctions

T-j	T-junction, a junction where you have to give way
X-roads	crossroads, a junction where you may or may not have to give way
offset X-roads	the four roads are not in the form of a perfect cross and you will have to turn left then right, or vice versa, to continue the route

Signs

'Placename 2'	words in quotation marks are those that appear on signposts; the numbers indicate distance in miles unless stated otherwise
NS	not signposted
trig point	a trigonometrical station

Instructions

An example of an easy instruction is:

4 *At the T-j at the end of Smith Road by the White Swan PH R on Brown Street 'Greentown 2, Redville 3'.*

There is more information in this instruction than you would normally need, but things do change: pubs may close down and signs may be replaced, removed or vandalized.

An example of a difficult instruction is:

8 *Shortly after the brow of the hill, soon after passing a telephone box on the right next L (NS).*

As you can see, there is no T-junction to halt you in your tracks, no signpost indicating where the left turn will take you, so you need to have your wits about you in order not to miss the turning.

Fact boxes

The introduction to each route includes a fact box giving useful information:

Start

This is the suggested start point coinciding with instruction 1 on the map. There is no reason why you should not start at another point if you prefer.

Distance and grade

The distance is, of course, that from the beginning to the end of the route. If you wish to shorten the ride, however, the maps enable you to do so.

The number of drinks bottles indicates the grade:

- Easy
- Moderate
- Strenuous

Page diagrams

The on-road routes occupy four pages of mapping each. The page diagrams on the introductory pages show how the map pages have been laid out, how they overlap and if any inset maps have been used.

This section of the route is shown on pages 92 and 93

This overlap area appears at the foot of pages 92 and 93 and at the top of pages 94 and 95

This area is shown as an inset on page 94

This section of the route is shown on pages 94 and 95

92 93 94 95

The grade is based on the amount of climbing involved and, for off-road rides, the roughness of the surface rather than the distance covered.

Remember that conditions may vary dramatically with the weather and seasons, especially along off-road routes

Terrain

This brief description of the terrain may be read in conjunction with the cross-profile diagram at the foot of the page to help you to plan your journey.

Nearest railway

This is the distance to the nearest station from the closest point on the route, not necessarily from the start. Before starting out you should check with British Rail for local restrictions regarding the carrying of bicycles.
(See page 15)

Refreshments

Pubs and teashops on or near the route are listed. The tankard symbols indicate pubs particularly liked by the author.

Before you go

Preparing yourself

Fitness

- Cycling uses muscles in a different way from walking or running, so if you are beginning or returning to it after a long absence you will need time to train your muscles and become accustomed to sitting on a saddle for a few hours. Build up your fitness and stamina gradually and make sure you are using a bicycle that is the right size for you and suits your needs.

Equipment

- Attach the following items to the bike: bell, pump, light-brackets and lights, lock-holder and lock, rack and panniers or elastic straps for securing things to the rack, map holder. Unless it is the middle of summer and the weather is guaranteed to be fine, you will need to carry extra clothes, particularly a waterproof, with you, and it is well worth investing in a rack for this purpose.
- Wearing a small pouch around your waist is the easiest and safest way of carrying small tools and personal equipment. The basics are: Allen keys to fit the various Allen bolts on your bike, chainlink extractor, puncture repair kit, reversible screwdriver (slot and crosshead), small adjustable spanner, spare inner tube, tyre levers (not always necessary with mountain bike tyres), coins and a phonecard for food and telephone calls, compass.
- Additional tools for extended touring: bottom bracket extractor, cone spanners, freewheel extractor, headset spanners, lubricant, socket spanner for pedals, spare cables, spoke-key.

Clothing

- What you wear when you are cycling should be comfortable, allowing you, and most especially your legs, to move freely. It should also be practical, so that it will keep you warm and dry if and when the weather changes.
- **Feet** You can cycle in just about any sort of footwear, but bear in mind that the chain has oil on it, so do not use your very best shoes. Leather tennis shoes or something similar, with a smooth sole to slip into the pedal and toe clip are probably adequate until you buy specialist cycling shoes, which have stiffer soles and are sometimes designed for use with specialist pedals.
- ***Legs*** Cycling shorts or padded cycling underwear worn under everyday clothing make long rides much more comfortable. Avoid tight, non-stretch trousers, which are very uncomfortable for cycling and will sap your energy, as they restrict the movement of your legs; baggy tracksuit

bottoms, which can get caught in the chain and will sag around your ankles if they get wet. Almost anything else will do, though a pair of stretch leggings is probably best.

- ***Upper body*** What you wear should be long enough to cover your lower back when you are leaning forward and, ideally, should have zips or buttons that you can adjust to regulate your temperature. Several thin layers are better than one thick layer.
- ***Head*** A helmet may protect your head in a fall.
- ***Wet weather*** If you get soaked to your skin and you are tired, your body core temperature can drop very quickly when you are cycling. A waterproof, windproof top is essential if it looks like rain. A dustbin bag would be better than nothing but obviously a breathable waterproof material is best.
- ***Cold weather*** Your extremities suffer far more when you are cycling than when you are walking in similar conditions. A hat that covers your ears, a scarf around your neck, a pair of warm gloves and a thermal top and bottom combined with what you would normally wear cycling should cover almost all conditions.
- ***Night and poor light*** Wearing light-coloured clothes or reflective strips is almost as important as having lights on your bike. Reflective bands worn around the ankles are particularly effective in making you visible to motorists.

Preparing your bicycle

- You may not be a bicycle maintenance expert, but you should make sure that your bike is roadworthy before you begin a ride.
- If you are planning to ride in soft, off-road conditions, fit fat, knobbly tyres. If you are using the bike around town or on a road route, fit narrower, smoother tyres.
- Check the tyres for punctures or damage and repair or replace if necessary or if you are in any doubt. Keep tyres inflated hard (recommended pressures are on the side wall of the tyre) for mainly on-road riding. You do not need to inflate tyres as hard for off-road use; slightly softer tyres give some cushioning and get better traction in muddy conditions.
- Ensure that the brakes work efficiently. Replace worn cables and brake blocks.
- The bike should glide along silently. Tighten and adjust any part that is loose or rubbing against a moving part. Using a good-quality bike oil lubricate the hubs, bottom bracket, pedals where they join the cranks, chain and gear-changing mechanism from both sides. If the bike still makes grating noises, replace the bearings.
- Adjust the saddle properly. You can raise or lower it, move it forwards or backwards or tilt it up or down. The saddle height should ensure that your legs are working efficiently: too low and your knees will ache; too high and your hips will be rocking in order for your feet to reach the pedals.
- Some women find the average bike saddle uncomfortable because the female pelvis is a different shape from the male pelvis and needs a broader saddle for support. Some manufacturers make saddles especially for women.

Cross-profiles

The introduction to each route includes a cross-profile diagram. The vertical scale is the same on each diagram but the horizontal scale varies according to the length of the route

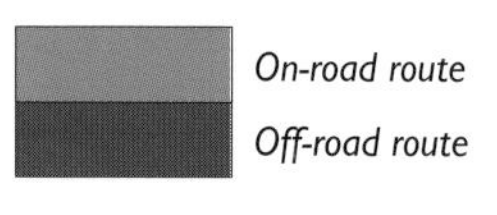

Corfe Castle
Start / finish
Blashenwell Farm
Kingston
Swyre Head
Kimmeridge

Tips for touring

The law

England and Wales have 120 000 miles of rights of way, but under the Wildlife and Countryside Act of 1968 you are allowed to cycle on only about 10 percent of them, namely on bridleways, by-ways open to all traffic (BOATS) and roads used as public paths (RUPPS).

The other 90 percent of rights of way are footpaths, where you may walk and usually push your bike, but not ride it. Local bylaws sometimes prohibit the pushing of bicycles along footpaths and although all the paths in this book have been checked, bylaws do sometimes change.

- You are not allowed to ride where there is no right of way. If you lose the route and find yourself in conflict with a landowner, stay calm and courteous, make a note of exactly where you are and then contact the Rights of Way Department of the local authority. It has copies of definitive maps and will take up the matter on your behalf if you are in the right.
- For further information on cycling and the law contact the Cyclists Touring Club (CTC) whose address can be found on the inside back cover.

Cycling techniques

If you are not used to cycling more than a few miles at a stretch, you may find initially that touring is tiring. There are ways of conserving your energy, however:

- Do not struggle in a difficult gear if you have an easier one. Let the gears help you up the hills. No matter how many gears a bike has, however, ultimately it is leg power that you need to get you up a hill. You may decide to get off and walk uphill with your bike to rest your muscles.
- You can save a lot of energy on the road by following close behind a stronger rider in his or her slipstream, but do not try this offroad. All the routes are circular, so you can start at any point and follow the instructions until you return to it. This is useful when there is a strong wind, as you can alter the route to go into the wind at the start of the ride, when you are fresh, and have the wind behind you on the return, when you are more tired.
- The main difference in technique between on-road and off-road cycling lies in getting your weight balanced correctly. When going down steep off-road sections, lower the saddle, keep the pedals level, stand up out of the saddle to let your legs absorb the bumps and keep your weight over the rear wheel. Control is paramount: keep your eyes on what lies ahead.

Traffic

The rides in this book are designed to minimize time spent on busy roads, but you will inevitably encounter some traffic. The most effective way to avoid an accident with a motor vehicle is to be highly aware of what is going on around you and to ensure that other road users are aware of you.

- Ride confidently.
- Indicate clearly to other road users what you intend to do, particularly when turning right. Look behind you, wait for a gap in the traffic, indicate, then turn. If you have to turn right off a busy road or on a difficult bend, pull in and wait for a gap in the traffic or go past the turning to a point where you have a clear view of the traffic in both directions, then cross and return to the turning.
- Use your lights and wear reflective clothing at night and in poor light.
- Do not ride two-abreast if there is a vehicle behind you. Let it pass. If it cannot easily overtake you because the road is narrow, look for a passing place or a gate entrance and pull in to let it pass.

Maintenance

Mountain bikes are generally stronger than road bikes, but any bike can suffer. To prevent damage as far as possible:

- Watch out for holes and obstacles.
- Clean off mud and lubricate moving parts regularly.
- Replace worn parts, particularly brake blocks.

Riders also need maintenance:

- Eat before you get hungry, drink before you get thirsty. Dried fruit, nuts and chocolate take up little space and provide lots of energy.
- Carry a water bottle and keep it filled, especially on hot days. Tea, water and well-diluted soft drinks are the best thirst-quenchers.

Breakdowns

The most likely breakdown to occur is a puncture.

- Always carry a pump.
- Take a spare inner tube so that you can leave the puncture repair until later.
- Make sure you know how to remove a wheel. This may require an adjustable spanner or, in many cases, no tool at all, as many bikes now have wheels with quick-release skewers that can be loosened by hand.

Security

Where you park your bike, what you lock it with and what you lock it to are important in protecting it from being stolen.

- Buy the best lock you can afford.
- Lock your bike to something immovable in a well-lit public place.
- Locking two bikes together is better than locking them individually.
- Use a chain with a lock to secure the wheels and saddle to the frame. Keep a note of the frame number and other details, and insure, photograph and code the bike.

Lost and Found

The detailed instructions and the Ordnance Survey mapping in this book minimize the chances of getting lost. However, if you do lose your way:

- Ask someone for directions.
- Retrace the route back to the last point where you knew where you were.
- Use the map to rejoin the route at a point further ahead.

Code of Conduct

- Enjoy the countryside and respect its life and work
- Only ride where you know you have a legal right
- Always yield to horses and pedestrians
- Take all litter with you
- Don't get annoyed with anyone; it never solves any problems
- Guard against all risk of fire
- Fasten all gates
- Keep your dogs under close control
- Keep to public paths across farmland
- Use gates and stiles to cross fences, hedges and walls
- Avoid livestock, crops and machinery or, if not possible, keep contact to a minimum
- Help keep all water clean
- Protect wildlife, plants and trees
- Take special care on country roads
- Make no unnecessary noise

Transporting your bike

There are three ways of getting you and your bike to the start of a ride:

Cycle to the start or to a point along a route near your home.

Take the train. Always check in advance that you can take the bike on the train. Some trains allow only up to two bikes and you may need to make a reservation and pay a flat fee however long the journey. Always label your bike showing your name and destination station.

Travel by motor vehicle. You can carry the bikes:

- Inside the vehicle. With the advent of quick release mechanisms on both wheels and the seatpost, which allow a quick dismantling of the bike, it is possible to fit a bike in even quite small cars. It is unwise to stack one bike on top of another unless you have a thick blanket separating them to prevent scratching or worse damage. If you are standing them up in a van, make sure they are secured so they cannot slide around.
- On top of the vehicle. The advantages of this method are that the bikes are completely out of the way and are not resting against each other, you can get at the boot or hatch easily and the bikes do not obscure the number plate or rear lights and indicators. The disadvantages are that you use up more fuel, the car can feel uncomfortable in a crosswind and you have to be reasonably tall and strong to get the bikes on and off the roof.
- On a rack that attaches to the rear of the vehicle. The advantages are that the rack is easily and quickly assembled and disassembled, fuel consumption is better and anyone can lift the bikes on and off. The disadvantages are that you will need to invest in a separate board carrying the number plate and rear lights if they are obstructed by the bikes, you cannot easily get to the boot or hatch once the bikes have been loaded and secured, and the bikes are resting against each other so you must take care that they don't scrape off paint or damage delicate parts.
- Whichever way you carry the bikes on the outside of the vehicle, ensure that you regularly check that they are secure and that straps and fixings that hold them in place have not come loose. If you are leaving the bikes for any length of time, be sure they are secure against theft; if nothing else lock them to each other.

Legend to 1:50 000 maps

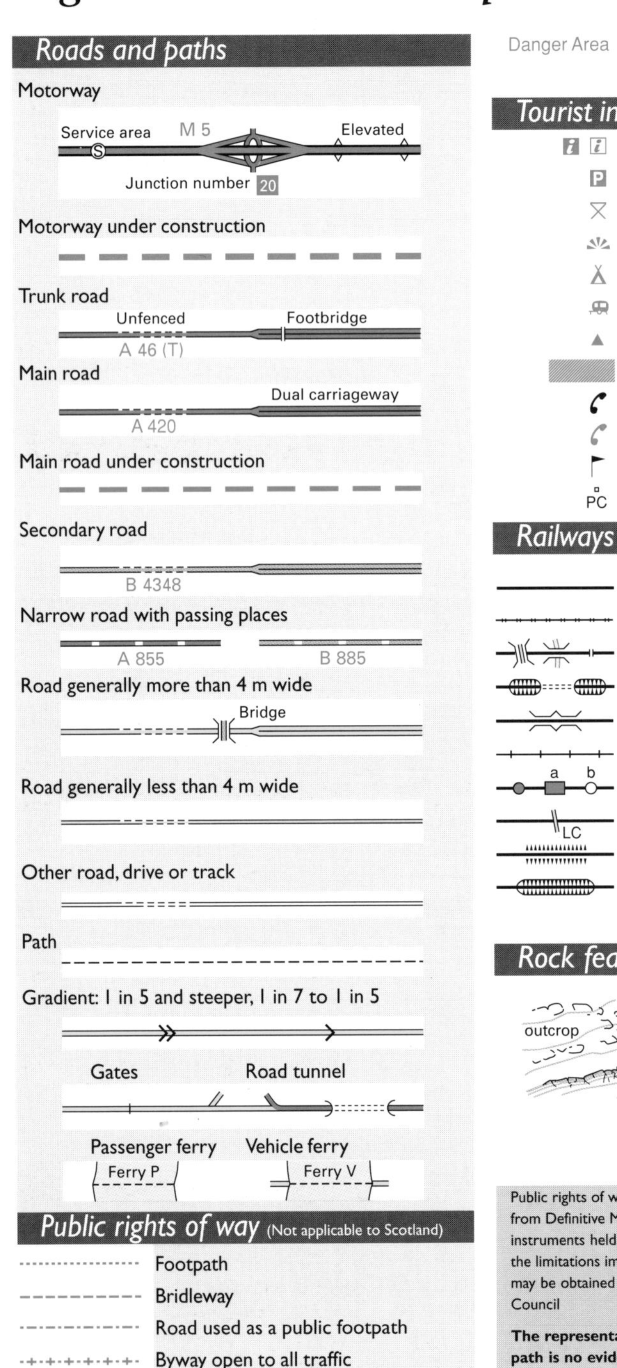

Danger Area — Firing and test ranges in the area. Danger! Observe warning notices

Tourist information

- Information centre, all year / seasonal
- Parking
- Picnic site
- Viewpoint
- Camp site
- Caravan site
- Youth hostel
- Selected places of tourist interest
- Public telephone
- Motoring organisation telephone
- Golf course or link
- PC Public convenience (in rural areas)

Railways

- Track: multiple or single
- Track: narrow gauge
- Bridges, footpath
- Tunnel
- Viaduct
- Freight line, siding or tramway
- a b Station, (a) principal, (b) closed to passengers
- LC Level crossing
- Embankment
- Cutting

Rock features

Public rights of way indicated by these symbols have been derived from Definitive Maps as amended by the latest enactments or instruments held by Ordnance Survey and are shown subject to the limitations imposed by the scale of mapping. Further information may be obtained from the appropriate County or London Borough Council

The representation on this map of any other road, track or path is no evidence of the existence of a right of way

Water features

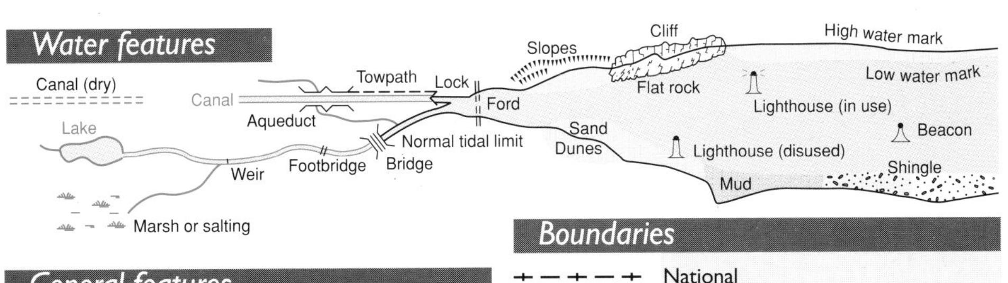

General features

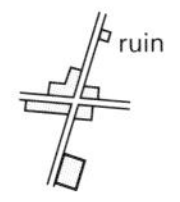	Buildings
	Electricity transmission line (with pylons spaced conventionally)
> - - > - - >	Pipeline (arrow indicates direction of flow)
ruin	Buildings
	Public buildings (selected)
	Bus or coach station
	Coniferous wood
	Non-coniferous wood
	Mixed wood
	Orchard
	Park or ornamental grounds
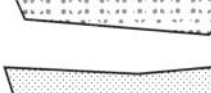	Quarry
	Spoil heap, refuse tip or dump
	Radio or TV mast
	Church or chapel with tower
	Church or chapel with spire
+	Church or chapel without tower or spire
o	Chimney or tower
	Glasshouse
+	Graticule intersection at 5' intervals
Ⓗ	Heliport
△	Triangulation pillar
	Windmill with or without sails
	Windpump

Boundaries

	National
	London borough
	National park or forest park
NT	National Trust — NT open access; NT limited access
	County, region or islands area
	District

Abbreviations

P	Post office
PH	Public house
MS	Milestone
MP	Milepost
CH	Clubhouse
PC	Public convenience (in rural areas)
TH	Town hall, guildhall or equivalent
CG	Coastguard

Antiquities

VILLA	Roman
Castle	Non-Roman
	Battlefield (with date)
☆	Tumulus
+	Position of antiquity which cannot be drawn to scale
	Ancient monuments and historic buildings in the care of the Secretaries of State for the Environment, for Scotland and for Wales and that are open to the public

Heights

50	Contours are at 10 metres vertical interval
·144	Heights are to the nearest metre above mean sea level

Heights shown close to a triangulation pillar refer to the station height at ground level and not necessarily to the summit

From St Neots to Grafham Water and south to Thurleigh

This ride visits Grafham Water: one of the most popular cycling attractions in the region. As with Rutland Water, some 30 miles to the northwest, a route has been designed around the reservoir, using improved existing rights of way and quiet lanes to form a most satisfying circular ride of appeal to everyone – from children just learning to ride to adults who may be returning to cycling after many years' absence. This ride follows the loop around the reservoir for about two thirds of its length before turning southwest along quiet lanes to Keysoe and Thurleigh. The route turns east here crossing gently undulating arable land to return via Duloe beneath the A1 back to St Neots.

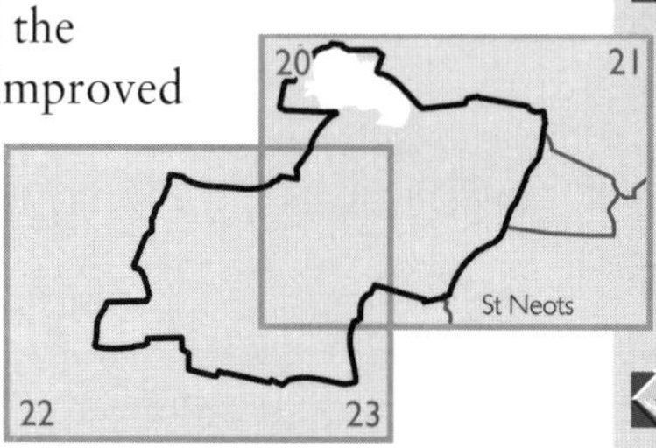

20 21 22 23 St Neots

Start

Bridge House PH, the Market Square, St Neots

P Several long stay car parks, follow signs

Distance and grade

37 miles

Easy

Terrain

No major hills. Lowest point – 75 feet (23 mts) at Great Staughton. Highest point – 270 feet (81 mts) at Thurleigh

Nearest railway

St Neots

Refreshments

*Plenty of choice, River Mill PH, **St Neots***
*The Horseshoe PH, The Swan PH, **Offord Cluny***
*Old Lion and Lamb PH, The Vine PH, The George PH, **Buckden***
*Plenty of choice around **Grafham Water***
*Chequers PH, **Keysoe***
*The Olde Plough PH, **Bolnhurst***
*The Wheatsheaf PH, **Roothams Green***

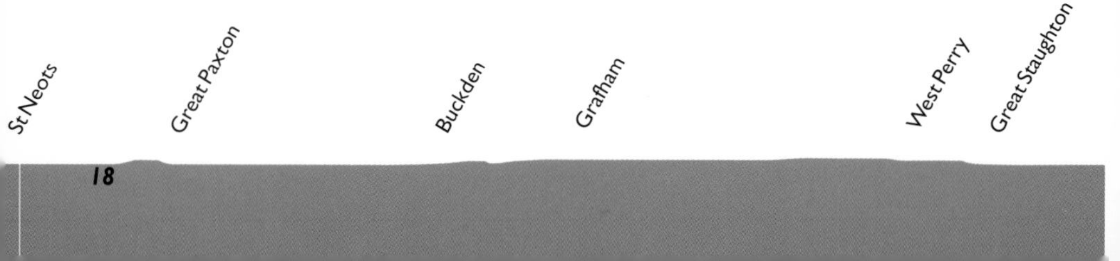

St Neots · Great Paxton · Buckden · Grafham · West Perry · Great Staughton

Places of interest

St Neots *1*
St Neots grew up around a 12th-century Benedictine Priory. In the 17th and 18th centuries there was much rebuilding in the town – the river was dredged and sluices were built enabling goods to be brought in by water. The magnificent church tower soars above the market square framed by Georgian houses backing onto the Great Ouse

Buckden Towers *4*
Former moated ecclesiastical palace of the Bishops of Lincoln with a splendid 15th-century gatehouse and tower. Queen Catherine of Aragon was imprisoned here before being taken to Kimbolton Castle

Grafham Water *5*
The circuit of the lake is one of the best family cycle routes in the region. It is also a woodland nature reserve providing nesting sites for lapwings, skylarks, wagtails, willow warblers and chiff chaffs

Kimbolton *(just off the route) 9*
A village with a Tudor manor remodelled in 1707 by Sir John Vanbrugh. Catherine of Aragon was imprisoned here after being divorced by Henry VIII. The church has some fine monuments

Bushmead Priory *(just off the route) 16*
A small Augustinian priory founded in 1195. Magnificent 13th-century timber roof of crown post construction with medieval wall paintings and stained glass

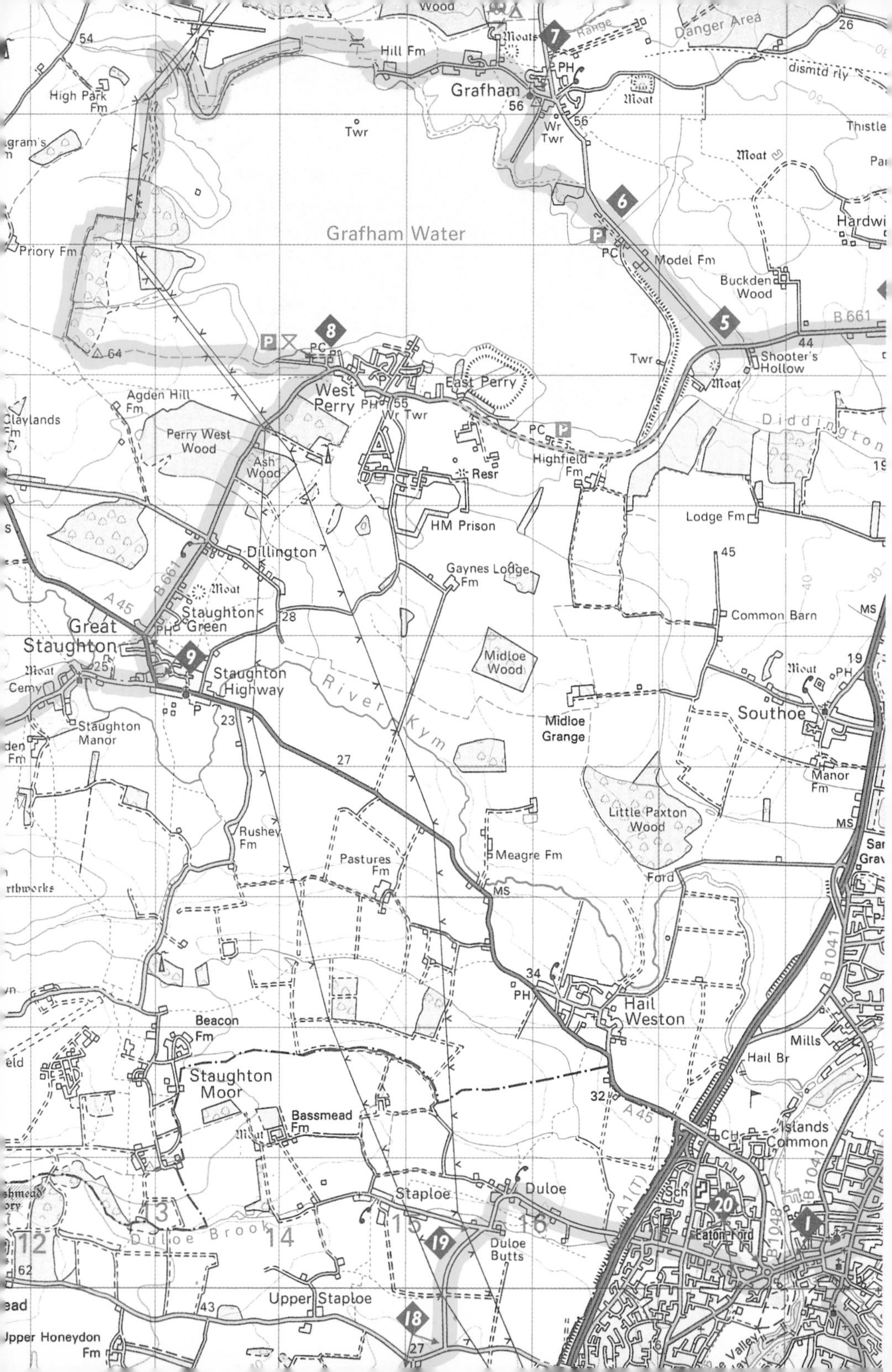

Grafham
Grafham Water
Hill Fm
High Park Fm
Priory Fm
Danger Area
Range
dismtd rly
Thistle
Hardwi
Buckden Wood
Model Fm
B 661
Shooter's Hollow
West Perry
East Perry
Agden Hill Fm
Claylands Fm
Perry West Wood
Ash Wood
Highfield Fm
HM Prison
Lodge Fm
Dillington
Gaynes Lodge Fm
Common Barn
Great Staughton
Staughton Green
Staughton Highway
Staughton Manor
Midloe Wood
Midloe Grange
River Kym
Southoe
Manor Fm
Little Paxton Wood
Rushey Fm
Pastures Fm
Meagre Fm
Ford
Hail Weston
Mills
Hail Br
Islands Common
Beacon Fm
Staughton Moor
Bassmead Fm
Staploe
Duloe
Duloe Brook
Duloe Butts
Upper Staploe
Upper Honeydon Fm
Eaton Ford
A 45
A1(T)
B 1041
B 1048
Diddington

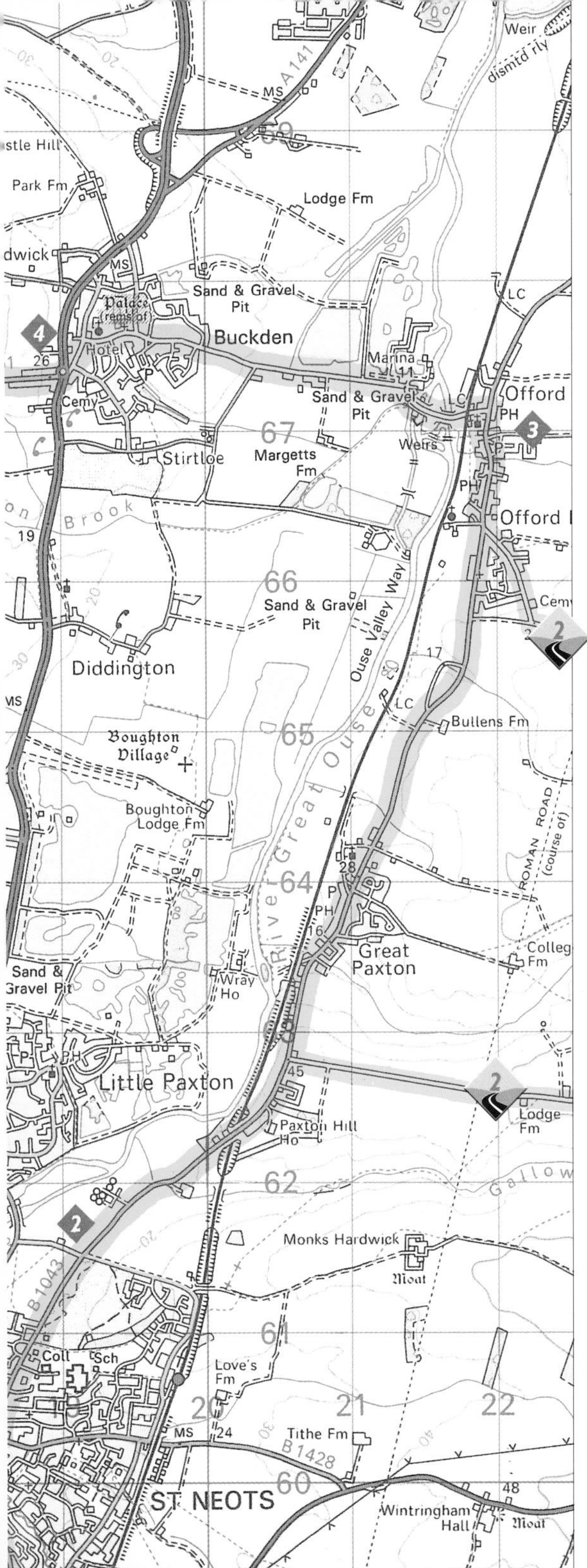

1 With back to Bridge House PH, Market Square, turn L away from the bridge. At 2nd major traffic lights (ie ignore pelican crossings) L onto Huntingdon Street 'Great Paxton. Priory Centre'

*2 At roundabout SA following signs for Great Paxton then Offord Cluny. (**Or** for links to route 2: R after Paxton Hill House or R through Offord)*

3 Go past The Horseshoe PH in Offord Cluny. Just by the Swan PH L 'Buckden 1½'

*4 At T-j in Buckden at the end of Church Street L (NS) then at roundabout with A1 SA 'Kimbolton B661'. **Take care** on the roundabout. Signal clearly and ride confidently*

5 After 1 mile 1st R 'Grafham 1½, Ellington 3'

6 At car park sign after 1 mile L into Marlow car park. Go SA towards lake and turn R on to the obvious cycle track

7 At T-j at the end of the track (Church Hill) in Grafham L and follow the tarmac to the end. Continue on the cycle track around the lake

8 At the car park (Mander Park) follow cycle signs to the main road. At the T-j with the B661 R (ie leave the round-the-lake ride at this point)

9 At T-j with the A45 L 'St Neots, Hail Weston' then on sharp LH bend 1st R 'Little Staughton, Pertenhall'

➜ page 22

18 At T-j R 'Eaton Socon 1, St Neots 3'. At next T-j R (same sign) then after 300 yards 1st L 'Duloe 1'

19 At T-j R 'Eaton Socon 1½, St Neots 2'

20 At X-roads SA onto Mill Hill Road. At mini-roundabout by Royce Court L then at major roundabout SA 'Town Centre B1428'

9 At T-j with the A45 L 'St Neots, Hail Weston' then on sharp LH bend 1st R 'Little Staughton, Pertenhall'

10 After 3 miles at T-j with B660 L 'Keysoe 1½, Bedford 11'

11 Ignore 1st right by Chequers Inn. Take next R near to the top of short hill onto Church Road 'Keysoe, Hatch End 1'

12 Ignore 1st right to Keysoe End West. Take next R by pair of thatched cottages onto Hatch Lane 'Thurleigh 2¾'

13 At T-j in Thurleigh L 'Bolnhurst 2¼, Keysoe 4¾'

14 At T-j with B660 R 'Bedford 6½, Bolnhurst Top End, Ravensden 3½'

15 After 1 mile 1st L on New Road 'Colmworth 1¾, Little Staughton 5'

16 At T-j at end of New Road L 'Colmworth 1, Bushmead 1¾, Little Staughton 3½' then after 300 yards 1st R on Mill Road 'Colesden 2½, Wyboston 4'

17 ***Easy to miss.*** *After 4 miles, on sharp RH bend, take the 2nd L 'Staploe 2½, Duloe 2½'*

18 At T-j R 'Eaton Socon 1, St Neots 3'. At next T-j R (same sign) then after 300 yards 1st L 'Duloe 1'

19 At T-j R 'Eaton Socon 1½, St Neots 2'

page 21

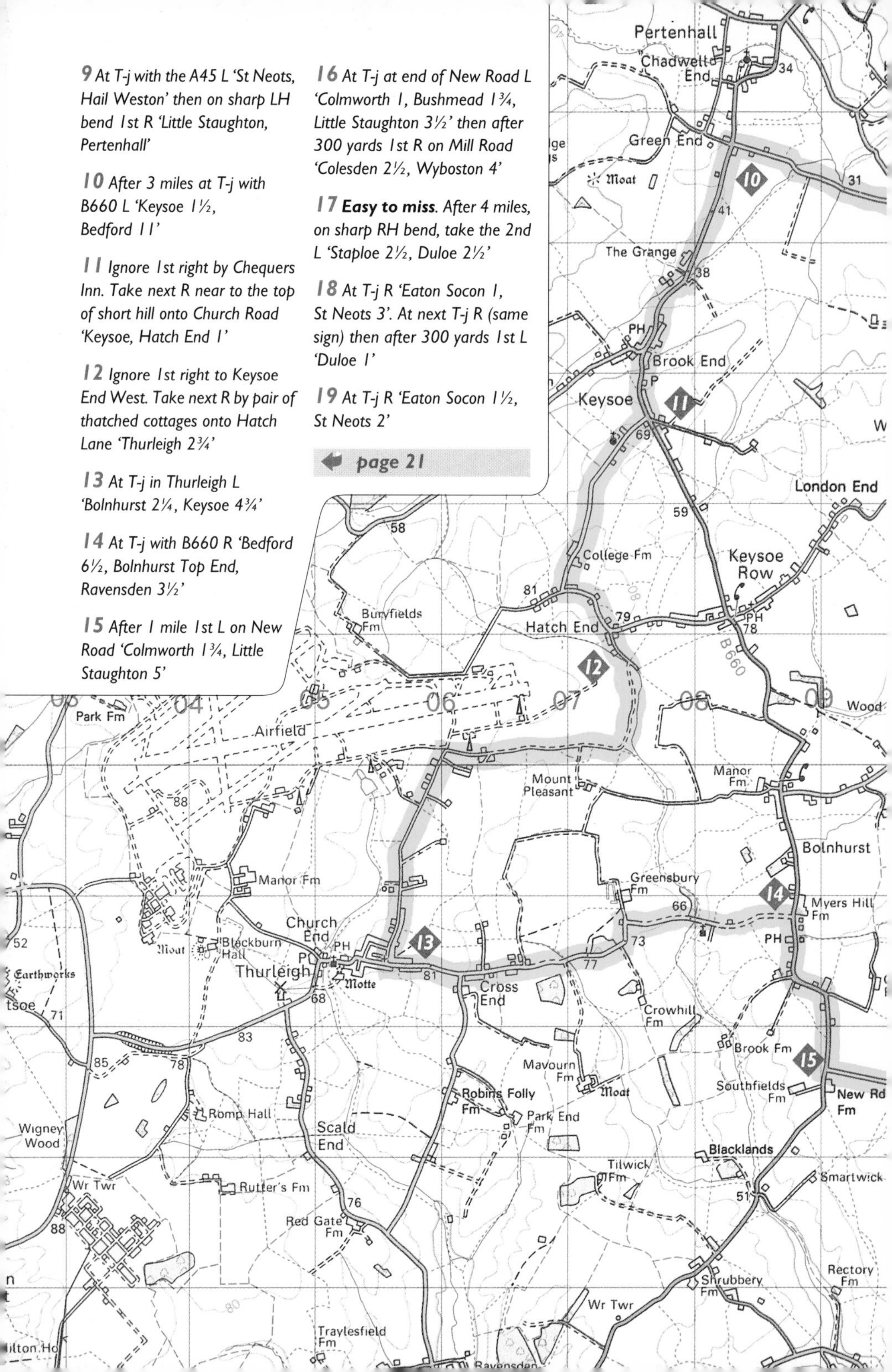

Dillington
Gaynes Lodge Fm
Hoo Fm
Moat
Staughton Green
Great Staughton
A45
B661
PH
65
28
Midloe Wood
Moat
Cemy
25
9
Staughton Highway
River Kym
Newpond Fm
33
New Fm
Staughton Manor
Garden Fm
Manor Fm
23
27
Midloe Grange
64
Rushey Fm
Pastures Fm
Meagre Fm
Green End
PH
ruin
Earthworks
63
Little Staughton
MS
West End
Grown Fm
65
34
PH
71
62
Moat
67
Beacon Fm
Airfield
Staughton Moor
The Wickey Fm
Bassmead Fm
Moat
61
Bushmead Priory
Staploe
Duloe
10
11
13
14
15
19
16
Duloe Brook
Wood End Fm
Bushmead Cross
12
Moats
62
Duloe Butts
60
Bushmead
43
Upper Staploe
18
Upper Honeydon Fm
27
City Fm
59
P
66
Honeydon
34
Church End
Colmworth
Manor Ho
Cherry Orchard Fm
55
Goodwick Fm
Chapel End
Coxfield
Tithe Fm
25
Begwary
16
Mill End
Brook Fm
Rootham's Green
Rd
PH
72
34
34
31
17
28
57
57
Begwary Brook
Top Fm
Low Fm
Channel's End
Moat
Wyboston
PH
Duck's Cross
38
Colesden Grange Fm
27
27
Moat
24
Chawston
56
Colesden
Colesden Lodge Fm
Resr
Bell Fm

2 East from St Neots through open farmland to Great Gransden and Conington

Gentle riding along quiet lanes through undulating arable country characterises this ride to the east of St Neots. The ride could easily be linked with the other ride from St Neots (route 1) to form a longer, sixty-mile ride through the countryside of Bedfordshire and Cambridgeshire.

Start

The Old Falcon Hotel, the Market Square, St Neots

P Several long stay car parks, follow signs

Distance and grade

33 miles
Easy

Terrain

No major hills. Lowest point – 35 feet (11 mts) at Hilton. Highest point – 230 feet (70 mts) northeast of Bourn

Nearest railway

St Neots

Refreshments

Plenty of choice, River Mill PH, ***St Neots***
Duncombe Arms PH, ***Waresley***
Crown and Cushion PH, ***Great Gransden***
Duke of Wellington PH, ***Bourn***
White Swan PH, ***Conington***
Three Horseshoes PH, ***Graveley***

St Neots Crane Hill Lily Hill Waresley Great Gransden Caxton Bourn

Places of interest

Bourn Windmill *7*
Pre-Civil War post mill which may well be the oldest of its type in England and was thoroughly restored in the 1980's

Conington *10*
The church of St Mary has a 14th-century tower, 18th-century nave and late 19th-century chancel. Monuments to the Cotton family include one by famous woodcarver Grinling Gibbons

Fenstanton *(just off the route) 11*
The landscape genius Capability Brown (1715-83) is buried in the 14th-century village church which stands among colour-washed cottages and Georgian houses

Hemingford Grey *(just off the route) 11*
A village of timber, thatch and brick cottages. The moated Norman manor house is said to be the oldest inhabited home in England. The upper section of the 12th-century church spire came down in a gale in 1741 and is believed to be at the bottom of the river

Background picture: Bourn Windmill

Knapwell
Fenstanton
Hilton
Graveley

1 *With back to the Old Falcon Hotel go through Market Square on one way system. At T-j by the Kings Head R then 1st R by the Woolpack PH and the church 'Biggleswade, B1043'*

2 *After 1 mile at roundabout L 'Industrial Estate, Abbotsley B1046' then 1st R 'Abbotsley, Waresley, The Gransdens'*

3 *Shortly after crossing bridges over the railway and A45 1st R on LH bend 'Abbotsley Golf Club'*

4 *After 3 miles, on sharp RH bend, 1st L 'Unsuitable for HGV'*

5 *At T-j in Waresley R (NS) then on sharp RH bend by church L 'Gt Gransden' onto Gamlingay Road*

6 *At T-j (with B1046) opposite Hall Farm House R 'Industrial Estate'. Ignore 1st left by the Crown and Cushion PH. Take the next L 'Caxton, Cambridge' then at mini-roundabout L 'Caxton 2¾, Cambridge'*

page 29

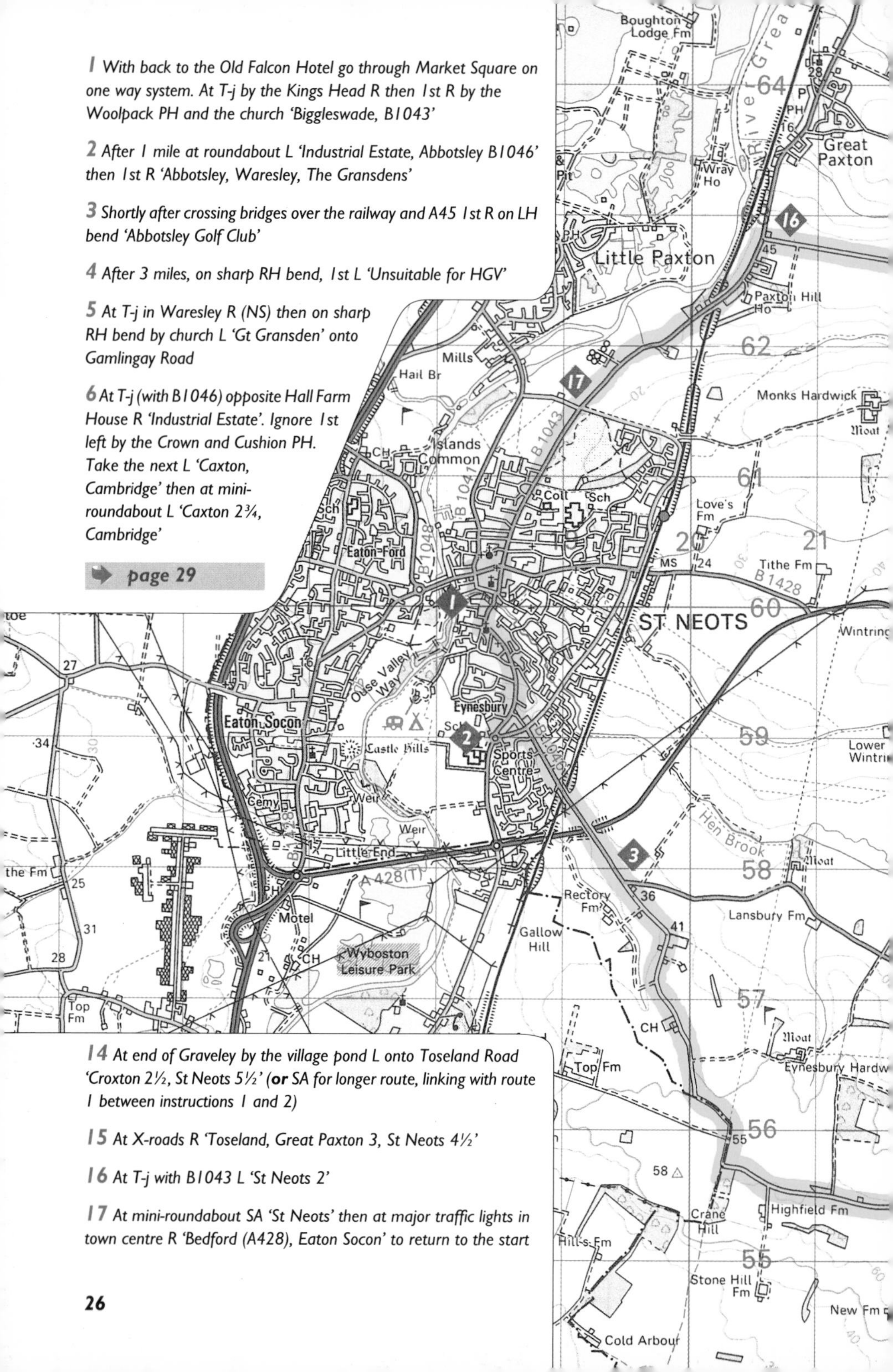

14 *At end of Graveley by the village pond L onto Toseland Road 'Croxton 2½, St Neots 5½' (**or** SA for longer route, linking with route 1 between instructions 1 and 2)*

15 *At X-roads R 'Toseland, Great Paxton 3, St Neots 4½'*

16 *At T-j with B1043 L 'St Neots 2'*

17 *At mini-roundabout SA 'St Neots' then at major traffic lights in town centre R 'Bedford (A428), Eaton Socon' to return to the start*

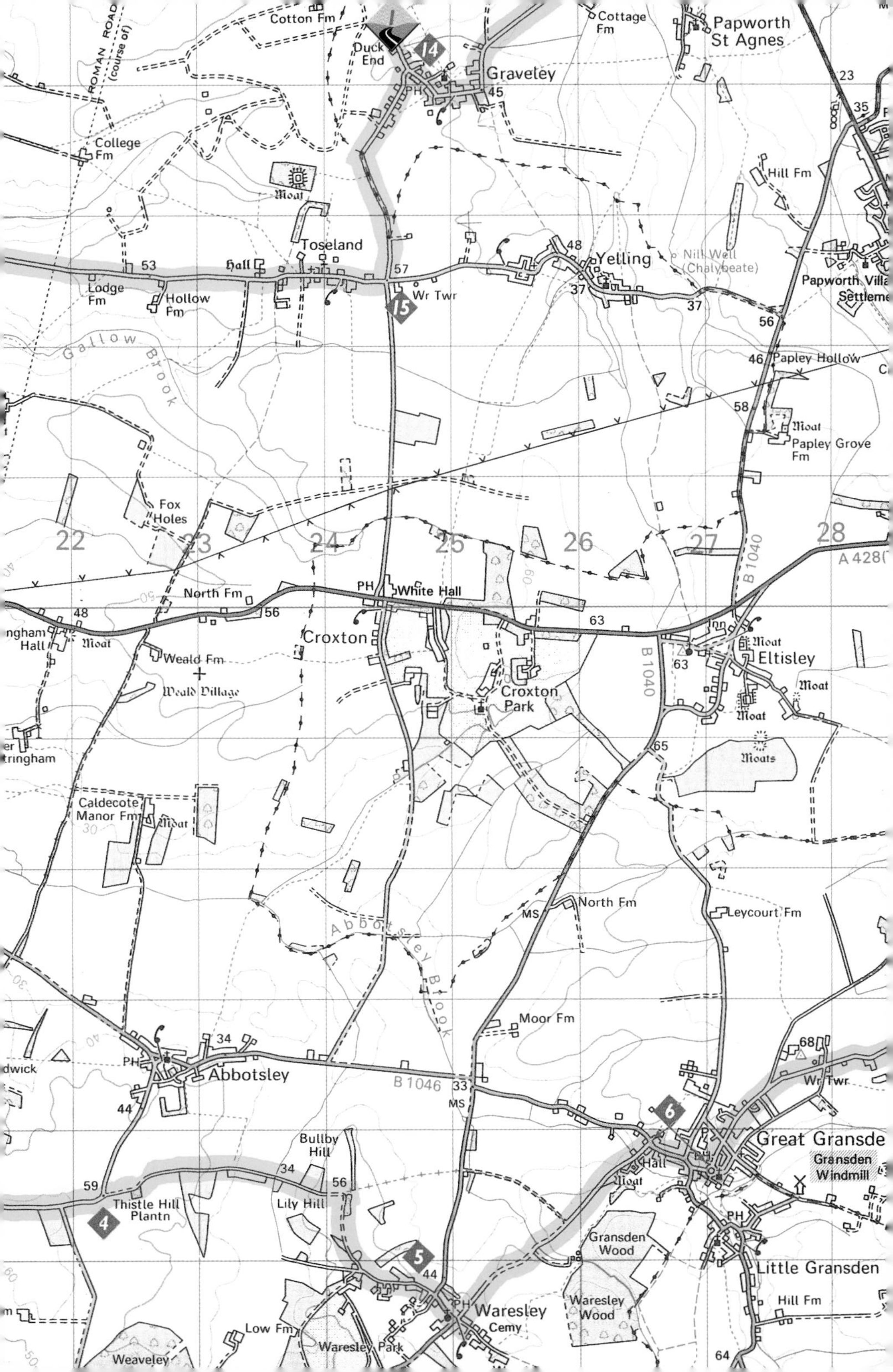

Cotton Fm
Cottage Fm
Papworth St Agnes
ROMAN ROAD (course of)
Duck End
Graveley
45
23
35
College Fm
Moat
Hill Fm
Toseland
48
Yelling
Nill Well (Chalybeate)
53
Hall
57
Lodge Fm
Hollow Fm
Wr Twr
37
37
Papworth Villa Settleme
56
Gallow Brook
46
Papley Hollow
58
Moat
Papley Grove Fm
Fox Holes
22
23
24
25
26
27
28
B 1040
A 428
North Fm
PH
White Hall
48
56
63
Moat
Croxton
Weald Fm
Weald Village
B 1040
63
Moat
Eltisley
Moat
Croxton Park
Moat
65
Moats
Caldecote Manor Fm
Moat
North Fm
MS
Leycourt Fm
Abbotsley Brook
Moor Fm
34
68
PH
Abbotsley
B 1046
33
MS
Wr Twr
44
Great Gransde
Bullby Hill
Hall
PH
Gransden Windmill
Moat
59
34
56
Thistle Hill Plantn
Lily Hill
PH
Gransden Wood
44
Little Gransden
Waresley Wood
PH
Waresley
Hill Fm
Low Fm
Cemy
Waresley Park
Weaveley
64

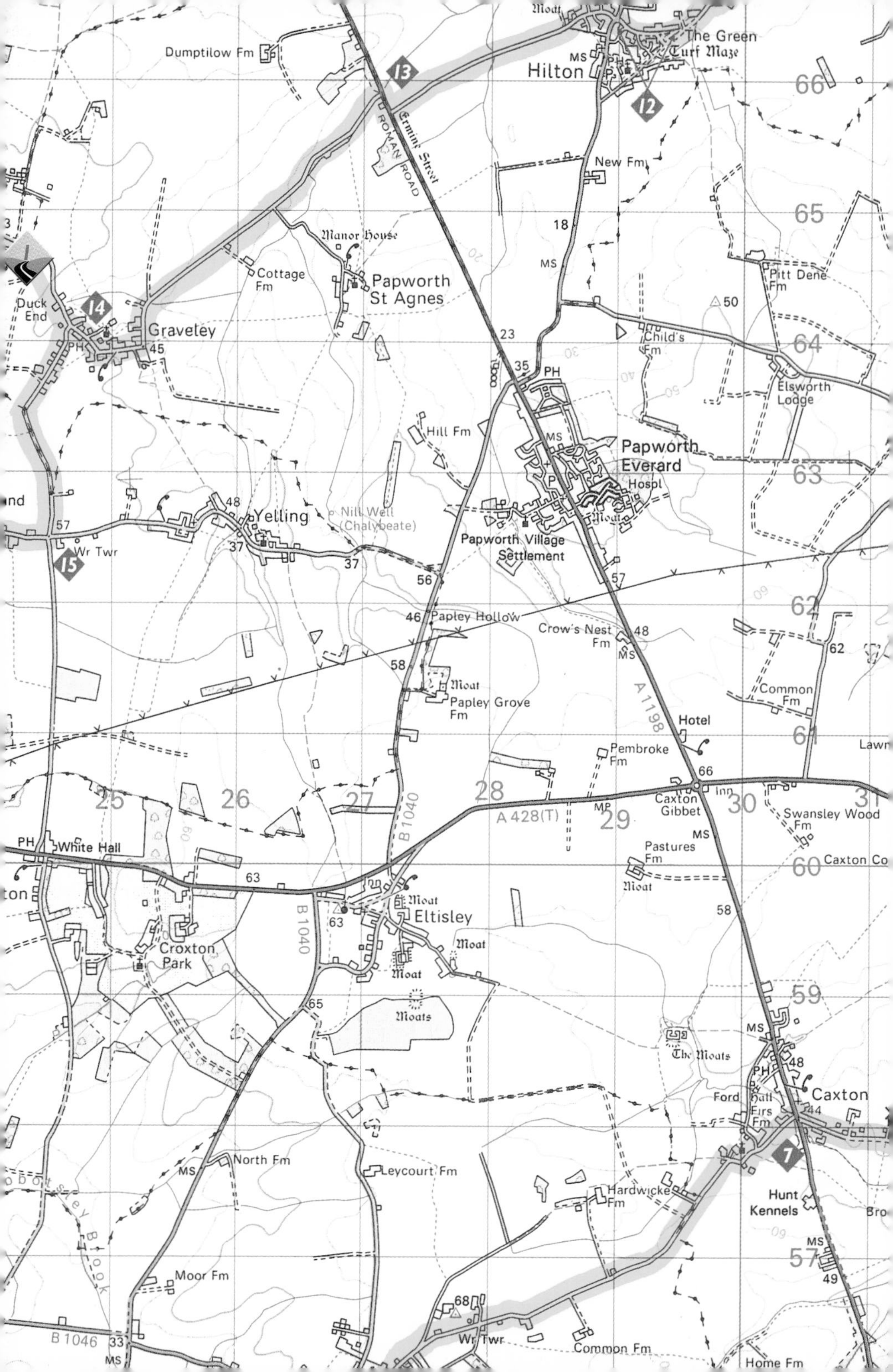

Moat
The Green
Turf Maze
Hilton
Dumptilow Fm
Ermine Street
ROMAN ROAD
New Fm
Manor House
Cottage Fm
Papworth St Agnes
Duck End
Graveley
Pitt Dene Fm
Child's Fm
Elsworth Lodge
Hill Fm
Papworth Everard
Hospl
Yelling
Nill Well (Chalybeate)
Wr Twr
Papworth Village Settlement
Papley Hollow
Crow's Nest Fm
Moat
Papley Grove Fm
A 1198
Hotel
Common Fm
Pembroke Fm
Caxton Gibbet
Inn
Swansley Wood Fm
A 428(T)
B 1040
White Hall
Pastures Fm
Caxton Co
Eltisley
Croxton Park
Moats
The Moats
Caxton
Ford Hall
Firs Fm
North Fm
Leycourt Fm
Hardwicke Fm
Hunt Kennels
Moor Fm
B 1046
Common Fm
Home Fm

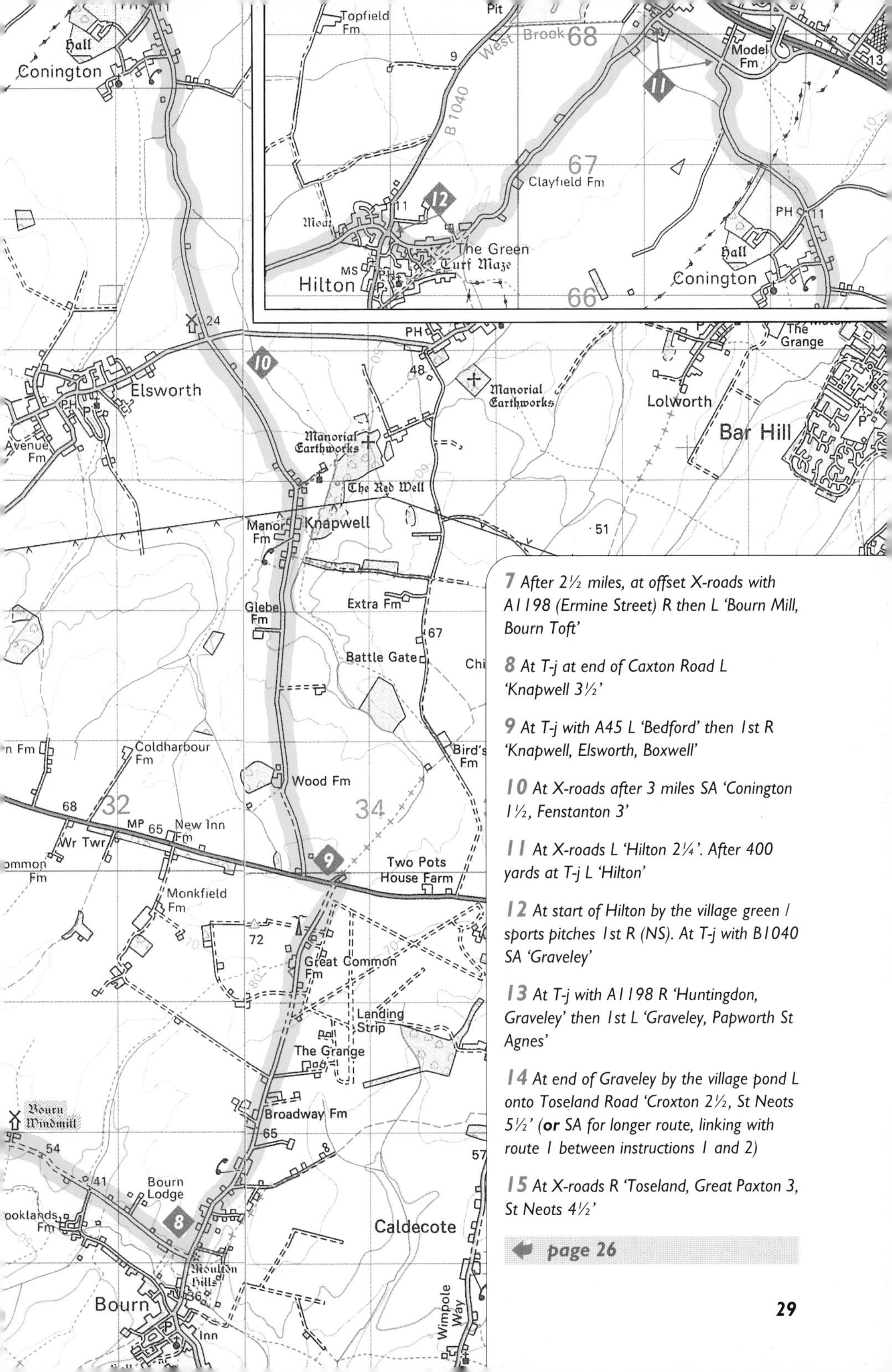

7 After 2½ miles, at offset X-roads with A1198 (Ermine Street) R then L 'Bourn Mill, Bourn Toft'

8 At T-j at end of Caxton Road L 'Knapwell 3½'

9 At T-j with A45 L 'Bedford' then 1st R 'Knapwell, Elsworth, Boxwell'

10 At X-roads after 3 miles SA 'Conington 1½, Fenstanton 3'

11 At X-roads L 'Hilton 2¼'. After 400 yards at T-j L 'Hilton'

12 At start of Hilton by the village green / sports pitches 1st R (NS). At T-j with B1040 SA 'Graveley'

13 At T-j with A1198 R 'Huntingdon, Graveley' then 1st L 'Graveley, Papworth St Agnes'

*14 At end of Graveley by the village pond L onto Toseland Road 'Croxton 2½, St Neots 5½' (**or** SA for longer route, linking with route 1 between instructions 1 and 2)*

15 At X-roads R 'Toseland, Great Paxton 3, St Neots 4½'

page 26

3 *Quiet Hertfordshire lanes through woods and farmland around Stevenage*

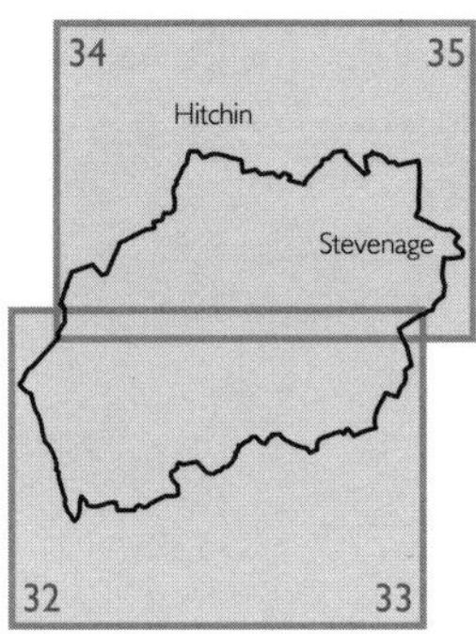

This ride appears to defy logic: all around are large centres of population such as Stevenage, Hitchin, Welwyn Garden City and Luton and yet more than eighty per cent of the ride is spent on tiny quiet lanes where you are as likely to see a pheasant as a motorist. There is a small price to pay for this: a plethora of instructions is needed to keep you away from the busy roads and lanes and on the quieter ones. Perhaps it is a ride that improves each time you ride it so that you need to spend less time looking at the instructions. The route passes through some lovely woodland sections and there are several fine views along the way. The culture stop is at the end: the house of George Bernard Shaw at Ayot St Lawrence.

Start

The Goat PH, High Street, Codicote, 5 miles south of Stevenage

P No specific parking. Park in the High Street, showing consideration

Distance and grade

37 miles

Moderate

Terrain

200 feet climb from Hooks Cross to Benington. 200 feet climb from Walkern to Warren's Green. 220 feet climb from Little Almshoe to Preston. Several more climbs up to 150 feet. Lowest point – 210 feet (64 mts) at the River Beane south of Benington. Highest point – 490 feet (147 mts) near Preston

Nearest railway

Knebworth, Watton at Stone and Hitchin are all just off the route

Codicote

Warren's Green

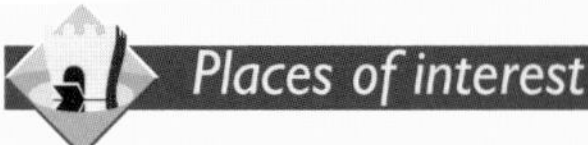

Places of interest

Knebworth House *2*
The ancestral home of the Lytton family with Gothic towers, turrets and a Tudor Great hall behind Victorian embellishments is set in 250 acres of formal gardens and deer park

Benington Lordship Gardens *8*
Hill-top gardens designed around an 18th-century manor house with Norman keep which include rock, water and walled kitchen gardens and a magnificent display of roses. The village of Benington is one of the prettiest in Hertfordshire with all the right ingredients – church, folly, stately home, pub, timbered cottages, village green and duck-pond

Walkern *9*
The village's claim to fame is that it was here in 1711 that the trial of Jane Wenham, the last person to be condemned to death for witchcraft in England, took place. She was accused, among other things, of bewitching sheep to death and appearing in the guise of a cat! There is an attractive Manor House with a vast 17th-century dovecote beside it. The prettiest part of the village is Church End, almost a separate village behind the Old Rectory

Ayot St Lawrence *26*
Peaceful village where George Bernard Shaw made his home, scarcely altered since his death in 1950. You can see a ruined 14th-century church and its 18th-century Grecian-style successor, timber-framed cottages and 17th-century Old Rectory

Refreshments

The Goat PH, The Globe PH, The Bell Inn PH, ***Codicote***
Robin Hood and Little John PH, ***Rabley Heath***
The Fox PH, ***Woolmer Green*** *The Bell PH,* ***Benington***
The White Lion PH, ***Walkern*** *The Anchor PH,* ***Warren Green***
Green Man PH, ***Great Wymondley*** *Red Lion PH,* ***Preston***
Cross Keys PH, ***Gustard Wood***
Brocket Arms PH, ***Ayot St Lawrence***

Great Wymondley
St Ippollitts
Preston
Whiteway Bottom
Ayot St Lawrence

1 With back to The Goat PH turn L down the main street in Codicote. At the end of the village L on to Rabley Heath Road 'Rabley Heath, Potters Heath'

2 At T-j by the Robin Hood and Little John PH R 'Potters Heath, Knebworth'. At next T-j L on to Spinney Lane 'Knebworth'

3 Cross bridge over A1(M). At T-j R 'Woolmer Green'. At T-j (with B197) at the end of Bridge Road in Woolmer Green R then 1st L just past the Post Office towards the Fox PH

4 After ¾ mile, bear R at fork (NS) and follow this lane round past Pound Farm. At T-j by triangle of grass R 'Datchworth' then after 400 yards 1st L on to Raffin Green Lane 'Raffin Green, Hooks Cross'

5 At T-j with A602 R 'Ware, Hertford', then 1st L 'White Hall'. This is a very busy road. Use the pavement with discretion

6 After ¾ mile at the bottom of a short hill 1st R 'White Hall'. At T-j L 'Walkern'

7 1st R at X-roads 'Benington 1, Benington Lordship'

page 34

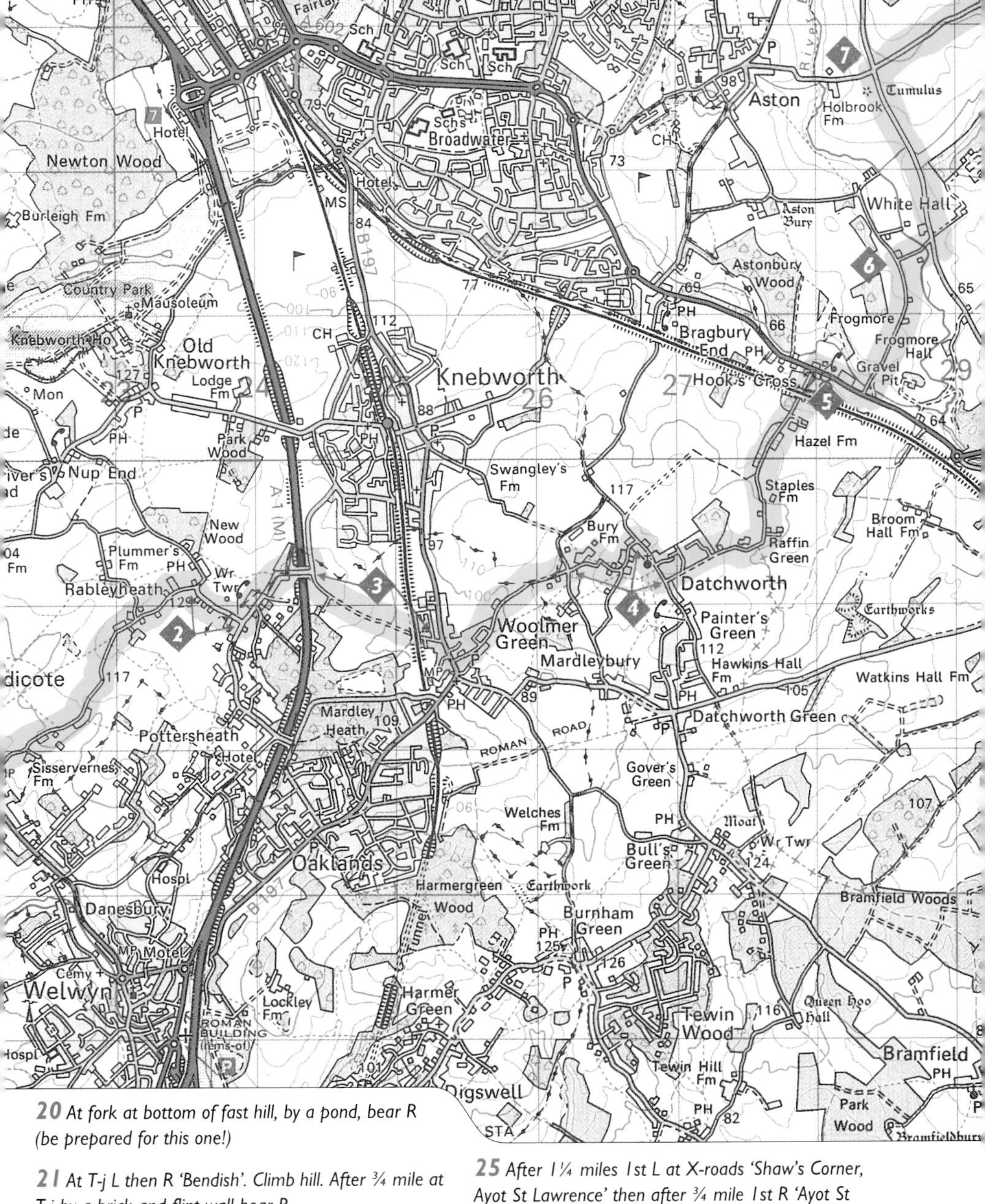

20 At fork at bottom of fast hill, by a pond, bear R (be prepared for this one!)

21 At T-j L then R 'Bendish'. Climb hill. After ¾ mile at T-j by a brick and flint wall bear R

22 At bottom of hill 1st L 'Kimpton'

23 At T-j L 'Kimpton' then bear R 'King's Walden'

24 At T-j with sharp bend in the road bear L downhill 'Kimpton' then at T-j with B652 R then L 'Gustard Wood, Blackmore End'

25 After 1¼ miles 1st L at X-roads 'Shaw's Corner, Ayot St Lawrence' then after ¾ mile 1st R 'Ayot St Lawrence, Shaw's Corner'

26 Follow signs for Ayot St Peter past Shaw's Corner and Brockets Arms PH. 1st L by triangle of grass on to Lordmead Lane 'Codicote, Kimpton'

27 At T-j with Kimpton Road, L 'Codicote'. At T-j by triangle of grass R 'Codicote' to return to the start

7 1st R at X-roads 'Benington 1, Benington Lordship'

8 At T-j in Benington L 'Walkern, Cottered'. After ½ mile, just after School Green and Benington Nurseries bear R on to concrete track 'Private Drive. Public bridleway only'. At T-j with road at the end of the track R

9 After 2 miles, at bottom of hill at a fork by a concrete-edged triangle of grass bear R. At T-j (with B1037) at the end of Winters Lane R

10 After ¾ mile 1st L 'Weston, Baldock'

11 **Easy to miss**. After 2 miles, in Hall's Green, 400 yards after passing beneath power lines, 1st L opposite houses on right

12 At T-j by the Anchor PH bear L. After 1 mile, on sharp LH bend by a triangle of grass bear R 'Graveley'

13 At T-j (with B197) in Graveley at the end of Church Lane R then 1st L 'Great Wymondley. 5 ton weight limit'

14 *At T-j at the end of Graveley Lane R 'Great Wymondley' then at offset X-roads with Willian Road L 'Stevenage 3'*

15 *At roundabout SA on to Blakemere End Road 'Titmore Green' (this section may be busy). At T-j R 'St Ippollitts ¾, Preston 2¾, Whitwell 4¾' then 1st L 'Preston, Little Almshoe'*

16 *At X-roads with B656 SA 'Preston'*

17 *After 1¼ miles at top of hill, R 'Preston, Breachwood Green'. At the village green in Preston by the Red Lion PH take the 2nd L 'King's Walden, Breachwood Green'*

18 *Ignore 1st left at X-roads after 400 yards. Take next L 'Whitwell'*

19 *At indistinct fork bear R then at T-j with black and white house ahead L 'Bendish, Whitwell'*

20 *At fork at bottom of fast hill, by a pond, bear R (be prepared for this one!)*

page 33

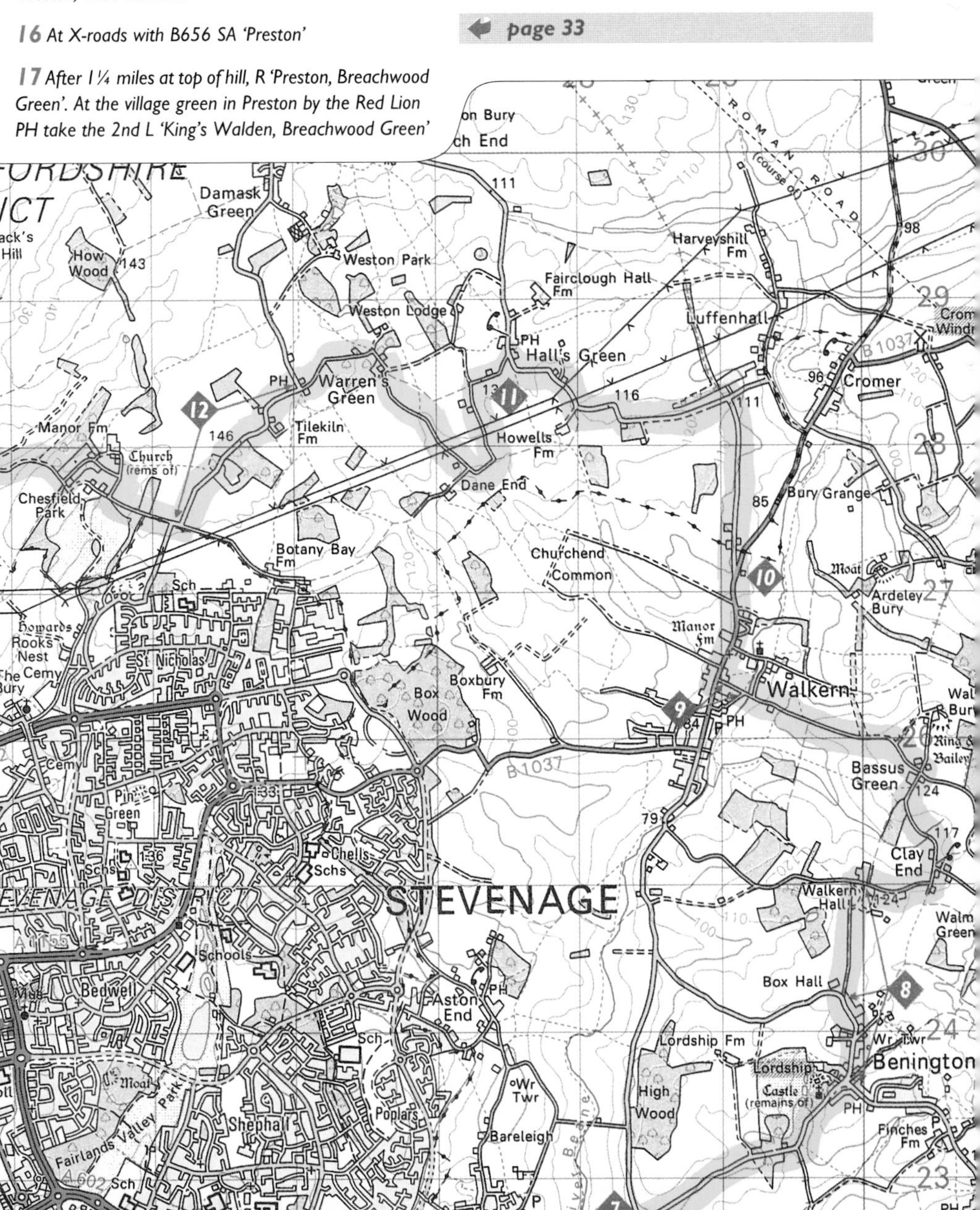

4 Northwest from Saffron Walden along the valley of the Cam to Barrington

Start

Cross Keys PH, near the traffic lights on the B184 Cambridge road, Saffron Walden, 18 miles southeast of Cambridge

P Long stay car park just off the B184 towards Cambridge

Distance and grade

33 miles
Easy / moderate

Terrain

240 feet climb west from Littlebury.
170 feet climb south from Haslingfield.
250 feet climb southeast from Fowlmere. Lowest point – 45 feet (14 mts) near to Haslingfield.
Highest point – 370 feet (112 mts) to the west of Littlebury

Nearest railway

Audley End Station to the west of Saffron Walden is just off the route

The course of the Icknield Way east from Royston represents the edge of the chalk and flint escarpment that runs from Dunstable to Newmarket and on to the coast. To the north and west of this lies the start of the lowlands that become the Fens further north. The River Cam or Rhee is crossed near Haslingfield at 45 feet above sea level, so the land to the north falls only 45 feet in the next 50 miles as the Cam joins the River Great Ouse and empties its waters into The Wash north of King's Lynn. The ride follows the string of villages along the River Cam or Granta to the north of Saffron Walden then crosses into the valley of the other main tributary of the Cam passing several fine pubs along the way. The cement works at Barrington strike an incongruous note in a ride along otherwise quiet lanes, through fine arable country. A steady climb south from Fowlmere takes you to over 300 feet before dropping down to the beautiful stately home at Audley End just to the west of the start.

40 41 38 39 Saffron Walden

Saffron Walden Littlebury Hinxton Whittlesford Newton Haslingfi

Places of interest

▼ *Pargeting on the old Sun Inn, Saffron Walden*

Saffron Walden 1

The town is dominated by the 193-feet spire of Essex's largest church. The Saffron crocus, grown for the yellow dye used to colour cloth and cakes, brought prosperity for 400 years. There are myriad 15th- and 16th-century buildings decorated with elaborate plasterwork known as 'pargeting'

Ickleton 5

The Normans made use of Roman tiles and columns when building the unusual parish church. There are strange beasts carved upon the pews and the churchyard wall

Duxford 10

The Imperial War Museum houses a superb collection of historic aircraft ranging from First World War fighters to the first Concorde ever flown

Docwra's Manor, Shepreth 15

Exotic plants spill out of raised beds, stone troughs and old sinks in 2 acres of inventive garden design

Fowlmere Nature Reserve 16

Oasis for resident warblers and kingfishers in an 85-acre fen reed bed with boardwalks and hides

Audley End 22

Mainly Georgian village with Jacobean almshouses. Audley End House was built in 1603 for the 1st Earl of Suffolk and has much fine decorative work by Adam. The classical grounds were landscaped by Capability Brown

Refreshments

Plenty of choice, Eight Bells PH, **Saffron Walden**
Ickleton Lion PH, **Ickleton**
Red Lion PH, **Hinxton**
Wheatsheaf PH, John
Barleycorn PH, **Duxford**
Bees in the Wall PH, **Whittlesford**
Queens Head PH, **Newton**
Royal Oak PH, **Barrington**
Chequers Inn PH, Swan Inn PH,
Queens Head PH, **Fowlmere**

Barrington Fowlmere Strethall

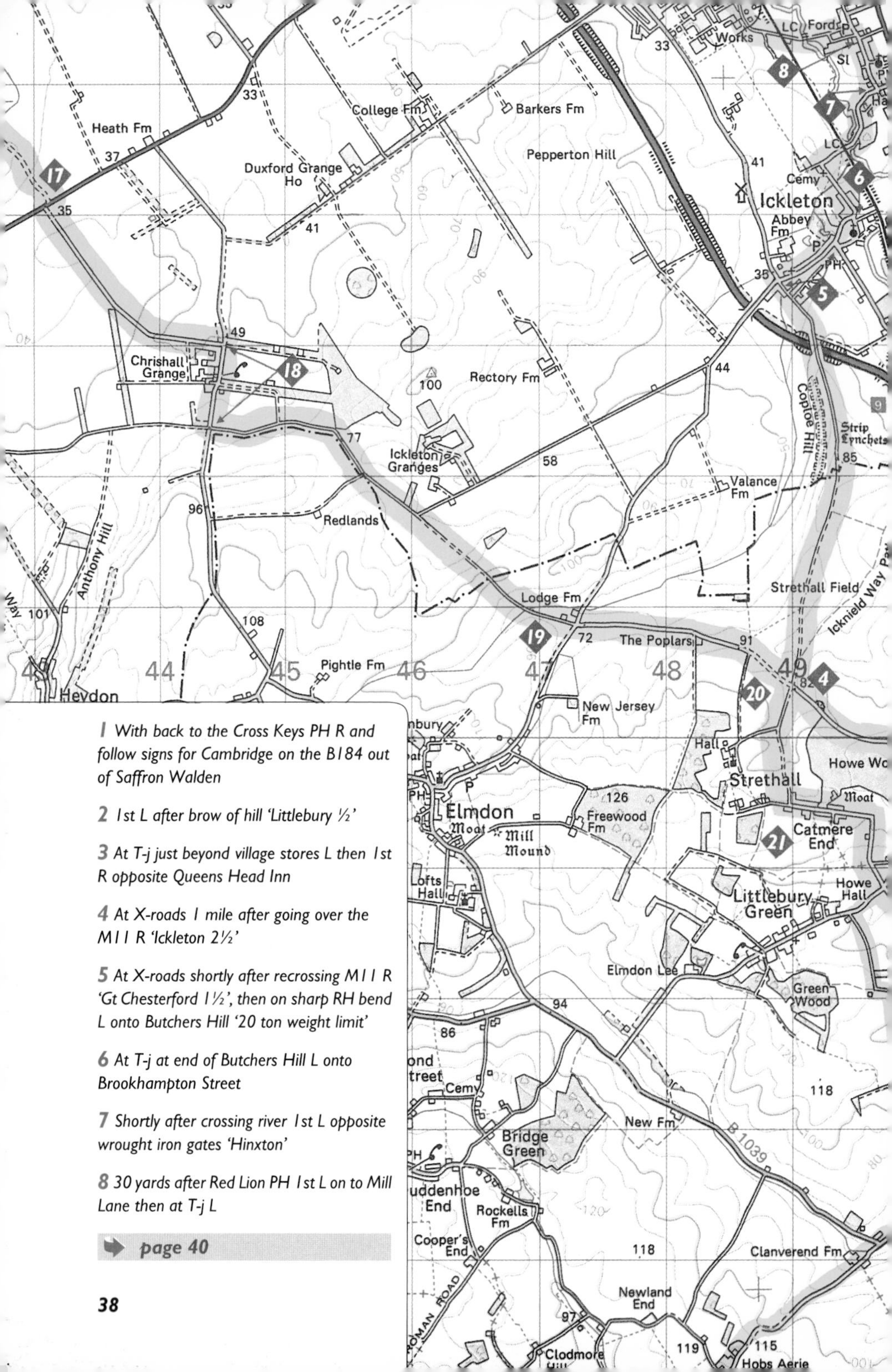

1 With back to the Cross Keys PH R and follow signs for Cambridge on the B184 out of Saffron Walden

2 1st L after brow of hill 'Littlebury ½'

3 At T-j just beyond village stores L then 1st R opposite Queens Head Inn

4 At X-roads 1 mile after going over the M11 R 'Ickleton 2½'

5 At X-roads shortly after recrossing M11 R 'Gt Chesterford 1½', then on sharp RH bend L onto Butchers Hill '20 ton weight limit'

6 At T-j at end of Butchers Hill L onto Brookhampton Street

7 Shortly after crossing river 1st L opposite wrought iron gates 'Hinxton'

8 30 yards after Red Lion PH 1st L on to Mill Lane then at T-j L

page 40

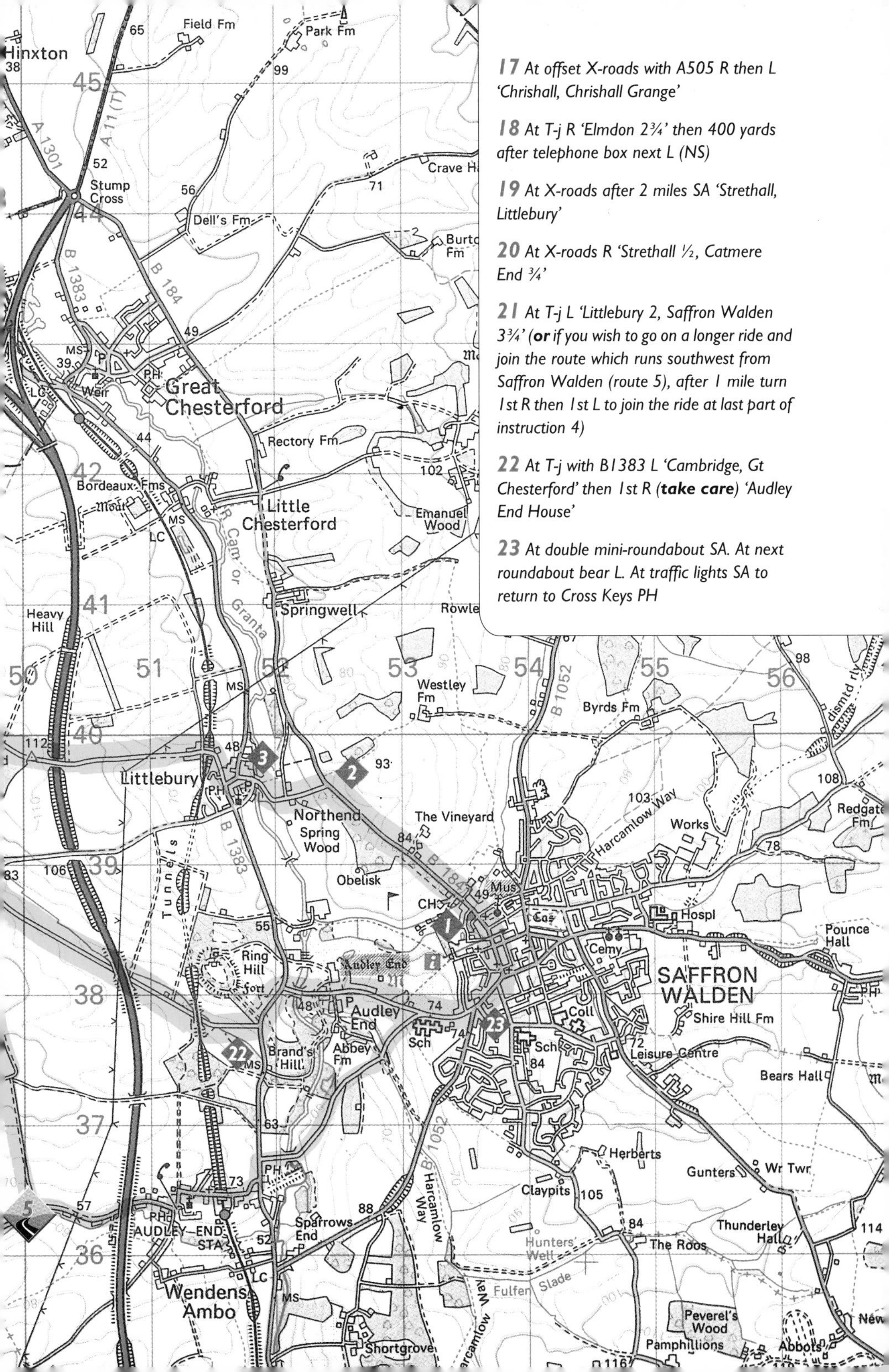

17 *At offset X-roads with A505 R then L 'Chrishall, Chrishall Grange'*

18 *At T-j R 'Elmdon 2¾' then 400 yards after telephone box next L (NS)*

19 *At X-roads after 2 miles SA 'Strethall, Littlebury'*

20 *At X-roads R 'Strethall ½, Catmere End ¾'*

21 *At T-j L 'Littlebury 2, Saffron Walden 3¾' (**or** if you wish to go on a longer ride and join the route which runs southwest from Saffron Walden (route 5), after 1 mile turn 1st R then 1st L to join the ride at last part of instruction 4)*

22 *At T-j with B1383 L 'Cambridge, Gt Chesterford' then 1st R (**take care**) 'Audley End House'*

23 *At double mini-roundabout SA. At next roundabout bear L. At traffic lights SA to return to Cross Keys PH*

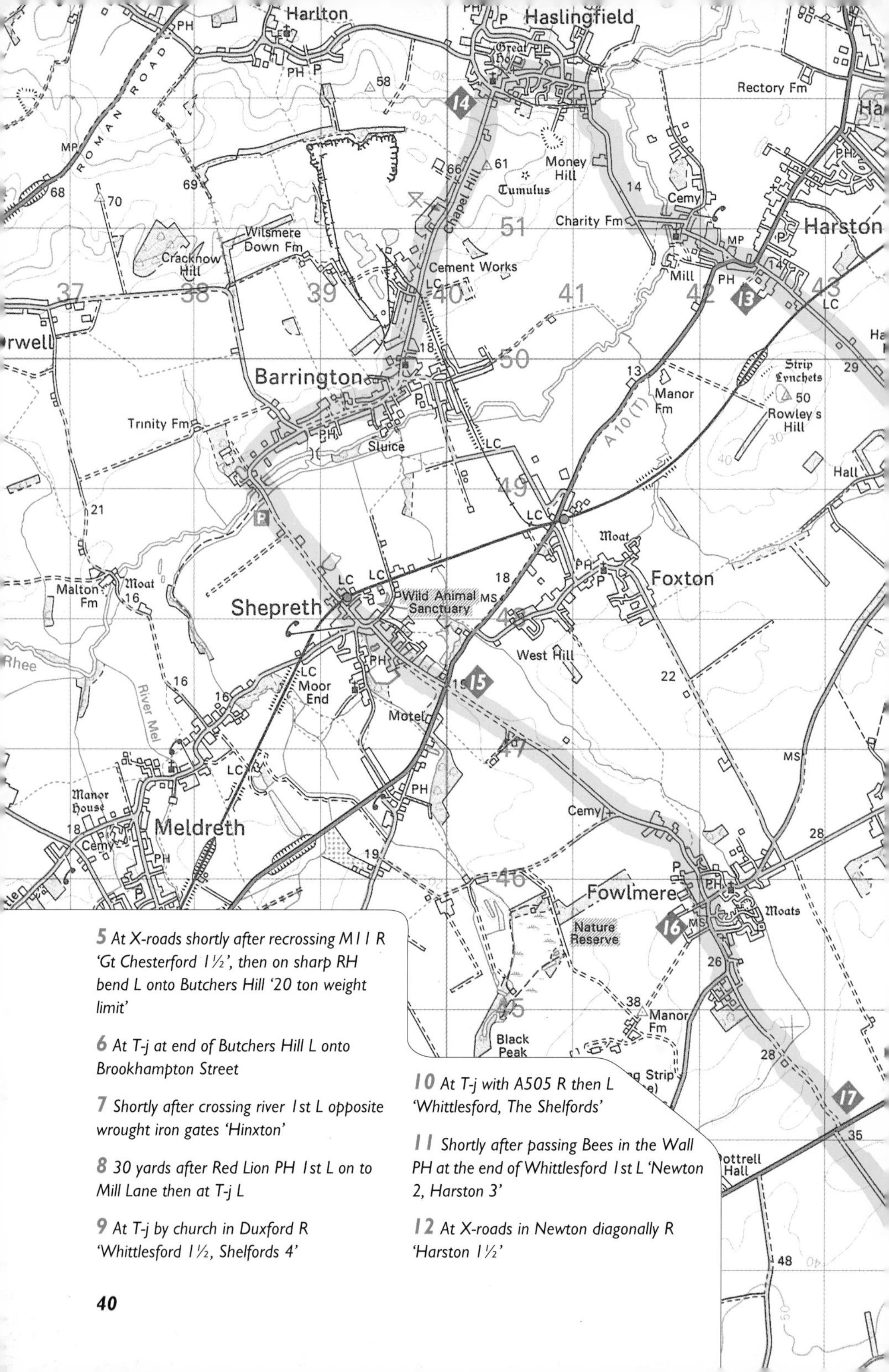

5 At X-roads shortly after recrossing M11 R 'Gt Chesterford 1½', then on sharp RH bend L onto Butchers Hill '20 ton weight limit'

6 At T-j at end of Butchers Hill L onto Brookhampton Street

7 Shortly after crossing river 1st L opposite wrought iron gates 'Hinxton'

8 30 yards after Red Lion PH 1st L on to Mill Lane then at T-j L

9 At T-j by church in Duxford R 'Whittlesford 1½, Shelfords 4'

10 At T-j with A505 R then L 'Whittlesford, The Shelfords'

11 Shortly after passing Bees in the Wall PH at the end of Whittlesford 1st L 'Newton 2, Harston 3'

12 At X-roads in Newton diagonally R 'Harston 1½'

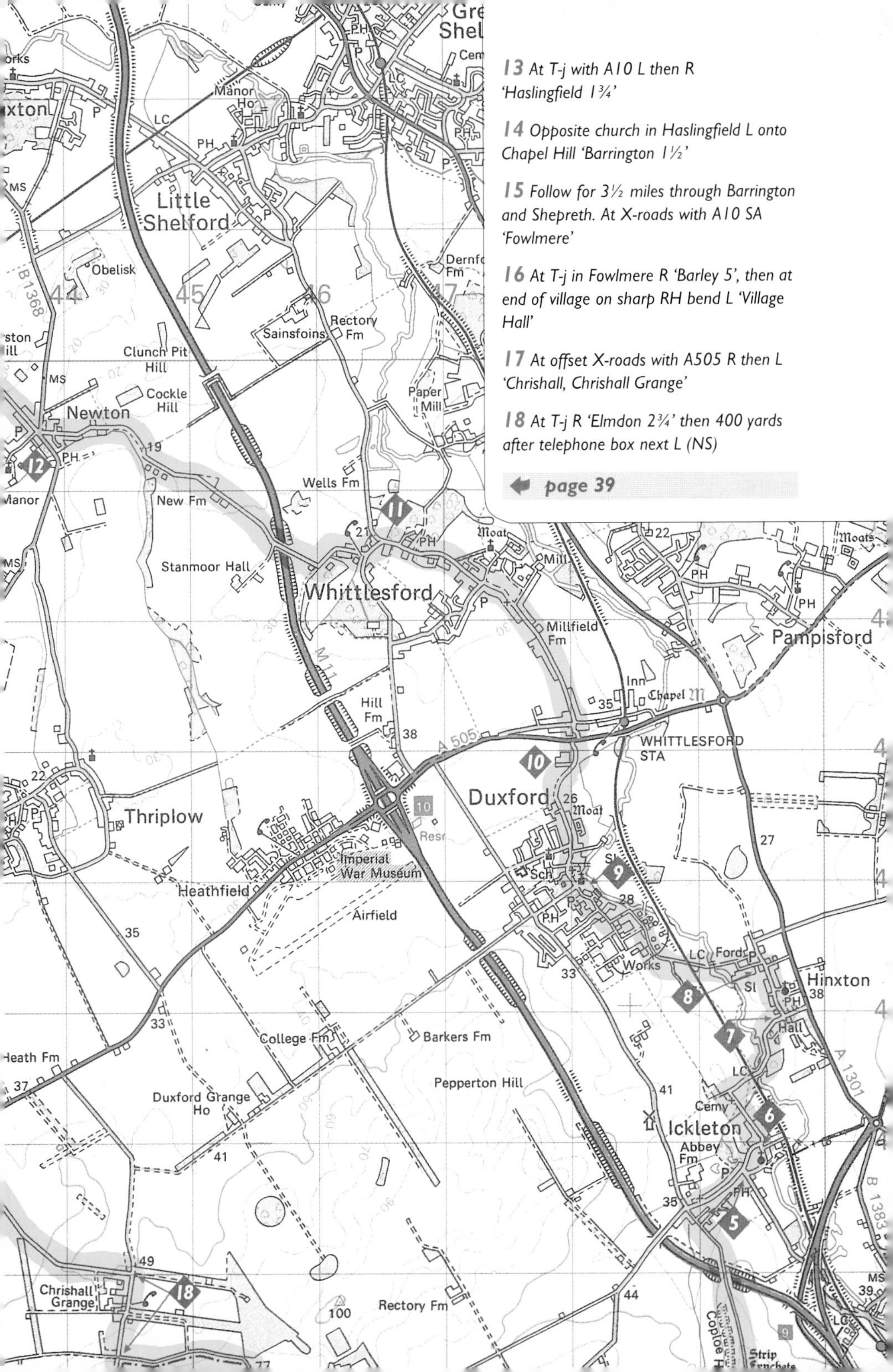

13 *At T-j with A10 L then R 'Haslingfield 1¾'*

14 *Opposite church in Haslingfield L onto Chapel Hill 'Barrington 1½'*

15 *Follow for 3½ miles through Barrington and Shepreth. At X-roads with A10 SA 'Fowlmere'*

16 *At T-j in Fowlmere R 'Barley 5', then at end of village on sharp RH bend L 'Village Hall'*

17 *At offset X-roads with A505 R then L 'Chrishall, Chrishall Grange'*

18 *At T-j R 'Elmdon 2¾' then 400 yards after telephone box next L (NS)*

page 39

5 *Southwest from Saffron Walden through pretty Essex villages of Arkesden, the Pelhams and Manuden*

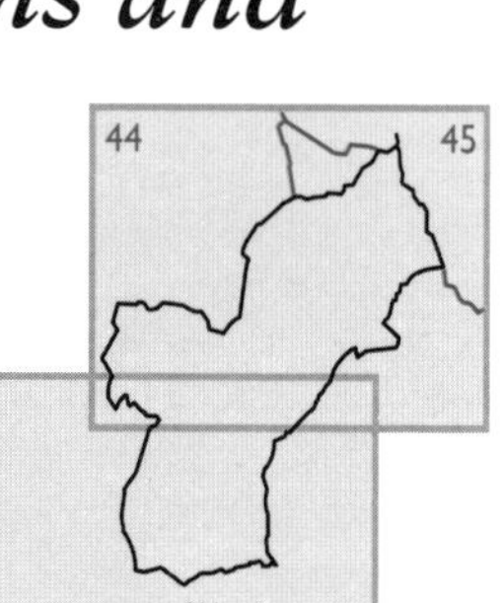

Exiting Saffron Walden to the southwest this ride soon reaches the lovely village of Arkesden, just the first in a string of attractive places along the way, most notably Clavering and Manuden, all of them boasting a sprinkling of thatched cottages and flint walls. Some tiny quiet lanes are used to link up these villages, most memorably from Further Ford End through the Pelhams to Manuden and Rickling. If on a mountain bike you may wish to try the sunken old lane that runs between Brent Pelham and Furneux Pelham. Otherwise you must be content with a short spell on the truly delightful (vehicle-free) lane that loops back on itself around Hartham Common south of Brent Pelham. After all these idyllic lanes the short section on the B183 comes as something of a shock but it is essentially downhill and you soon escape to the attractive village of Widdington before heading back to the start.

Start

Cross Keys PH, near the traffic lights on the B184 Cambridge road, Saffron Walden, 18 miles southeast of Cambridge

P Long stay car park just off the B184 towards Cambridge

Distance and grade

34 miles

Easy / moderate

Terrain

190 feet climb from Audley End towards Arkesden, several climbs of 100 feet. Lowest point – 165 feet (50 mts) near Audley End. Highest point – 430 feet (130 mts) near to Brent Pelham

Nearest railway

Audley End Station to the west of Saffron Walden is just off the route

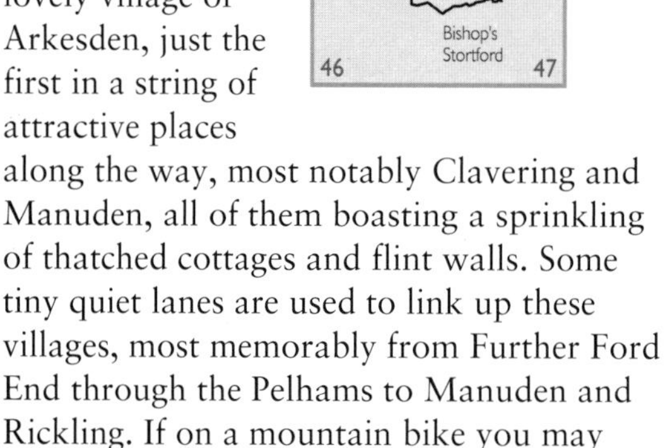

Places of interest

▲ *Thatchers at work in Arkesden*

Clavering *6*
A village of old cottages with moat encircling meadow where the Sherriff of Essex built a castle in 1052. One of Britain's smallest houses stands by the river

Brent Pelham *9*
The local hero is a certain Piers Shonks, famed for dragon-slaying, who was buried in the church walls. An inscription in the church reads:

'Shonks one serpent kills, t'other defies,
And in this wall as in a fortress lies'

Brent Pelham has medieval stocks and a whipping post

Furneux Pelham *(just off the route) 11*
The largest of the three Pelham villages once owned by the Norman family. The gloriously restored 15th-century church has windows by Morris and Burne-Jones. There is also a brewery and an adjacent pub, The Brewery Tap

Prior's Hall Barn, Widdington *19*
Splendid aisled barn built from unseasoned oak beams, little altered since the 14th century

Mole Hall *19*
Unusual mixture of animals from home and abroad, including wallabies, chimpanzees and otters. Wildfowl nest in the moat of the 13th-century manor house and there is a butterfly pavilion

Refreshments

*Plenty of choice, Eight Bells PH, **Saffron Walden***
*Axe and Compasses PH, **Arkesden***
*The Cricketers Inn PH, Fox and Hounds PH, **Clavering***
*Black Horse PH, **Brent Pelham***
*The Cock PH, **Stocking Pelham***
*Brewery Tap PH, **Furneux Pelham,** (just off the route)*
*Catherine Wheel PH, **Gravesend***
*Three Horseshoes PH, Yew Tree PH, **Manuden***
*Cricketers Arms PH, **Rickling Green***
*Fleur de Lys PH, **Widdington***

Level's Green
Manuden
Quendon
Widdington
Debden Manor

1 With back to the Cross Keys PH L. At traffic lights SA up hill. At mini-roundabout SA. At next double mini-roundabout SA 'Audley End'

2 Just past the school on the left 1st L 'Wenden'

3 At T-j with B1383 L 'Newport, Bishop's Stortford' then 1st R on B1039 'Wendens Ambo, Royston 11'

4 At mini-roundabout SA over railway bridge then underneath motorway. ¾ mile after going under M11, on sharp RH bend, next L 'Arkesden 1½'

5 At T-j by triangle of grass in Arkesden L 'Wicken Bonhunt, Clavering, Newport'

6 Follow signs for Clavering. At T-j with B1308 R 'Clavering ¾, Buntingford 9' then 2nd R in Clavering after the Fox and Hounds PH 'Ford'

7 Ignore two turnings to the right. 2 miles out of Clavering 1st proper L 'Further Ford End. Unsuitable for motors'

8 At T-j by triangle of grass L 'Meesden, Brent Pelham'

9 At church and junction with B1038 bear L 'Newport' then 1st R 'Ford. Unsuitable for motors'

*10 After ¾ mile 1st L sharply back on yourself (**or** if you have a mountain bike you could go straight ahead and rejoin the route further south). At T-j R (NS)*

11 At T-j in Stocking Pelham by The Cock PH R 'Furneux Pelham, Albury, Little Hadham'

➡ **page 46**

16 At T-j in Rickling Green L then 1st R 'Quendon ¼, Newport 3, Saffron Walden 6¼'

17 At T-j with B1383 L 'Newport, Saffron Walden'. Busy road

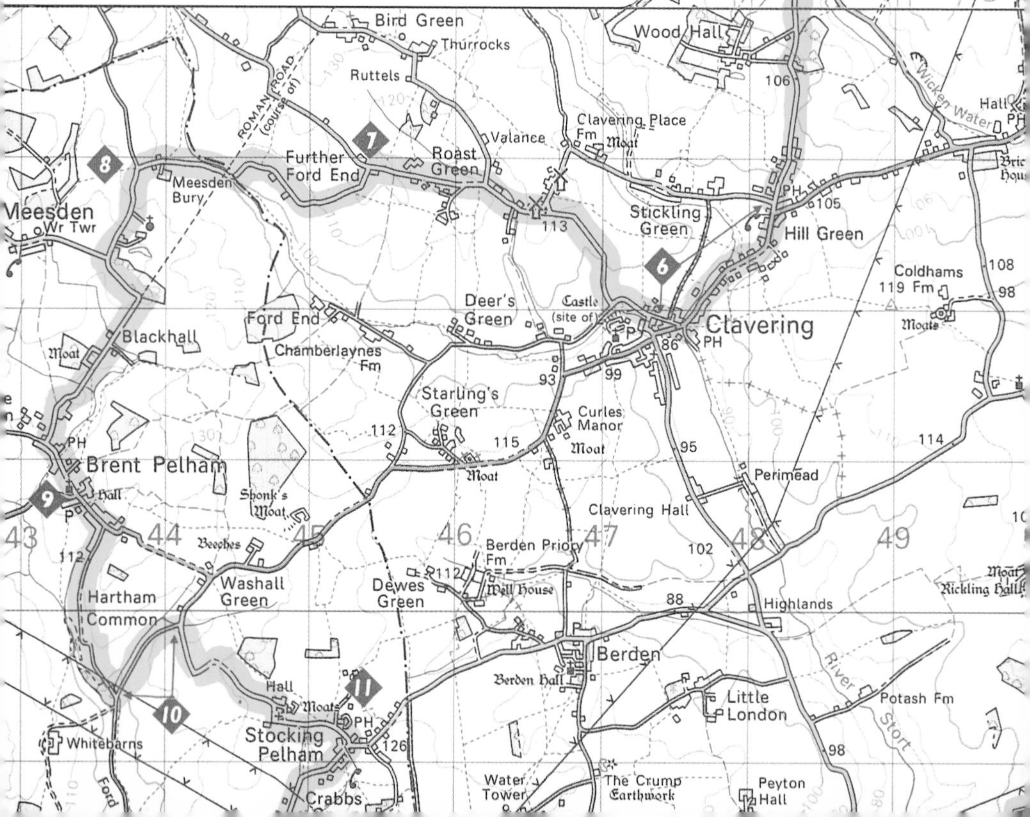

18 Immediately after going over motorway 1st R 'Henham 3, Elsenham 3' then 1st L 'Widdington'

19 ½ mile after Fleur de Lys PH in Widdington 1st R (NS)

20 At T-j R 'Debden 1'

*21 1st L at X-roads 'Saffron Walden' (**or** turn right 'Debden' for a longer ride, linking with route 6 at instruction 3)*

22 At roundabout at end of Debden Road, R downhill and at traffic lights SA to return to the start

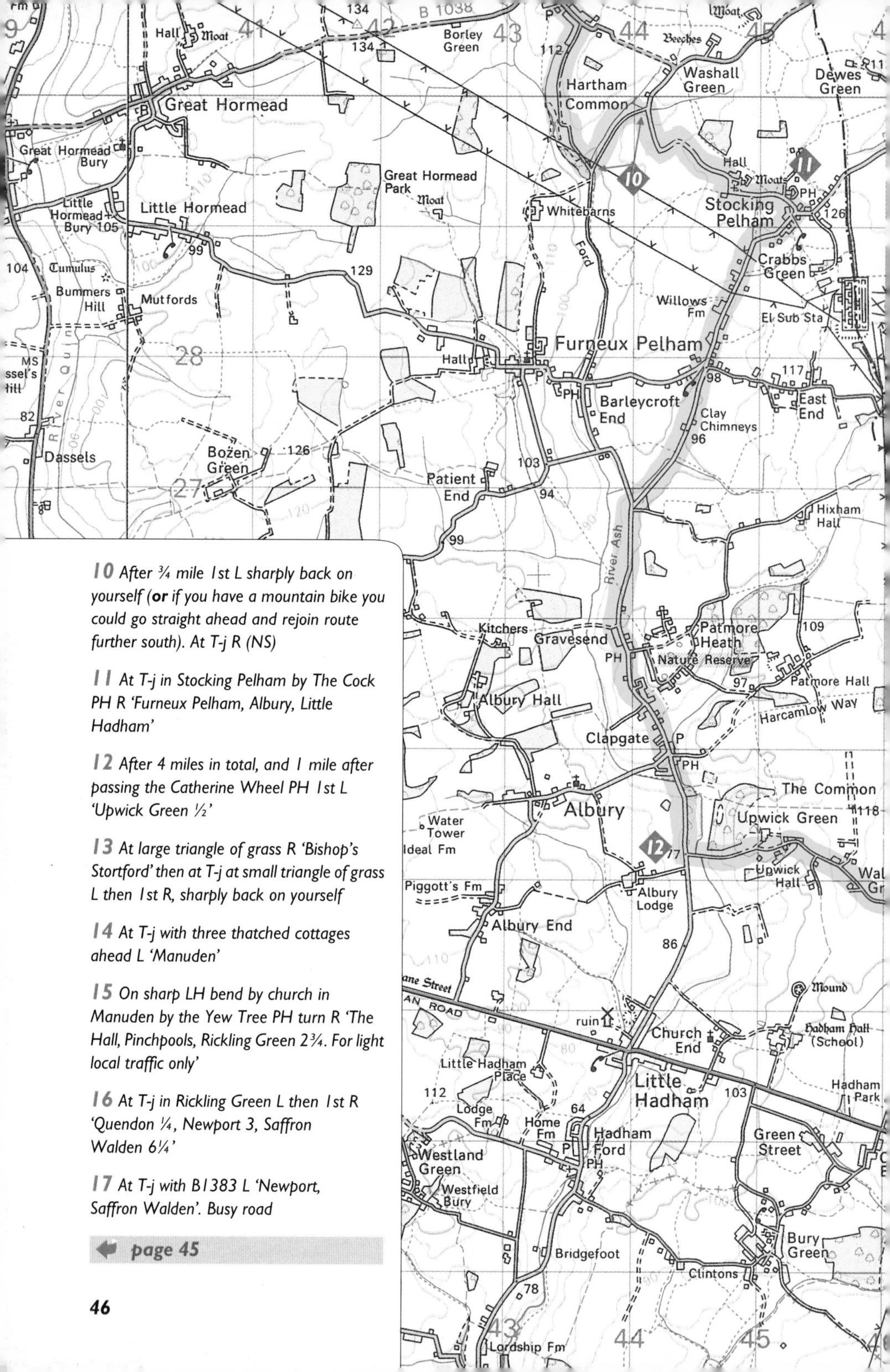

__10__ After ¾ mile 1st L sharply back on yourself (__or__ if you have a mountain bike you could go straight ahead and rejoin route further south). At T-j R (NS)

__11__ At T-j in Stocking Pelham by The Cock PH R 'Furneux Pelham, Albury, Little Hadham'

__12__ After 4 miles in total, and 1 mile after passing the Catherine Wheel PH 1st L 'Upwick Green ½'

__13__ At large triangle of grass R 'Bishop's Stortford' then at T-j at small triangle of grass L then 1st R, sharply back on yourself

__14__ At T-j with three thatched cottages ahead L 'Manuden'

__15__ On sharp LH bend by church in Manuden by the Yew Tree PH turn R 'The Hall, Pinchpools, Rickling Green 2¾. For light local traffic only'

__16__ At T-j in Rickling Green L then 1st R 'Quendon ¼, Newport 3, Saffron Walden 6¼'

__17__ At T-j with B1383 L 'Newport, Saffron Walden'. Busy road

page 45

Quendon
Rickling Hall
Rickling Green
Quendon Wood
Berden Priory Fm
Wall House
Highlands
Berden
Berden Hall
Little London
Potash Fm
River Stort
Harcamlow Way
Broom Wood
Water Tower
The Crump Earthwork
Peyton Hall
Ugley
Park Green
Brick House End
Battle's Wood
Parsonage Fm
Wades Hall
Fieldgate
Gravel Pit
Maggots End
Pinchpools
Bollington Hall
Quaremead
Ugley Green
Mount Pleasant
Orford Ho
Mallows Green
The Hall
Manuden Ho
Manuden
Strip Lynchets
Alsa Lodge
Alsa Wood
Uppend
Parsonage Fm
Norman Ho
Bentfield Bury
Bentfield Green
Stansted Ho
Farnham Green
Lincolns
Hole Fm
Hall
Chatter End
Hassobury (School)
STANSTED MOUNTFITCHET
Castle
Farnham
Moat
Hazel End
Level's Green
Stansted Hall
Bailey Hills
Forest Hall
Parsonage Fm
Bourne Brook
Wickham Hall
Foxdells Fm
Birchanger
Bury Lodge
Duck End
Hall Fm
Water Tower
Whitehall
Blacklands
Hotel
Cradle End
Start Hill
BISHOP'S STORTFORD
Tilekiln Green
Hockerill
Harps Fm
Bedlar's

6 East from Saffron Walden through Thaxted, Finchingfield and the Bumpsteads

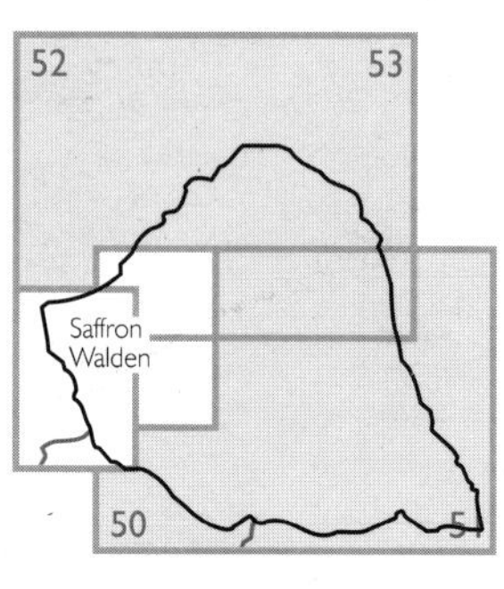

Three climbs south from Saffron Walden, one either side of the curiously named stream 'Fulfen Slade' and one from the crossroads north of Debden take you to the attractive village of Thaxted with its very fine Guildhall. The ride heads west to two further pretty Essex villages – Great Bardfield and Finchingfield. The section on tiny lanes between the two villages is one of the highlights of the ride. The route turns north to Helions Bumpstead and Castle Camps before heading for home through Castle Camps and Ashdon. This ride could easily be linked with the ride starting in Thaxted (route 7).

Start

Cross Keys PH, near the traffic lights on the B184 Cambridge road, Saffron Walden, 18 miles southeast of Cambridge

P Long stay car park just off the B184 towards Cambridge

Distance and grade

32 miles

Easy / moderate

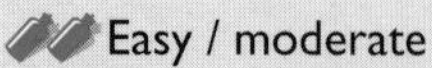

Terrain

190 feet climb from Audley End to Arkesden, 160 feet climb southwest from Ashdon. Several shorter climbs. Lowest point – 165 feet (50 mts) at Audley End. Highest point – 400 feet (123 mts) at Castle Camps

Nearest railway

Audley End Station to the west of Saffron Walden is just off the route

Saffron Walden — Debden — Cutlers Green — Thaxted — Great Bardfield

Places of interest

▼ *Thaxted Guildhall*

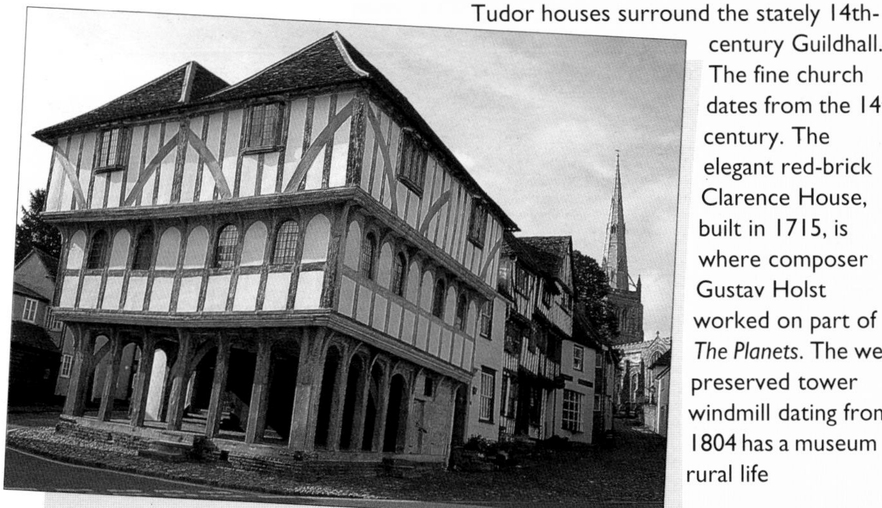

Thaxted *3*
Tudor houses surround the stately 14th-century Guildhall. The fine church dates from the 14th century. The elegant red-brick Clarence House, built in 1715, is where composer Gustav Holst worked on part of *The Planets*. The well-preserved tower windmill dating from 1804 has a museum of rural life

Great Bardfield *5*
One of three Bardfield villages huddled by the River Pant, with medieval and Georgian houses, restored windmill, mainly 14th-century church, cottage museum and village lock-up

Finchingfield *8*
Jumble of medieval cottages and Georgian houses around the village green

Refreshments

White Hart PH, Plough PH, ***Debden***
Plenty of choice Swan PH, Star PH, ***Thaxted***
The Bell PH, The Vine PH, ***Great Bardfield***
Red Lion PH, Finchingfield Inn PH, Fox PH, ***Finchingfield***
Three Horseshoes PH, ***Helions Bumpstead***
Rose and Crown PH, ***Ashdon***

Hempstead Wood
Helions Bumpstead
Castle Camps
Ashdon

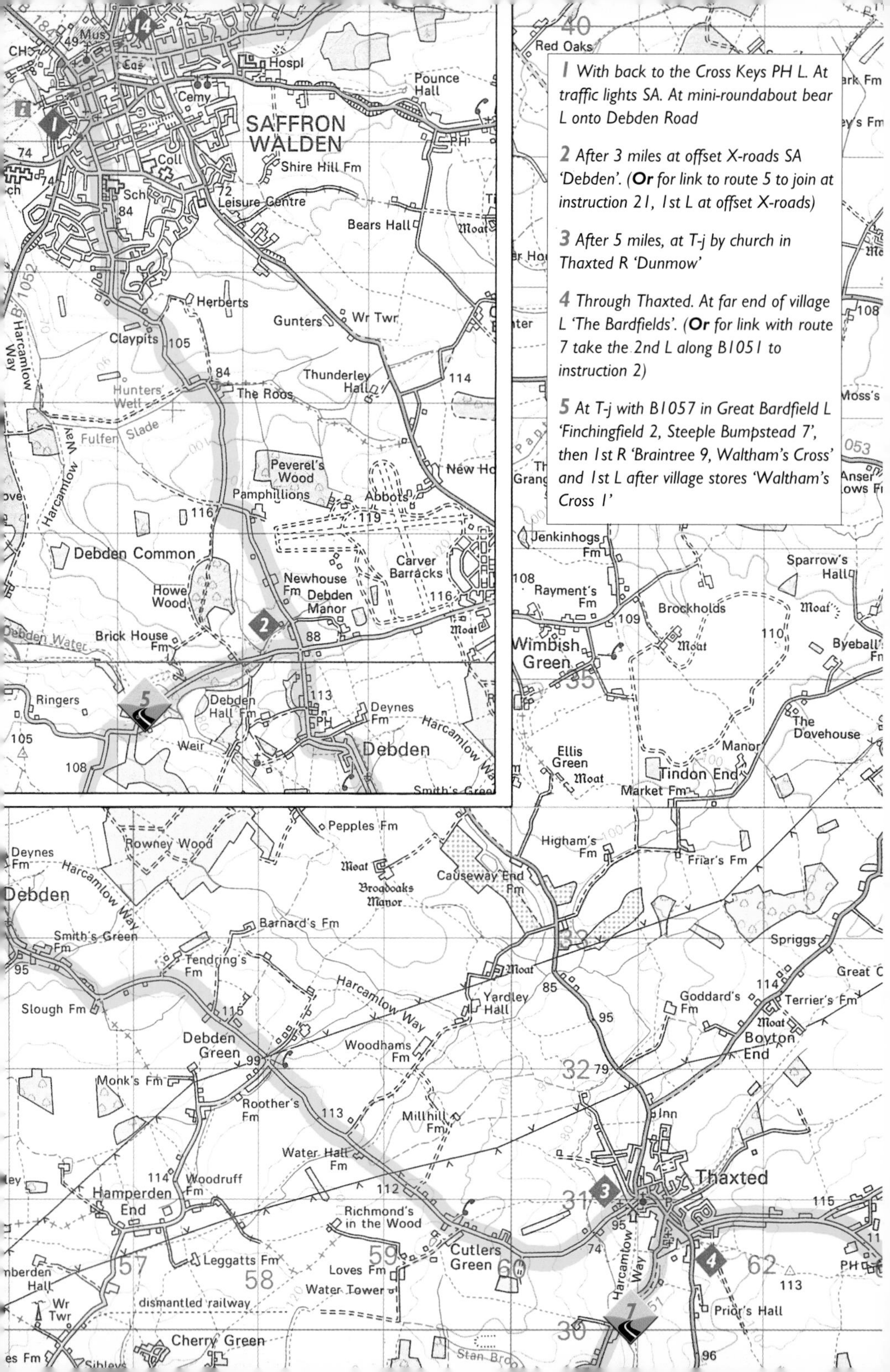

1 With back to the Cross Keys PH L. At traffic lights SA. At mini-roundabout bear L onto Debden Road
2 After 3 miles at offset X-roads SA 'Debden'. (Or for link to route 5 to join at instruction 21, 1st L at offset X-roads)
3 After 5 miles, at T-j by church in Thaxted R 'Dunmow'
4 Through Thaxted. At far end of village L 'The Bardfields'. (Or for link with route 7 take the 2nd L along B1051 to instruction 2)
5 At T-j with B1057 in Great Bardfield L 'Finchingfield 2, Steeple Bumpstead 7', then 1st R 'Braintree 9, Waltham's Cross' and 1st L after village stores 'Waltham's Cross 1'
SAFFRON WALDEN
Hospl
Pounce Hall
Cemy
Coll
Shire Hill Fm
Leisure Centre
Bears Hall
Herberts
Gunters
Wr Twr
Claypits
Hunters' Well
The Roos
Thunderley Hall
Fulfen Slade
Harcamlow Way
Peverel's Wood
Pamphillions
Abbots
New Ho
Debden Common
Carver Barracks
Howe Wood
Newhouse Fm
Debden Manor
Brick House Fm
Debden Water
Ringers
Debden Hall Fm
Weir
Deynes Fm
Debden
Smith's Green
Red Oaks
Jenkinhogs Fm
Rayment's Fm
Wimbish Green
Brockholds
Sparrow's Hall
Byeball's Fm
The Dovehouse
Ellis Green
Tindon End
Manor
Market Fm
Higham's Fm
Friar's Fm
Pepples Fm
Rowney Wood
Broadoaks Manor
Causeway End Fm
Barnard's Fm
Tendring's Fm
Spriggs
Yardley Hall
Goddard's Fm
Terrier's Fm
Boyton End
Slough Fm
Debden Green
Woodhams Fm
Monk's Fm
Roother's Fm
Millhill Fm
Inn
Water Hall Fm
Thaxted
Woodruff Fm
Hamperden End
Richmond's in the Wood
Cutlers Green
Leggatts Fm
Loves Fm
Water Tower
Prior's Hall
dismantled railway
Cherry Green

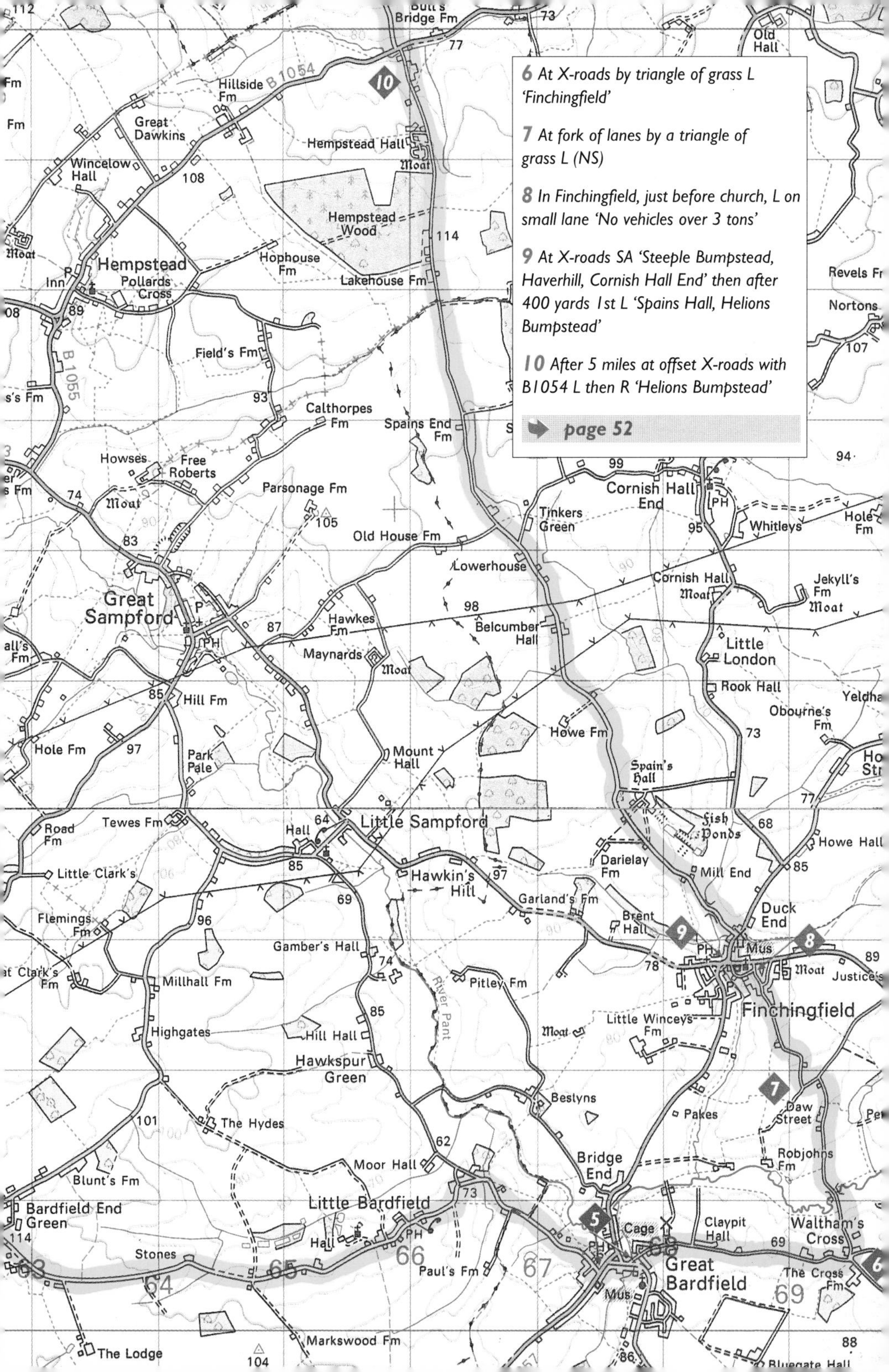

6 At X-roads by triangle of grass L 'Finchingfield'
7 At fork of lanes by a triangle of grass L (NS)
8 In Finchingfield, just before church, L on small lane 'No vehicles over 3 tons'
9 At X-roads SA 'Steeple Bumpstead, Haverhill, Cornish Hall End' then after 400 yards 1st L 'Spains Hall, Helions Bumpstead'
10 After 5 miles at offset X-roads with B1054 L then R 'Helions Bumpstead'
page 52
Bull's Bridge Fm
Old Hall
B 1054
Hillside Fm
Great Dawkins
Wincelow Hall
Hempstead Hall
Moat
Hempstead Wood
Hempstead
Inn
Pollards Cross
Hophouse Fm
Lakehouse Fm
Field's Fm
B 1055
Calthorpes Fm
Spains End Fm
Howses
Free Roberts
Parsonage Fm
Old House Fm
Revels Fm
Nortons
Cornish Hall End
Tinkers Green
Whitleys
Hole Fm
Lowerhouse
Cornish Hall
Jekyll's Fm
Great Sampford
Hawkes Fm
Belcumber Hall
Maynards
Little London
Rook Hall
Hill Fm
Obourne's Fm
Howe Fm
Hole Fm
Park Pale
Mount Hall
Spain's Hall
Road Fm
Tewes Fm
Little Sampford
Fish Ponds
Howe Hall
Little Clark's
Hawkin's Hill
Darielay Fm
Mill End
Flemings Fm
Garland's Fm
Brent Hall
Duck End
Gamber's Hall
Mus
Justice's
Millhall Fm
Pitley Fm
River Pant
Finchingfield
Highgates
Hill Hall
Little Winceys Fm
Hawkspur Green
Beslyns
Daw Street
The Hydes
Pakes
Moor Hall
Robjohns Fm
Blunt's Fm
Bridge End
Bardfield End Green
Little Bardfield
Claypit Hall
Waltham's Cross
Cage
Stones
Hall
Paul's Fm
Great Bardfield
The Cross Fm
Markswood Fm
The Lodge
Bluegate Hall

10 *After 5 miles at offset X-roads with B1054 L then R 'Helions Bumpstead'*

11 *Through X-roads in Helions Bumpstead following signs for Camps and Bartlow*

12 *Through Castle Camps following signs for Bartlow and Linton. 2 miles after Castle Camps, with two left turns in quick succession, turn L on the second of these 'Ashdon 1½'*

13 *At T-j in Ashdon L 'Saffron Walden, Radwinter'*

14 *After 3½ miles, back in Saffron Walden, at mini-roundabout SA on to Church Street. At T-j at end of Church Street L to return to the start*

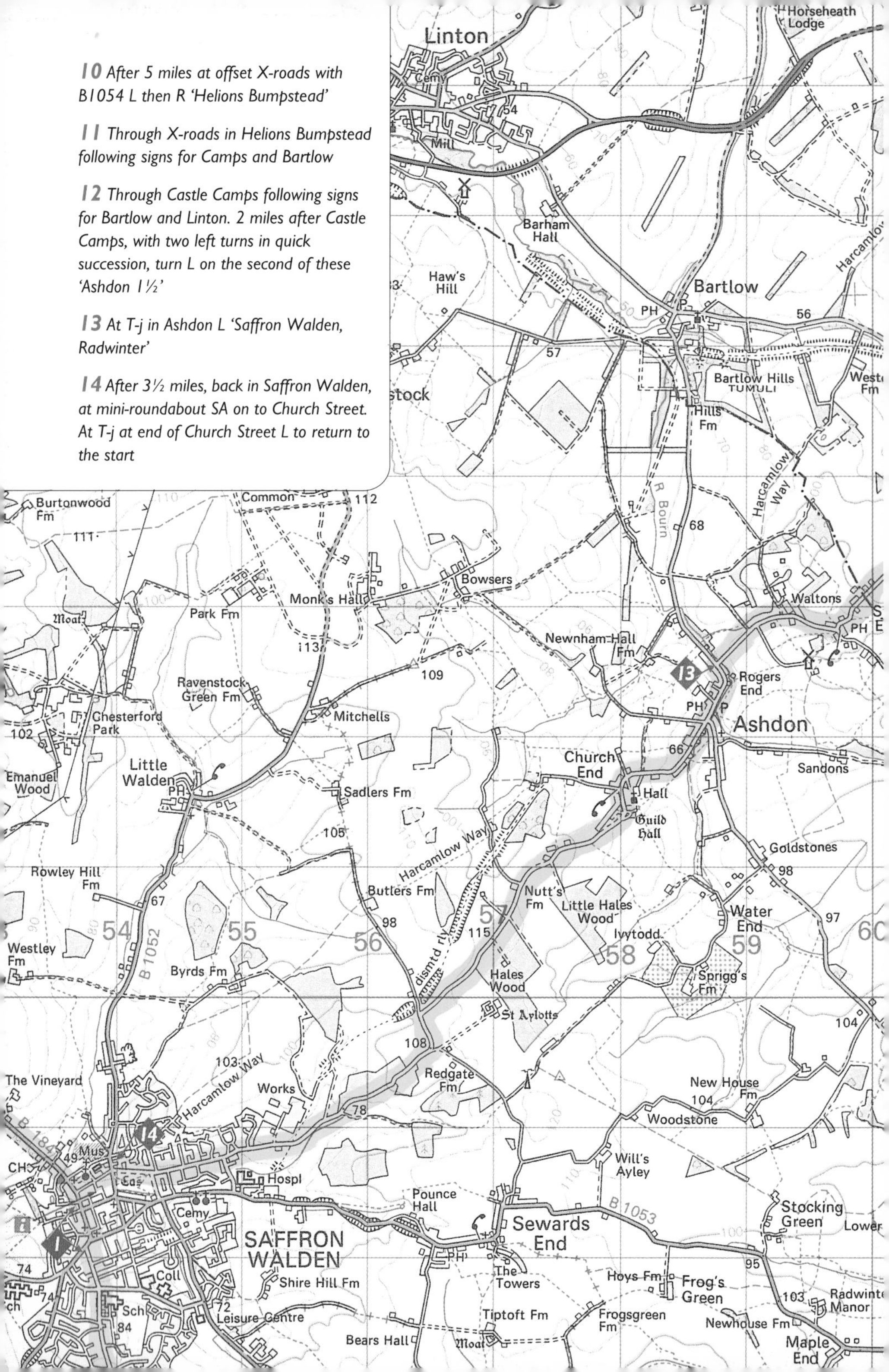

Horseheath
Horseheath Park
Silver Street Fm
Hall Fm
Norney Plantn
Howe Wood
Manor Fm
Inn
A 604
Cardinal's Green
Hanchet End
Hanchet Hall
Moat
Shardelow's Fm
dismtd rly
Barsey Fm
Mill Green
Wr Twr
Tumulus
Hazel Stub
Sch
Cemy
Shudy Camps Park
Shudy Camps
Nosterfield End
Industrial Estate
Haverhill Hall
Moon Hall
Horseham Hall
Copy Fm
Castle Camps
Whitensmere Fm
Camps Hall
Steveton End
Moat Fm
Langley Wood
Castle Fm
Draper's Fm
Motte & Bailey
Wiggens Green
Pale Green
Camps End
Cooper's Fm
Helions Bumpstead
Browning's Fm
Helions
Bumpstead Hall
Winsey Fm
Little Biggin Common
Olmstead Green
Olmstead Hall
Bourne Fm
Great Bendysh Wood
Boblow
Smith's Green
Bull's Bridge Fm
Red Oaks Hill
Swan's Fm
Little Bendysh Wood
Radwinter End
Park Fm
Hillside Fm
B 1054
Godfrey's Fm
Great Dawkins
Bendysh Hall
Hempstead Hall
Wincelow Hall
Hempstead Wood
Cowlass Hall
Hophouse Fm
Hempstead
Pollards Cross
Lakehouse Fm
Selland's Fm
Radwinter
Field's Fm

7 *South from Thaxted through the heart of Essex*

Thaxted is one of Essex's most attractive villages with a large square boasting the very fine half-timbered Guildhall. The ride heads south along the valley of the River Chelmer from which Chelmsford derives its name. Great Dunmow is the one town encountered en route and could easily be used as an alternative starting point. The straight roads leading to and from the town give an indication of the Roman settlements that abounded in this area north of London. Fine pubs are passed at High Easter and Pleshey before the route turns north through Felsted, Little Dunmow and Stebbing on its way back to a well-earned tea stop in Thaxted. This ride could easily be linked to route 6 which starts from Saffron Walden and passes through Thaxted.

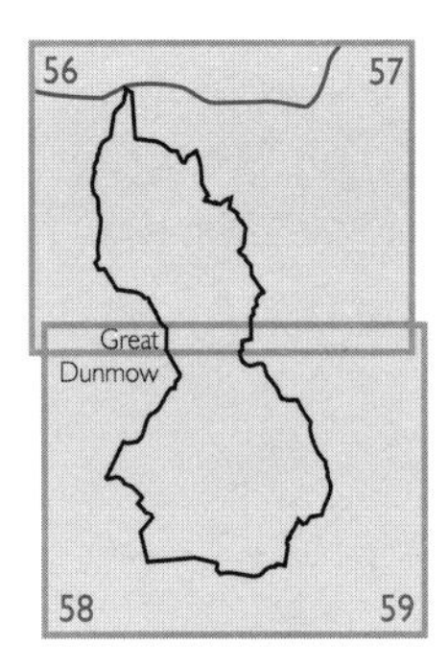

Start

The Guildhall, Thaxted, 10 miles northeast of Bishop's Stortford

P Long stay car park on Town Street at the bottom of the square in Thaxted

Distance and grade

33 miles

Easy

Terrain

No real hills. Lowest point – 130 feet (39 mts) the River Chelmer south of Felsted. Highest point – 340 feet (102 mts) northwest of Lindsell

Nearest railway

Braintree, 7 miles east of the route at Stebbing

Thaxted
Little Easton
Great Dunmow
High Easter

Places of interest

Little Dunmow *(just off the route) 5*
The Dunmow Flitch trial is held here every four years to find a man and his wife who have not had a domestic brawl or wished to be unmarried for 12 months and a day. A flitch of bacon is presented to the couple able to prove this enviable state of affairs! The records of the awarding of the flitch in the 18th century are hung on the church walls

The Rodings *9*
Eight villages and hamlets bear the name: Abbess, Aythorpe, Beauchamp, Berners, High, Leaden, Margaret and White Roding

Pleshey *13*
Ancient Britons settled the site, hacking out a 40-acre enclosure; the Romans displaced them and added their own entrenchments; and the Saxons called it Tumblestoun from the ancient mounds that were left. The Normans in turn took over: today, the village, encircled by the massive Norman earthworks which formed their castle bailey, is most picturesque. A short walk to the castle mound over the amazing 15th-century, single-span, brick bridge is rewarded with fine views

Stebbing *17*
Well-preserved buildings date from the Middle Ages and a handsome 18th-century water mill straddles the brook. The Great Mount earthwork is the site of a castle built by Richard De Vark in 1086. The moated Porter's Hall on Stebbing Green is an early 17th-century farmhouse

Refreshments

Plenty of choice, Swan PH, Star PH, ***Thaxted***
The Stag PH, ***Little Easton***
Green Man PH, ***Great Easton,*** *(just off the route)*
Plenty of choice in ***Great Dunmow***
Cock and Bell Inn PH, ***High Easter***
The White Horse PH, The Leather Bottle PH, ***Pleshey***
The Swan Hotel PH, ***Felsted***
Flitch of Bacon PH, ***Little Dunmow,*** *(just off the route)*
Red Lion PH, Kings Head PH, White Hart PH, ***Stebbing***

Pleshey Felsted Stebbing Lindsell

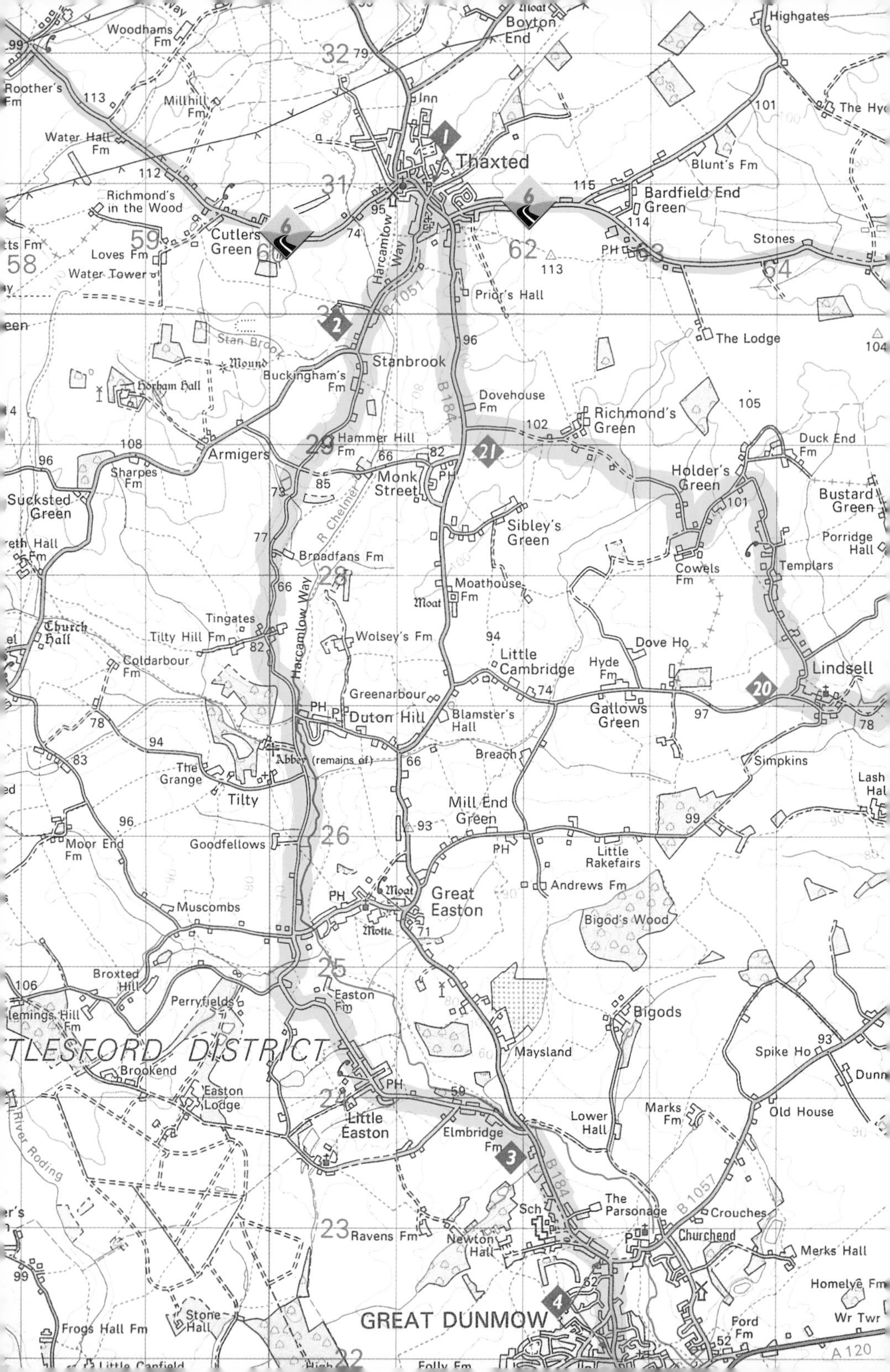

Woodhams Fm
Boyton End
Highgates
Roother's Fm
Millhill Fm
Inn
Water Hall Fm
Thaxted
Blunt's Fm
Richmond's in the Wood
Bardfield End Green
Cutlers Green
Loves Fm
Water Tower
Stones
Prior's Hall
The Lodge
Stan Brook
Stanbrook
Mound
Buckingham's Fm
Horham Hall
Dovehouse Fm
Richmond's Green
Hammer Hill Fm
Armigers
Duck End Fm
Monk Street
Holder's Green
Sharpes Fm
Sucksted Green
Bustard Green
Sibley's Green
R Chelmer
Porridge Hall
Broadfans Fm
Cowels Fm
Templars
Moathouse Fm
Moat
Tingates
Tilty Hill Fm
Church Hall
Wolsey's Fm
Dove Ho
Little Cambridge
Hyde Fm
Lindsell
Coldarbour Fm
Greenarbour
Duton Hill
Blamster's Hall
Gallows Green
Abbey (remains of)
Breach
Simpkins
The Grange
Tilty
Mill End Green
Lash Hall
Goodfellows
Moor End Fm
Little Rakefairs
Andrews Fm
Great Easton
Muscombs
Motte
Bigod's Wood
Broxted Hill
Perryfields
Easton Fm
Flemings Hill Fm
Bigods
UTTLESFORD DISTRICT
Maysland
Spike Ho
Brookend
Easton Lodge
Lower Hall
Marks Fm
Old House
Little Easton
Elmbridge Fm
River Roding
The Parsonage
Crouches
Sch
Churchend
Ravens Fm
Newton Hall
Merks Hall
Homelye Fm
Stone Hall
Frogs Hall Fm
GREAT DUNMOW
Wr Twr
Ford Fm
Little Canfield
Folly Fm
Harcamlow Way
B 1051
B 184
B 1057
A 120

1 *With back to the Guildhall in Thaxted go down through the square on the B184 towards Great Dunmow, then 1st R at the end of the square on to Park Street (B1051) 'Broxted 3, Elsenham 6'*

2 *After 1 mile, on sharp RH bend L by triangle of grass 'Duton Hill 2, The Eastons 3'*

3 *Follow signs for Dunmow for 4½ miles. At T-j with B184 R 'Dunmow 1'*

4 *At mini-roundabout SA 'Town Centre'. At T-j by Saracens Head Hotel L 'Chelmsford (A130)'*

➡ **page 59**

16 *At T-j with A120 R 'Chelmsford' then 1st L 'Stebbing 1'. Very busy section.* **Take care**

17 *After 1 mile 1st L in Stebbing by memorial cross 'Lindsell, Great Bardfield, Stebbing Village'*

18 *At T-j with B1507 R 'Lindsell 2¼, Great Bardfield 4¼'*

19 *After 1½ miles, 1st L 'Lindsell'*

20 *At the end of buildings in Lindsell 1st R by triangle of grass 'Thaxted'*

21 *At T-j with B184 R 'Saffron Walden'. (***Or** *for link with route 6 1st R after Prior's Hall to join at instruction 4)*

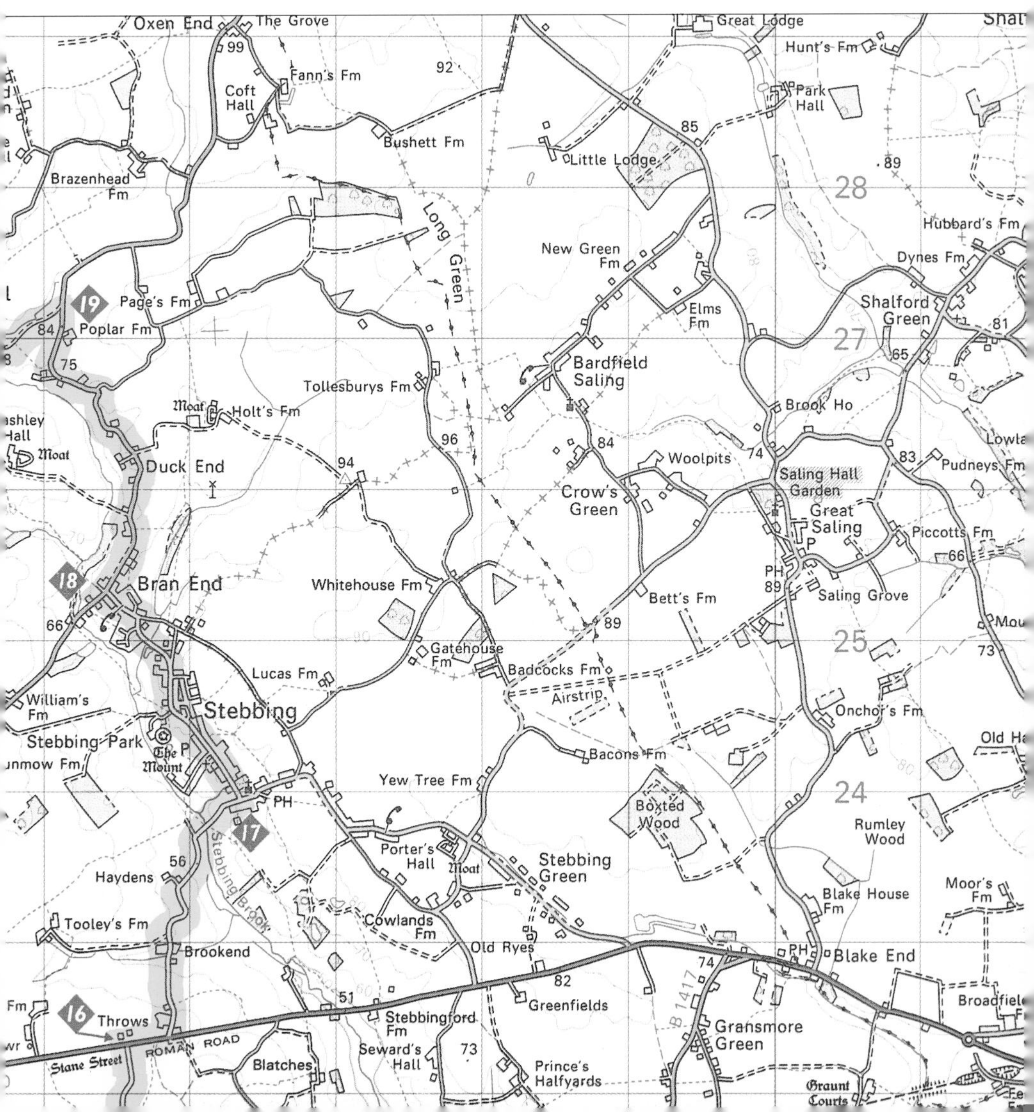

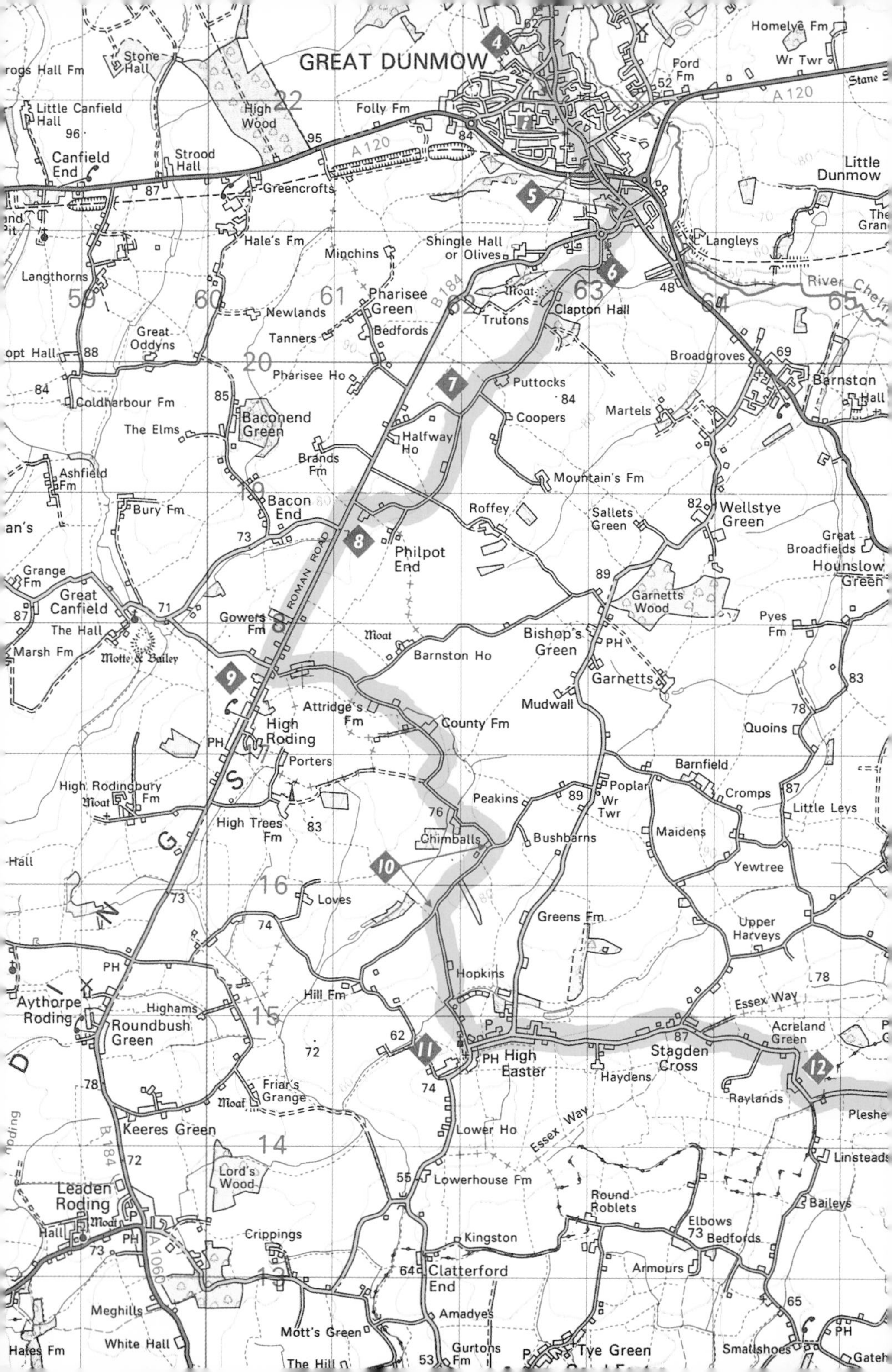
GREAT DUNMOW
Little Canfield Hall
Canfield End
Stone Hall
High Wood
Strood Hall
Folly Fm
A 120
Greencrofts
Hale's Fm
Minchins
Shingle Hall or Olives
Langthorns
Pharisee Green
Newlands
Tanners
Bedfords
Great Oddyns
Pharisee Ho
Coldharbour Fm
Baconend Green
The Elms
Ashfield Fm
Brands Fm
Halfway Ho
Bacon End
Bury Fm
Philpot End
ROMAN ROAD
Grange Fm
Great Canfield
The Hall
Marsh Fm
Motte & Bailey
Gowers Fm
Moat
Barnston Ho
Attridge's Fm
High Roding
County Fm
Porters
High Rodingbury Fm
High Trees Fm
Peakins
Chimballs
Bushbarns
Loves
Greens Fm
Hopkins
Hill Fm
Aythorpe Roding
Highams
Roundbush Green
High Easter
Friar's Grange
Keeres Green
Lord's Wood
Lower Ho
Lowerhouse Fm
Leaden Roding
Hall
Crippings
Kingston
Clatterford End
Meghills
Amadyes
White Hall
Mott's Green
Hales Fm
The Hill
Gurtons Fm
Tye Green
Homelye Fm
Wr Twr
Ford Fm
Stane St
Little Dunmow
Langleys
River Chelmer
Trutons
Clapton Hall
Moat
Broadgroves
Barnston
Hall
Puttocks
Coopers
Martels
Mountain's Fm
Roffey
Sallets Green
Wellstye Green
Great Broadfields
Hounslow Green
Garnetts Wood
Bishop's Green
PH
Garnetts
Mudwall
Pyes Fm
Quoins
Barnfield
Poplar
Wr Twr
Cromps
Little Leys
Maidens
Yewtree
Upper Harveys
Essex Way
Acreland Green
Stagden Cross
Haydens
Raylands
Pleshey
Linsteads
Round Roblets
Baileys
Elbows
Bedfords
Armours
Smallshoes
B 184
A 1060

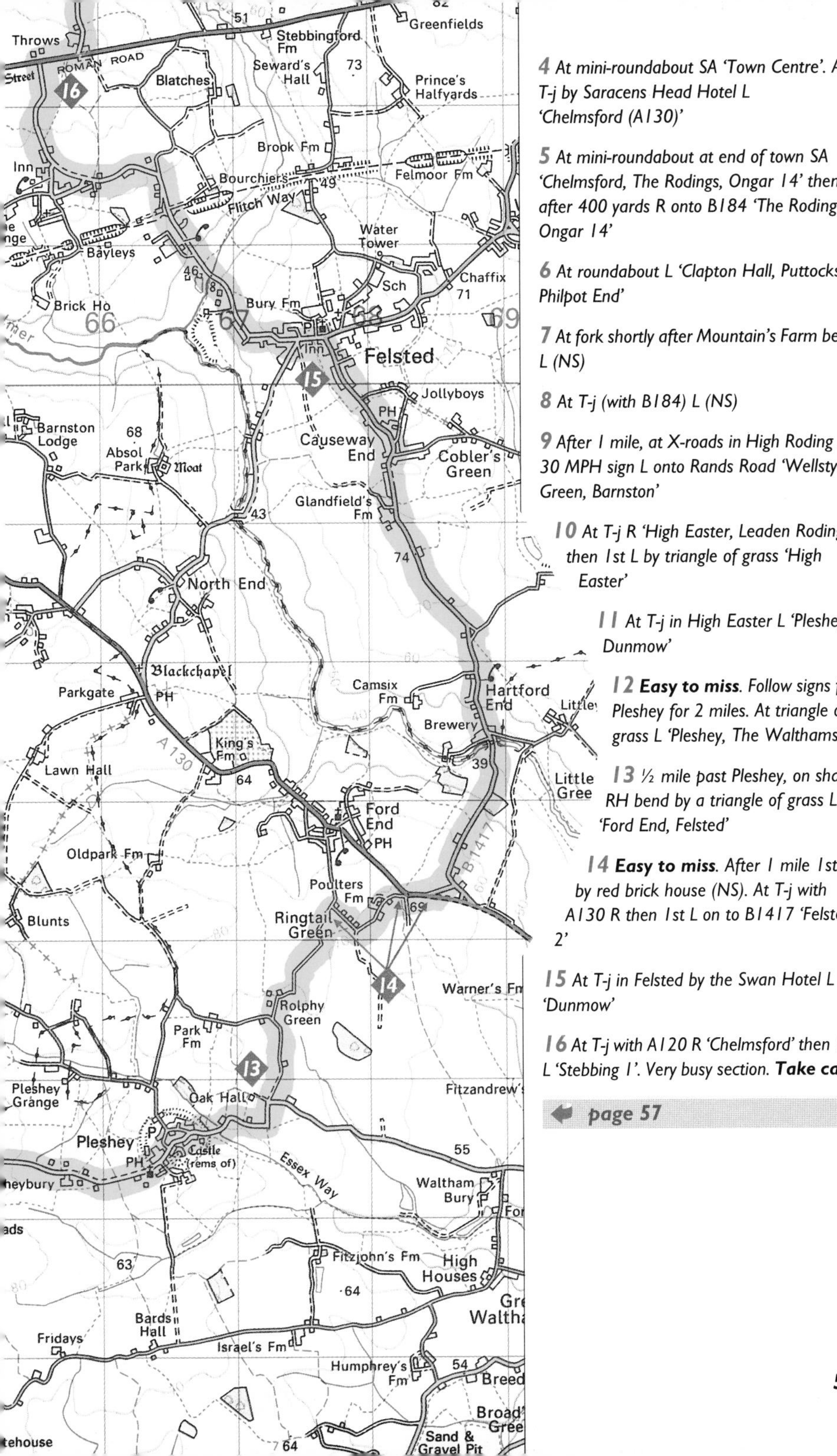

4 *At mini-roundabout SA 'Town Centre'. At T-j by Saracens Head Hotel L 'Chelmsford (A130)'*

5 *At mini-roundabout at end of town SA 'Chelmsford, The Rodings, Ongar 14' then after 400 yards R onto B184 'The Rodings, Ongar 14'*

6 *At roundabout L 'Clapton Hall, Puttocks, Philpot End'*

7 *At fork shortly after Mountain's Farm bear L (NS)*

8 *At T-j (with B184) L (NS)*

9 *After 1 mile, at X-roads in High Roding by 30 MPH sign L onto Rands Road 'Wellstye Green, Barnston'*

10 *At T-j R 'High Easter, Leaden Roding' then 1st L by triangle of grass 'High Easter'*

11 *At T-j in High Easter L 'Pleshey, Dunmow'*

12 ***Easy to miss****. Follow signs for Pleshey for 2 miles. At triangle of grass L 'Pleshey, The Walthams'*

13 *½ mile past Pleshey, on sharp RH bend by a triangle of grass L 'Ford End, Felsted'*

14 ***Easy to miss****. After 1 mile 1st R by red brick house (NS). At T-j with A130 R then 1st L on to B1417 'Felsted 2'*

15 *At T-j in Felsted by the Swan Hotel L 'Dunmow'*

16 *At T-j with A120 R 'Chelmsford' then 1st L 'Stebbing 1'. Very busy section.* ***Take care***

page 57

8 Southeast from Newmarket past the gallops and the studs in the heart of horseracing country

The whole area around Newmarket is dominated by its role as the centre of horseracing and breeding. Traffic often stops entirely to let a group of frisky thoroughbreds cross the road and you may well be rewarded with the sight of scores of horses out training on the gallops either side of the Moulton Road. This is where the ride starts and it would take a strong cyclist to keep up with the horses as they canter up the slope towards the woods. You pass the fine old packhorse bridge in Moulton as the route heads east. There is a short busy section either side of Horringer preceding a climb to Suffolk's loftiest summits(!) near to Rede. From Wickhambrook onwards the signs of horseracing multiply as each mile is covered bringing you closer to Newmarket. The ride ends with a long, gentle descent into the town centre.

Start

The Clocktower at the end of the High Street, Newmarket

P Follow long stay car park signs on the B1063 Clare and Moulton road

Distance and grade

36 miles

Easy / moderate

Terrain

3 climbs of between 150 and 200 feet, several shorter climbs. Lowest point – 100 feet (30 mts) Newmarket. Highest point – 385 feet (116 mts) at Rede

Nearest railway

Newmarket

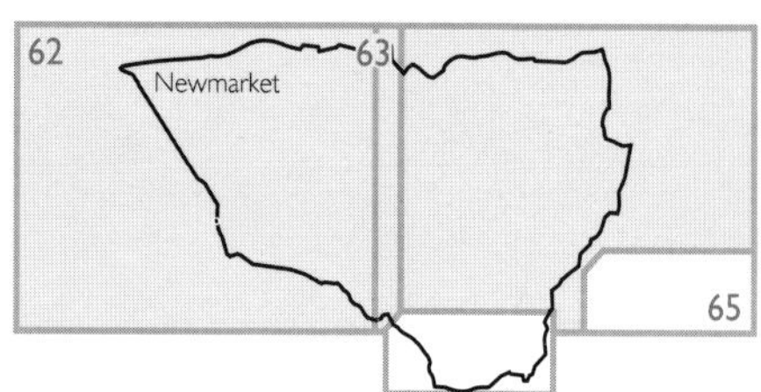

Newmarket
Moulton
Gazeley
Barrow
Little Saxham
Horringer

Places of interest

Newmarket *1*
Headquarters of British horseracing since the 17th century. Beside the heath the National Stud houses some of the world's finest stallions. The National Horseracing Museum has paintings by Stubbs and Munnings. Nell Gwynne's House in Palace Street survived the 1683 fire that destroyed most of the town

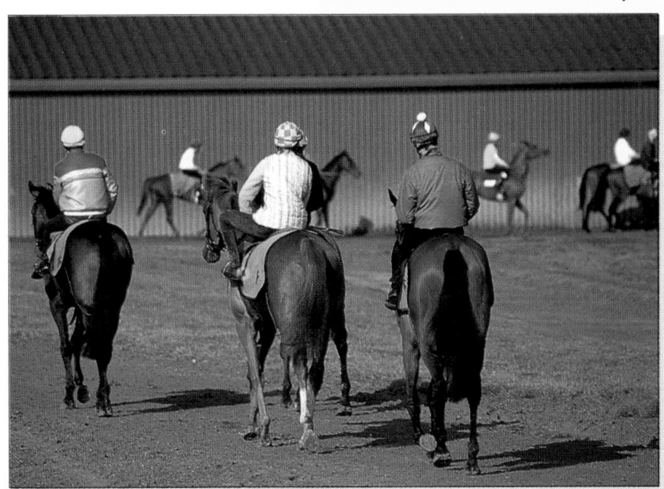

▲ *Racehorse training at Newmarket*

Ickworth House *7*
An extravagant rotunda house begun in 1794 and completed in 1830, commissioned by the eccentric 4th Earl of Bristol and Bishop of Derry to house his art collection. The magnificent grounds were landscaped by Capability Brown

Wickhambrook *14*
Noted for Gifford's Hall, a gabled and timber-framed manor house dating from 1480

Refreshments

Plenty of choice in ***Newmarket***
Kings Head PH, ***Moulton***
The Chequers PH, ***Gazeley***
Weeping Willow PH, ***Barrow***
Six Bells PH, Beehive PH♦♦*,*
Horringer
White Horse PH♦*, between*
Horringer and Rede

Rede Hawkedon Wickhambrook Kirtling

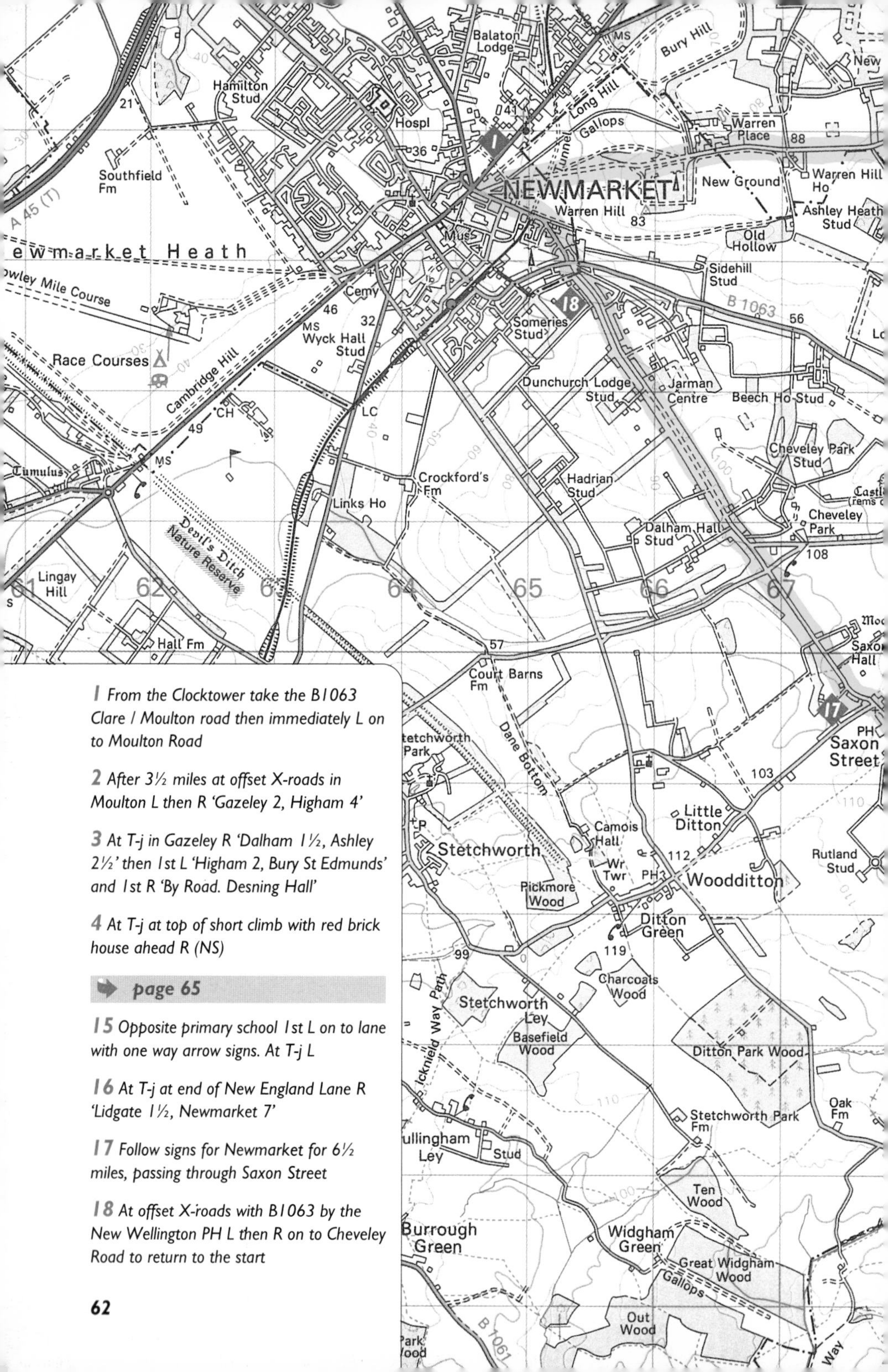

1 From the Clocktower take the B1063 Clare / Moulton road then immediately L on to Moulton Road

2 After 3½ miles at offset X-roads in Moulton L then R 'Gazeley 2, Higham 4'

3 At T-j in Gazeley R 'Dalham 1½, Ashley 2½' then 1st L 'Higham 2, Bury St Edmunds' and 1st R 'By Road. Desning Hall'

4 At T-j at top of short climb with red brick house ahead R (NS)

page 65

15 Opposite primary school 1st L on to lane with one way arrow signs. At T-j L

16 At T-j at end of New England Lane R 'Lidgate 1½, Newmarket 7'

17 Follow signs for Newmarket for 6½ miles, passing through Saxon Street

18 At offset X-roads with B1063 by the New Wellington PH L then R on to Cheveley Road to return to the start

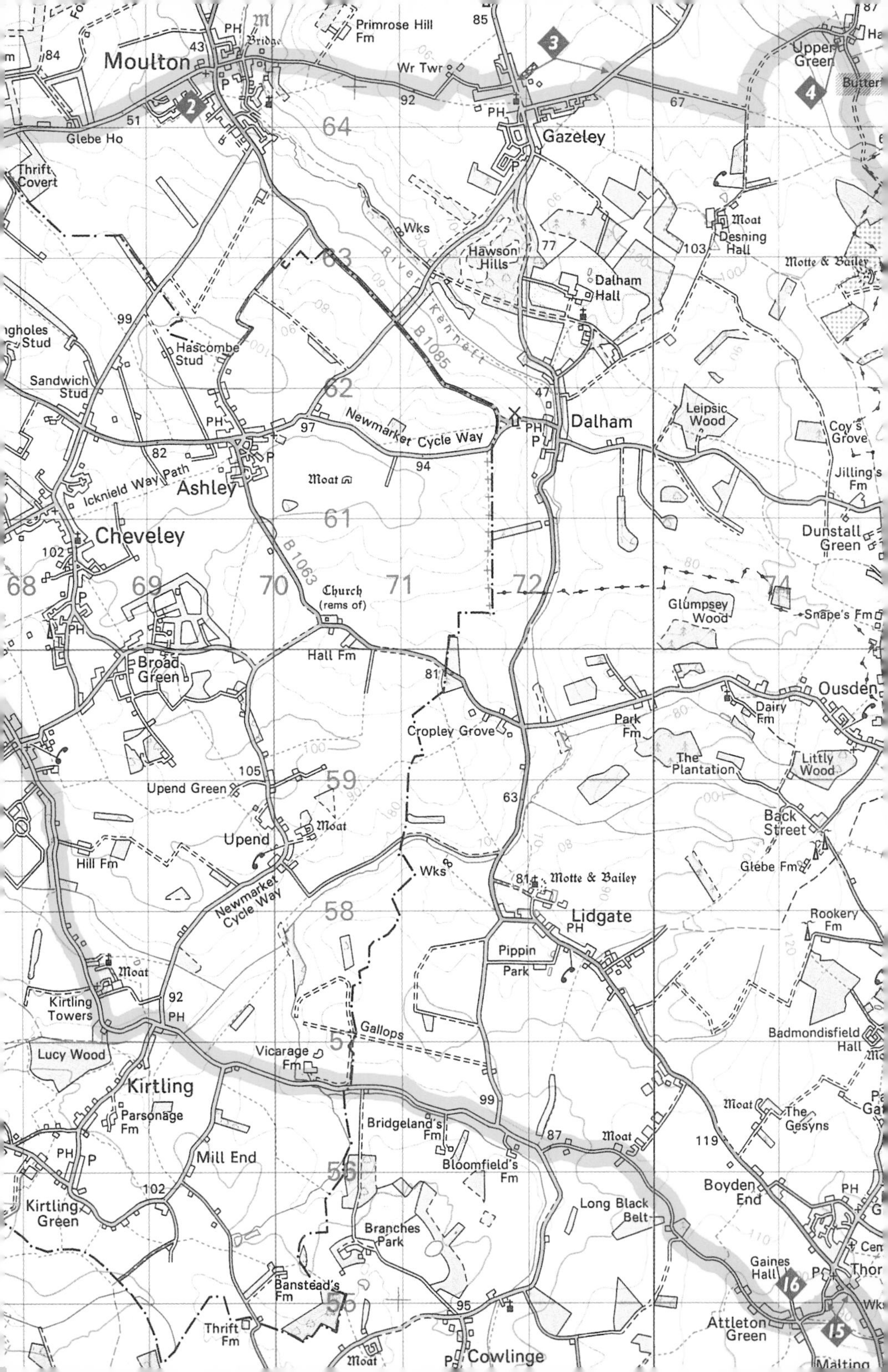
Moulton
Primrose Hill Fm
Wr Twr
Upper Green
Glebe Ho
Thrift Covert
Gazeley
Wks
Hawson Hills
Moat
Desning Hall
Dalham Hall
Motte & Bailey
River Kennett
B1085
Hascombe Stud
Sandwich Stud
Newmarket Cycle Way
Dalham
Leipsic Wood
Coy's Grove
Jilling's Fm
Icknield Way Path
Ashley
Cheveley
Dunstall Green
B1063
Church (rems of)
Glumpsey Wood
Snape's Fm
Broad Green
Hall Fm
Ousden
Dairy Fm
Cropley Grove
Park Fm
The Plantation
Littly Wood
Upend Green
Back Street
Upend
Hill Fm
Glebe Fm
Lidgate
Rookery Fm
Pippin Park
Kirtling Towers
Gallops
Badmondisfield Hall
Lucy Wood
Vicarage Fm
Kirtling
Parsonage Fm
The Gesyns
Bridgeland's Fm
Mill End
Bloomfield's Fm
Boyden End
Kirtling Green
Long Black Belt
Branches Park
Gaines Hall
Banstead's Fm
Thrift Fm
Attleton Green
Cowlinge

Upper Green
Hall
Tropical Butterfly House
Fishpond
Cemy
Hatchery Ho
Hall
Moat
Moat
Burthorpe
Frog Hall
Mound
97
67
PH
Feltons
Barrow
Sewage Wks
Twite's Fm
53
Honeyhill Fm
Warren Lodge
79
Windsor Wood
64
Little Saxham
Lodge Fm
82
Moats
ST EDMUND
Lower Fm
Denham End
Motte & Bailey
Denham Castle
Wilsummer Wood
Great Saxham
Hall
63
Dairy Wood
Twist Wood
101
Wolfe Hall
Hearse Wood
Frizzeler's Green
Cobb's Hall
62
P
Horsepool Fm
Coy's Grove
Hall
Moat
Denham
101
Jilling's Fm
Abbot's Fm
Willow Fm
101
Park Wood
Jennison's Plantn
Downter's Wood
77
Dunstall Green
Hargrave Hall
The Wash
Birds End
79
Chevington Lodge Fm
Chevington Hall Fm
75
76
77
78
80
Lownde Wood
Snape's Fm
Stonehall Fm
Moat
PH
Great Southwood Park Fm
Hargrave
Chevington
60
Mon
Ousden
Moat
113
110
Lady's Green
111
Broad Green
PH
College Fm
Hollybu Green
Littly Wood
PH
The Grove
Tan Office Green
Hill Fm
59
Ruffin's Ho
Witham's Fm
Stonehouse Fm
Wks
Little Knowles Green
120
Fm
Baxter's Green
Easterwood Fm
Rookery Fm
Chedburgh
58
Moat
Genesis Green
Busses Fm
Easter Wood
Gate House
123
Wr Twr
PH
119
Rede Hall
Black Horse Fm
Wks
Hall Fm
125
Depden Green
Hall
Moat
Depden
Hall
57
Lodge Fm
Park Gate
The Gesyns
114
Francis Wood
Aldersfield Hall
Elms Fm
PH
Meeting Green
116
Ashfield Green
Great Wood
Rede
PH
Cemy
A143
Pykards H
Thorns
Dodd's Fm
95
Coblands Fm
Gatesbury's Fm
55
Wickhambrook
Clopton Hall
Black Wood
Malting
Clopton Green
Scoles Gate
4
5
10
14
15
16

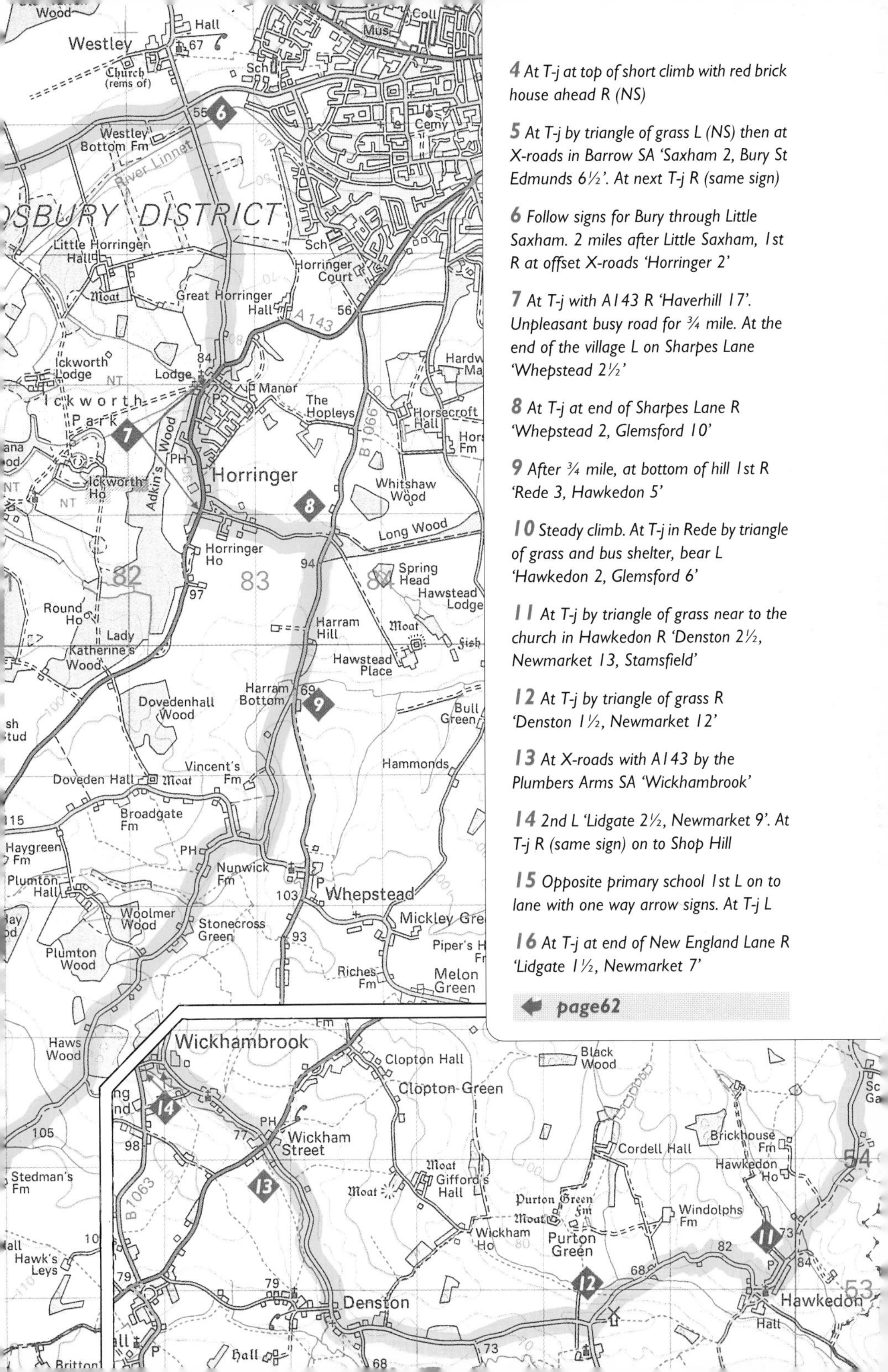

4 At T-j at top of short climb with red brick house ahead R (NS)

5 At T-j by triangle of grass L (NS) then at X-roads in Barrow SA 'Saxham 2, Bury St Edmunds 6½'. At next T-j R (same sign)

6 Follow signs for Bury through Little Saxham. 2 miles after Little Saxham, 1st R at offset X-roads 'Horringer 2'

7 At T-j with A143 R 'Haverhill 17'. Unpleasant busy road for ¾ mile. At the end of the village L on Sharpes Lane 'Whepstead 2½'

8 At T-j at end of Sharpes Lane R 'Whepstead 2, Glemsford 10'

9 After ¾ mile, at bottom of hill 1st R 'Rede 3, Hawkedon 5'

10 Steady climb. At T-j in Rede by triangle of grass and bus shelter, bear L 'Hawkedon 2, Glemsford 6'

11 At T-j by triangle of grass near to the church in Hawkedon R 'Denston 2½, Newmarket 13, Stamsfield'

12 At T-j by triangle of grass R 'Denston 1½, Newmarket 12'

13 At X-roads with A143 by the Plumbers Arms SA 'Wickhambrook'

14 2nd L 'Lidgate 2½, Newmarket 9'. At T-j R (same sign) on to Shop Hill

15 Opposite primary school 1st L on to lane with one way arrow signs. At T-j L

16 At T-j at end of New England Lane R 'Lidgate 1½, Newmarket 7'

page62

9 *North from Lavenham towards Bury St Edmunds and east to the village of Rattlesden*

Lavenham is the loveliest village in Suffolk and is probably best appreciated out of season. There are many fine pubs and tea shops and every street has fine old timbered buildings which are best seen on a walking tour of the village before or after the ride. The route follows the Chad Brook from Bridge Street towards Shimpling then climbs to the dizzy heights of almost 350 feet north of Hartest before dropping past the handsome house at Bryers near to Hawstead Green. A short section of the busy A134 is negotiated near to Sicklesmere before a steady climb towards the Nature Reserve at Bradfield Woods and the delightful church at Rattlesden. Quiet lanes take you south to the pretty thatched cottages of Kettlebaston and back to Lavenham where the climb up Prentice Street is the hardest of the day. Why not walk and take a closer look at the fine old buildings.

68 69 70 71

Start

The Tourist Information Centre, Lavenham, 10 miles southeast of Bury St Edmunds

P Follow signs for long stay car park just off the B1071 Sudbury road

Distance and grade

33 miles
Easy / moderate

Terrain

Gently rolling landscape. 4 climbs of 150 feet and several of between 50 and 100 feet. The steepest hill is right at the end as you climb Prentice Street back to the starting point. Lowest point – 140 feet (42 mts) at Sicklesmere. Highest point – 330 feet (100 mts) north of Hartest

Nearest railway

Bury St Edmunds, 4 miles northwest of the route at Sicklesmere

Places of interest

***Lavenham** 1*

Resplendent Suffolk wool town reflects the prosperous Middle Ages – the telegraph lines are hidden underground to preserve the character of over 300 listed buildings. Tudor houses sag with age and the cathedral-like church on the hill is the greatest of all East Anglia's medieval 'wool' churches. The old Wool Hall is now part of the Swan Hotel. The Museum of Weaving Industry is displayed in the Tudor Guildhall

▼ *Lavenham*

***The Priory, Lavenham** 1*

Medieval Benedictine Priory, later a Tudor clothier's residence. Recently rescued from a derelict ruin with a Great Hall, Jacobean staircase, courtyard, aromatic herb garden, kitchen garden, orchard and pond

***Long Melford** (just off the route) 3*

The main street of the village runs along the former Roman highway. Pepperpot towers distinguish the 16th-century mansion of Melford Hall. The 16th-century Bull Inn is reputed to be haunted. The moated manor of Kentwell Hall has a Tudor-rose maze and rare breeds of domestic farm animals

***Bradfield Woods Nature Reserve** 12*

A diversity of soils gives a wide variety of plants, regularly coppiced native trees and shrubs with unusual fungi in autumn. The reserve is home to four kinds of deer, small mammals, butterflies and migrant birds. There is also a visitor centre

Refreshments

Plenty of choice ***in Lavenham***
Rose and Crown PH, ***Bridge Street***
The Crown PH, ***Hartest***
Metcalfe Arms PH, ***Hawstead Green***
Fox and Hounds PH, ***Maypole Green***
Brewers Arms PH, ***Rattlesden***
Six Bells PH, ***Preston St Mary***

Gedding

Rattlesden

1 With back to the Tourist Information Centre L downhill. At T-j R then at next T-j L 'Long Melford 4, Sudbury 6'

2 Shortly after church on right, on a sharp LH bend, bear R 'Bridge St 3'

3 After 2½ miles, at offset X-roads with A134, R then L 'Shimpling 2, Chadacre 3' then 1st R on to Aveley Lane 'Shimpling 2'

4 At T-j after 2 miles at the end of Aveley Lane by a letter box L 'Stanstead 3, Hartest 2'

➡ page 70

12 **Easy to miss**. Follow signs for Gedding and Felsham for 5 miles. 1 mile after passing Bradfield Woods Nature Reserve on your right, turn L by a triangle of grass 'Drinkstone 2½, Rattlesden 2½'

13 1st R by telephone box 'Felsham ¾, Rattlesden 2'. At T-j L 'Ratlesden 1½, Stowmarket 6¼'

14 After 2 miles, just past the Brewers Arms PH in Rattlesden, on a sharp LH bend, R onto Birds Green

15 1st R by triangle of grass 'Poystreet Green' then at T-j L 'Hitcham 4, Hadleigh 11'

16 Do **not** take the 1st R to Lavenham. After 1 mile at T-j R (NS)

17 Ignore right and left turns. Follow signs for Hitcham. At X-roads SA 'Bildeston 3, Hadleigh 8'

18 At T-j by triangle of grass L 'Hitcham ½, Bildeston 2'

19 At bottom of hill on double bend R 'Kettlebaston 1'

20 At T-j by triangle of grass and a letter box R (sign broken)

21 At T-j L 'Lavenham 2'

22 At X-roads on the outskirts of Lavenham L 'Local traffic only' then 4th R on to Prentice Street. A steep climb past lovely houses to return to the start

Copdoe's Fm
Manor Fm
Brook
Cocks
PH
Cook's
Dutmos Woods
Newhall F
Harrow Green
house
59
84
Maypole Green
PH
Rawhall Wood
Pitcher's Green
Chensil Grove
Laurel Fm
Bradfield St Clare
58
The Lodge
97
Wr Twr
Hedge Wood
Moat Hall
Car
Bush Green
Sutton Hall
57
Moat
Elmgreen Fm
Woo Fm
Smallbridge Fm
hall Green
Moat
PH
56
Great Green
ppers Hall
Colchester Green
93
Upper Church Fm
Moat
Cemy
Palmers Fm
Bull's Wood
P
Cockfield
A1141
Hall
Bullswood Fm
87
54
Vall
Perrydown Fm
69
Earl's Hall Fm
90
Clipt Bushes Fm
PH
Button's Green
88
53
Knights Hill Fm
Stow's Hill
Malting Fm
83
Shimpling Street
Moat
PH
90
Slough Hill
Midway Fm
Shimpling Park Fm
80
Smithwood Green
63
Mount Fm
52
Mill Hill
4
82
60
Moat
Hunt's Moat
87
Elms Fm
Likely Hill
Wr Twr
Roo Gre
Shimplingthorne
Lavenham Lodge
58
Shimpling
80
Lavenham Hill Fm
wage Wks
70
Alpheton
Clapstile Fm
51
Lavenham Park Fm
Aveley Wood
Hall
87
88
89
Melford Park Fm
90
91
72
92
Frog's Hall
Moneyho Corner
86
53
Chad Brook
84
50
Moat
22
MS
Nether Hall
Rowhedge Fm
3
Bright's Fm
1
Lavenham
79
Dunton's Fm
Nature Reserve
i
P
Mus
48
Clayhill Fm
Bridge Street
PH
Ford Hall
Slough Fm
49
2
PH
NT
P
Sewage Wk

Smallwood Green
Gedding Hall
Moat
Rattlesden
PH
Wood Hall
Moat
Hill Fm
14
15
55
Abbot's Hall
White House Fm
Moat
12
94
Gedding
Grange Fm
62
Brook Fm
Peystreet Green
Hollybush Fm
PH
13
Bradfield Woods Nature Reserve
Felsham Ho
Moat
Cockerells Hall
Hill Fm
Hollybush Fm
Leffey Hall
Felsham Hall
PH
Lower Green
Rookery Fm
Moore's Fm
Hightown Green
16
Mullett's Fm
Fasbourn Hall
Manor Fm
67
94
Moat
Brooke Hall
The Grange
Moat
94
Moat
Castle Fm
Landing Strip
Moat
ROMAN ROAD
93
Felsham Wood
Burnt House Fm
Castle Fm
World's End
Thorpe Wood
Lower Fm
Home Fm
98
97
PH
Grove Fm
89
Ryece Hall
Thorpe Green
Potash Fm
Moat
93
Brettenham
Moat
P
The Well Ho
Stanstead Hall
Moat
17
Thorpe Morieux
72
P
Almshouse Green
85
Cook's Green
The Plains Fm
84
Park Fm
Birds Fm
Hall
92
Cross Green
Sch
The Wash
81
Popples
Devil's Hill Wood
Blox Hall
Dale Fm
Hill Fm
Manor Fm
Moat
Causeway House Fm
62
87
Home Wood
Hill Fm
P
18
Charity Fm
Down Hall
52
Rushbrooke Fm
Brickhouse Fm
PH
Hitcham
82
Mortimer's Fm
76
80
70
High House Fm
Wetherden Hall
Moat
57
19
Fen Fm
21
Priory Fm
Moat
Preston St Mary
95
College Fm
Hitcham Ho
81
Boxtree Fm
Riverside Fm
99
Bentons
94
96
97
98
PH
Hall
Moat
Kettlebaston
51
20
Whelp Street
Swifts Manor
Chapel Fm
Hillhouse Fm
Collier's Fm
Bildeston
Inn
Church Fm
66
P
Spragg's Wood
Wagger Fm
74
39
37

4 At T-j after 2 miles at the end of Aveley Lane by a letter box L 'Stanstead 3, Hartest 2'

5 After 1 mile, just after black timber house on the left, 1st R 'Hartest'

*6 Fast descent. Just **before** the bridge R '13 ton weight limit'*

7 At T-j by triangle of grass L on to Golden Lane 'Whepstead 2' then after ½ mile 1st R on to Folly Lane 'Hawstead 2½'

8 At the end of Folly Lane bear L (keep an eye out for the lovely timbered house called Bryers on your left)

9 At T-j at the end of Whepstead Road L 'Nowton 2, Bury St Edmunds 4'

10 After 1½ miles, at the bottom of a fast descent and at the end of a double bend turn R 'Sicklesmere'

11 At T-j with the main road (A134) R then 1st L (use the pavement with discretion to avoid the traffic) 'Little Welnetham, Bradfield St George'

page 68

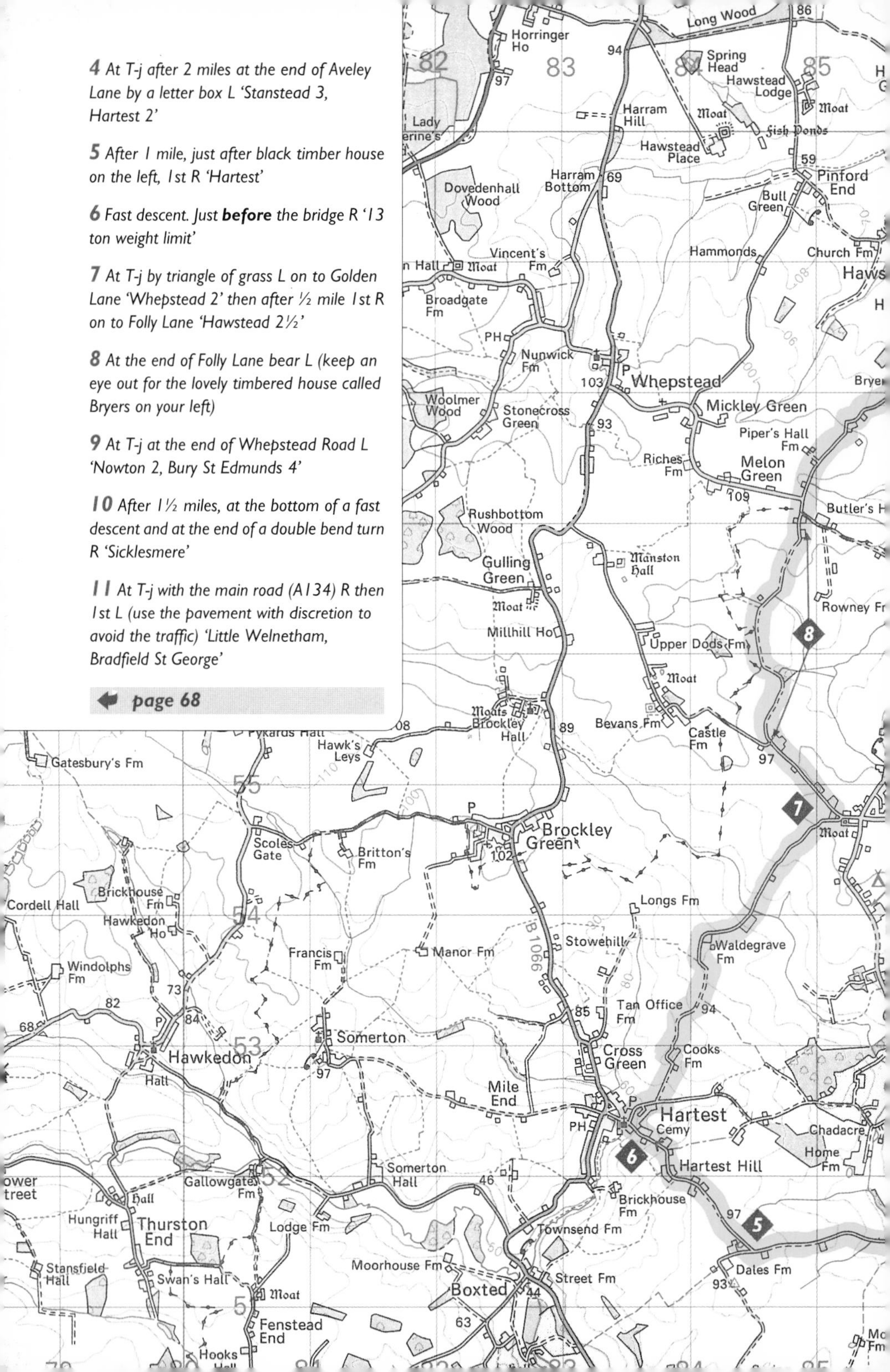

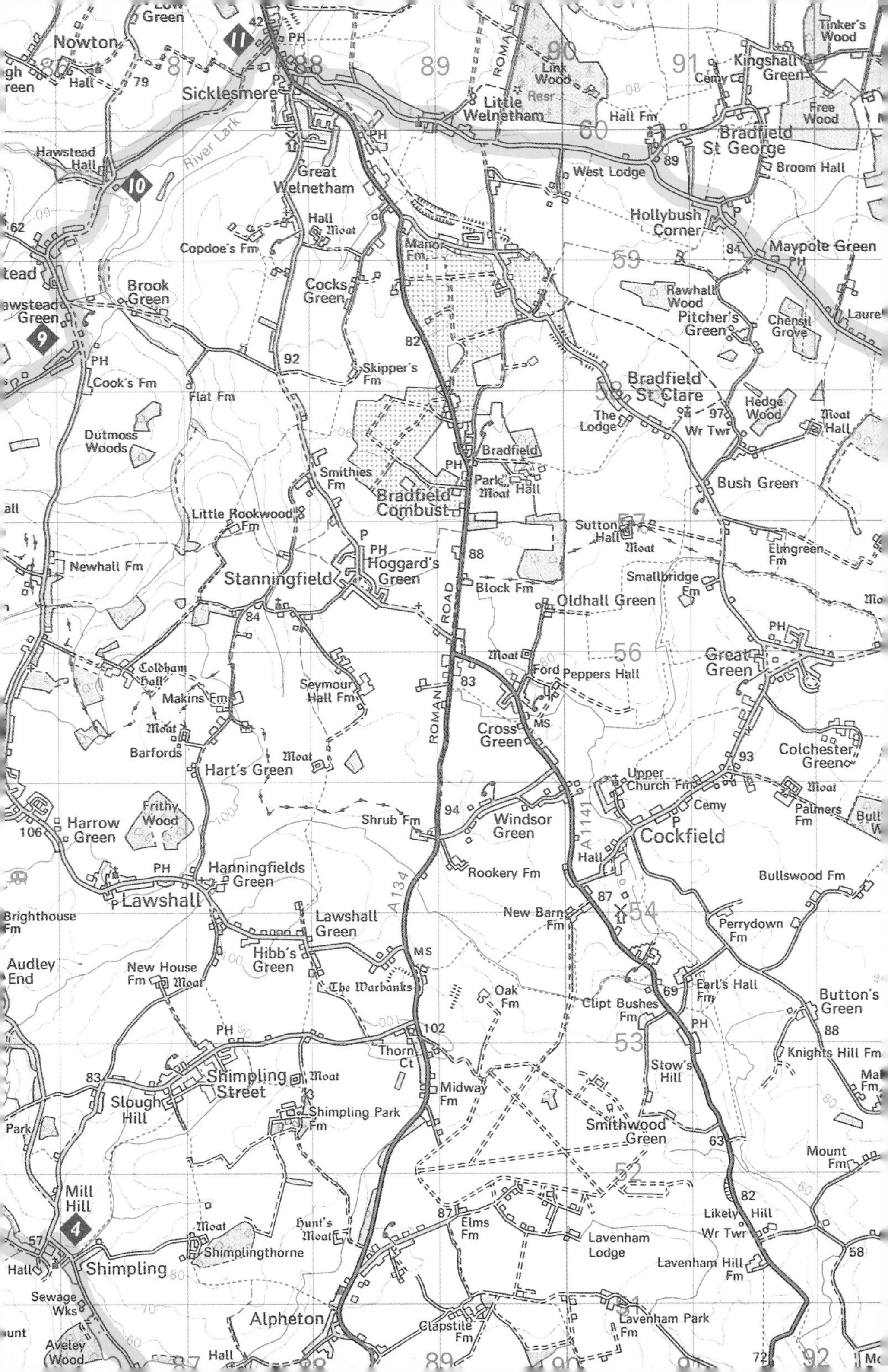

Green
Nowton
Hall
79
Sicklesmere
42
PH
88
89
ROMAN
90
Link Wood
Resr
Little Welnetham
60
Hall Fm
91
Cemy
Kingshall Green
Tinker's Wood
Free Wood
Bradfield St George
89
Broom Hall
West Lodge
Hawstead Hall
River Lark
10
Great Welnetham
Hall
Moat
Copdoe's Fm
Manor Fm
Hollybush Corner
84
Maypole Green
59
Rawhall Wood
Pitcher's Green
Chensil Grove
62
Brook Green
Cocks Green
Hawstead Green
9
82
92
Skipper's Fm
PH
Cook's Fm
Flat Fm
Bradfield St Clare
The Lodge
97
Wr Twr
Hedge Wood
Moat Hall
Dutmoss Woods
Bradfield
Park Hall
Moat
Smithies Fm
Bradfield Combust
Bush Green
Little Rookwood Fm
Sutton Hall
Moat
Elmgreen Fm
Newhall Fm
P
PH
Hoggard's Green
88
Stanningfield
Block Fm
Smallbridge Fm
Oldhall Green
84
ROAD
PH
56
Moat
Ford
Peppers Hall
Great Green
Coldham Hall
Makins Fm
Seymour Hall Fm
83
Cross Green
MS
Moat
Barfords
Hart's Green
Moat
ROMAN
Colchester Green
93
Upper Church Fm
Moat
Palmers Fm
Cemy
Frithy Wood
Harrow Green
106
Shrub Fm
94
Windsor Green
A1141
P
Cockfield
Hall
PH
Hanningfields Green
Lawshall
Rookery Fm
Bullswood Fm
A134
87
New Barn Fm
54
Brighthouse Fm
Lawshall Green
Perrydown Fm
Audley End
New House Fm
Moat
Hibb's Green
MS
The Warbanks
Oak Fm
69
Earl's Hall Fm
Clipt Bushes Fm
Button's Green
PH
88
PH
102
Thorn Ct
53
Knights Hill Fm
83
Slough Hill
Shimpling Street
Moat
Stow's Hill
Midway Fm
Shimpling Park Fm
Park
Smithwood Green
63
Mount Fm
52
Mill Hill
4
Moat
Hunt's Moat
87
Elms Fm
Lavenham Lodge
82
Likely Hill
Wr Twr
58
57
Shimplingthorne
Hall
Shimpling
Lavenham Hill Fm
Sewage Wks
Alpheton
Clapstile Fm
Lavenham Park Fm
Aveley Wood
Hall
72
92

10 Southwest from Sudbury to Castle Hedingham and the Belchamps

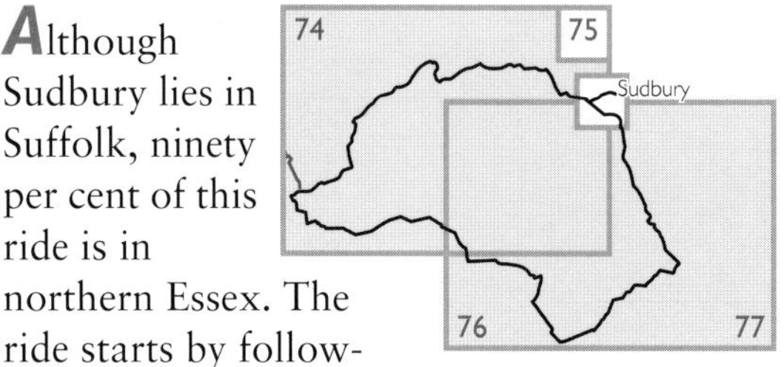
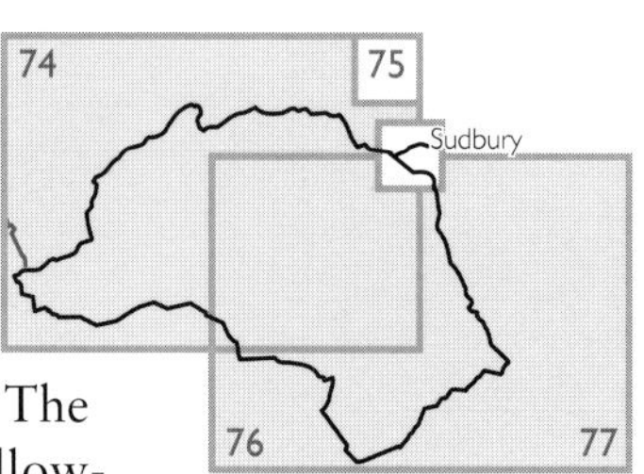

Although Sudbury lies in Suffolk, ninety per cent of this ride is in northern Essex. The ride starts by following the valley of the River Stour south through Henny Street, Lamarsh and the attractive village of Bures. Some of the farms on the tiny lanes southwest from Bures through Daw's Cross to Colne Engaine you feel sure might have inspired Gainsborough, who was born in Sudbury. Halstead has few attractions for the cyclist and is avoided in favour of lanes which skirt to the north via the Maplesteads and Castle Hedingham. The route heads west as far as Toppesfield before returning towards Sudbury via the Belchamps.

Start

The long stay car park by the Leisure Pool in Sudbury, 15 miles northwest of Colchester

P As above. Follow signs

Distance and grade

33 miles

Easy / moderate

Terrain

Several climbs up to 100 feet. Lowest point – 75 feet (23 mts) at Lamarsh. Highest point – 285 feet (86 mts) near to Belchamp St Paul

Nearest railway

Sudbury

Sudbury
Daw's Hall
Bures
Colne Engaine
Little Maplestead

Places of interest

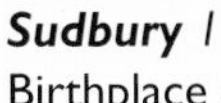

Sudbury *1*
Birthplace of the painter Thomas Gainsborough in 1727. Half-timbered Gainsborough's House dates from 1480, with an added Georgian front. It is now a museum with portraits and landscapes illustrating the artist's career

Castle Hedingham *11*
The village is dominated by the towering Norman keep of Hedingham Castle, built around 1140 by the De Vere family who lived here for 500 years. Well-preserved banqueting hall and minstrels' gallery

Colne Valley Railway *12*
Vintage steam trains take passengers along a lovingly restored section of the Old Colne Valley and Halstead railway. There is a wildlife conservation area and picnic site

▲ *The Colne Valley Railway*

Refreshments

Plenty of choice, Waggon and Horses PH, ***Sudbury***
The Henny Swan PH, ***Henny Street***
The Red Lion PH, ***Lamarsh***
The Swan PH, The Eight Bells PH, ***Bures***
The Bell PH, ***Castle Hedingham***
Waggon and Horses PH, The White Hart PH, ***Great Yeldham***
Cherry Tree PH, ***Knowl Green***
Half Moon PH, ***Belchamp St Paul***
Red Lion PH, ***Belchamp Otter***

Castle Hedingham

Great Yeldham

Belchamp Otten

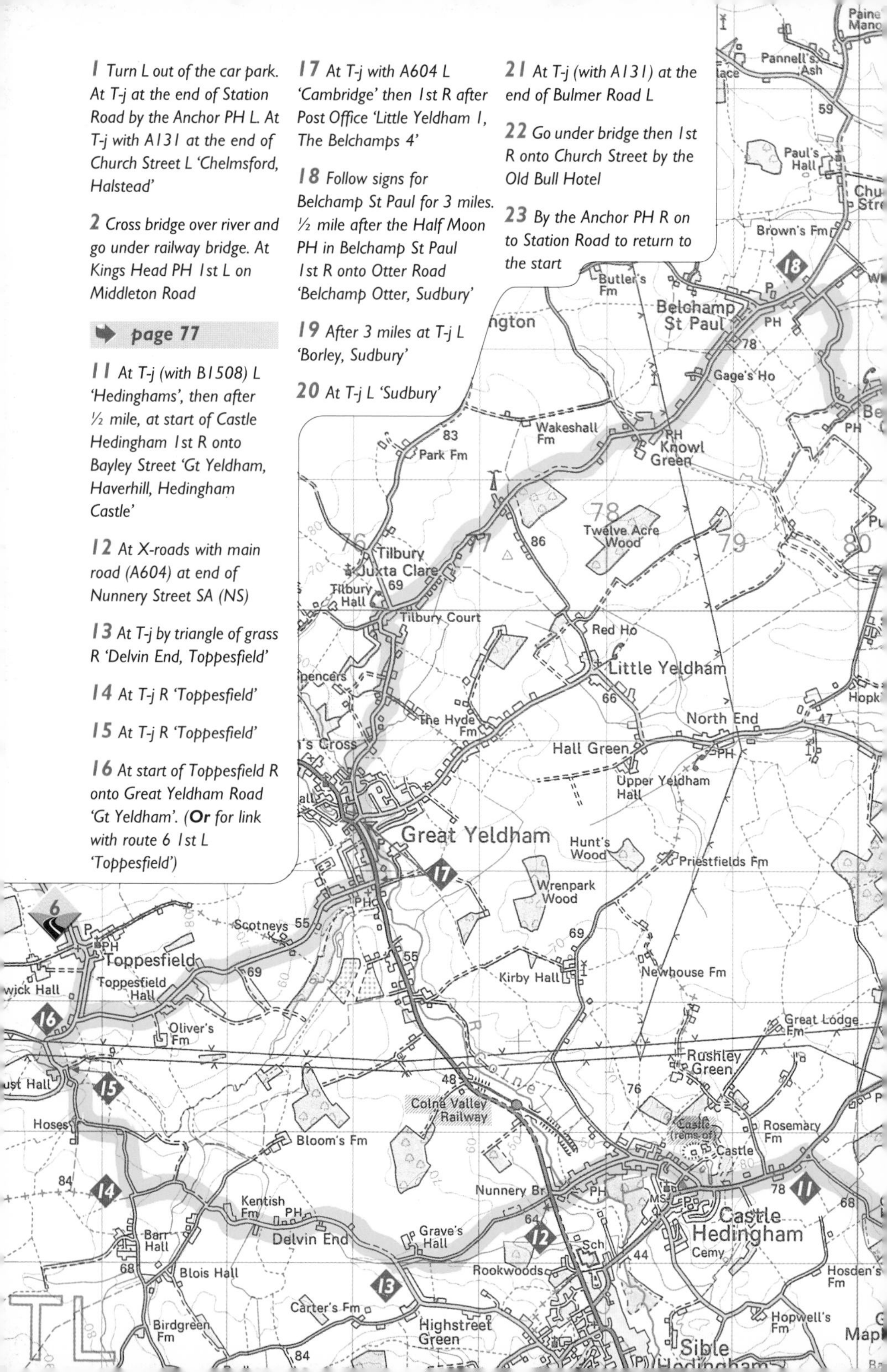

1 Turn L out of the car park. At T-j at the end of Station Road by the Anchor PH L. At T-j with A131 at the end of Church Street L 'Chelmsford, Halstead'

2 Cross bridge over river and go under railway bridge. At Kings Head PH 1st L on Middleton Road

➡ page 77

11 At T-j (with B1508) L 'Hedinghams', then after ½ mile, at start of Castle Hedingham 1st R onto Bayley Street 'Gt Yeldham, Haverhill, Hedingham Castle'

12 At X-roads with main road (A604) at end of Nunnery Street SA (NS)

13 At T-j by triangle of grass R 'Delvin End, Toppesfield'

14 At T-j R 'Toppesfield'

15 At T-j R 'Toppesfield'

16 At start of Toppesfield R onto Great Yeldham Road 'Gt Yeldham'. (**Or** for link with route 6 1st L 'Toppesfield')

17 At T-j with A604 L 'Cambridge' then 1st R after Post Office 'Little Yeldham 1, The Belchamps 4'

18 Follow signs for Belchamp St Paul for 3 miles. ½ mile after the Half Moon PH in Belchamp St Paul 1st R onto Otter Road 'Belchamp Otter, Sudbury'

19 After 3 miles at T-j L 'Borley, Sudbury'

20 At T-j L 'Sudbury'

21 At T-j (with A131) at the end of Bulmer Road L

22 Go under bridge then 1st R onto Church Street by the Old Bull Hotel

23 By the Anchor PH R on to Station Road to return to the start

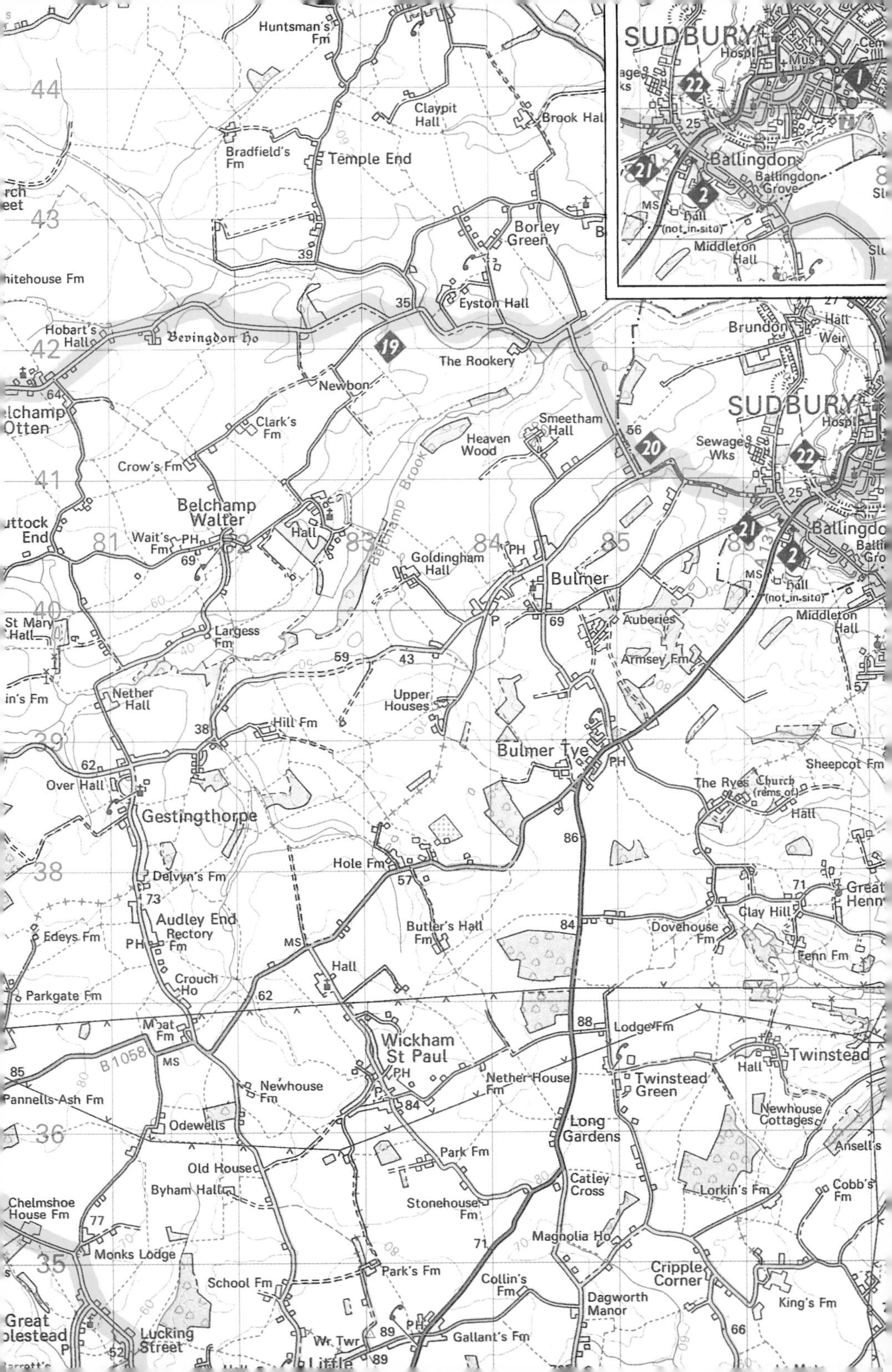

SUDBURY
Hospl
Mus
Ballingdon
Ballingdon Grove
Hall (not in situ)
Middleton Hall
Huntsman's Fm
Claypit Hall
Brook Hall
Bradfield's Fm
Temple End
Borley Green
Whitehouse Fm
Eyston Hall
Hobart's Hall
Bevingdon Ho
The Rookery
Newbon
Brundon
Weir
Belchamp Otten
Clark's Fm
Smeetham Hall
Heaven Wood
Sewage Wks
Crow's Fm
Belchamp Walter
Belchamp Brook
Buttock End
Wait's Fm
Hall
Goldingham Hall
Bulmer
St Mary Hall
Largess Fm
Auberies
Armsey Fm
Nether Hall
Upper Houses
Hill Fm
Bulmer Tye
Over Hall
Gestingthorpe
Sheepcot Fm
The Ryes
Church (rems of)
Hole Fm
Delvyn's Fm
Great Henny
Audley End
Rectory Fm
Butler's Hall Fm
Clay Hill
Dovehouse Fm
Edeys Fm
Fenn Fm
Crouch Ho
Parkgate Fm
Moat Fm
Lodge Fm
Wickham St Paul
Twinstead
B1058
Newhouse Fm
Nether House Fm
Twinstead Green
Pannells Ash Fm
Odewells
Long Gardens
Newhouse Cottages
Ansell's
Park Fm
Old House
Byham Hall
Catley Cross
Lorkin's Fm
Cobb's Fm
Chelmshoe House Fm
Stonehouse Fm
Monks Lodge
Magnolia Ho
Park's Fm
Cripple Corner
School Fm
Collin's Fm
Dagworth Manor
King's Fm
Great Yeldham
Lucking Street
Wr Twr
Gallant's Fm
Little

Ballingdon
Ballingdon Grove
Bulmer
Goldingham Hall
Wait's Fm
Hall (not in situ)
Middleton Hall
Auberies
Armsey Fm
Largess Fm
Nether Hall
Upper Houses
Hill Fm
Bulmer Tye
Over Hall
Gestingthorpe
The Ryes
Church (rems of)
Hall
Sheepcot Fm
Hole Fm
Delvyn's Fm
Great Henny
Clay Hill
Audley End
Rectory Fm
Edeys Fm
Butler's Hall Fm
Dovehouse Fm
Fenn Fm
Hall
Crouch Ho
Moat Fm
Wickham St Paul
Lodge Fm
Twinstead
B1058
Newhouse Fm
Nether House Fm
Twinstead Green
Odewells
Long Gardens
Newhouse Cottages
Ansell's Fm
Old House
Park Fm
Byham Hall
Catley Cross
Lorkin's Fm
Cobb's Fm
Stonehouse Fm
Monks Lodge
Magnolia Ho
Cripple Corner
School Fm
Park's Fm
Collin's Fm
Dagworth Manor
King's Fm
Lucking Street
Wr Twr
Gallant's Fm
Hall
Little Maplestead
Le Mote Hall
Birchleys
Cross End
Oak Fm
Stapleford's Fm
Pebmarsh
Montague's Fm
Hampers
Gage's
Greathouse Fm
Byndes
Spoon's Hall
Dyne's Hall
Dean's Hall
Stanley Hall
Moat
Valiants
Marvel's Garden
Bennett's Fm
Fitz John's Fm
Hunt's Hall
Hill Ho
Bentall's Fm
Ashford Lodge
Stoneylands
Worlds End Fm
Hungary Hill
Doe's Corner
Oxley Wood
The Cangle
Baggarett's
The Howe
Star Stile
Peverall's Fm
Elm Tree Fm
Brick House Fm
A131
Abbot's Shrubs
Countess Cross
Hospl
Schs
Boose's Green
Over Hall
Inn
Cemy
Sch
Westwood Fm
Bunting's Green
Colne Engaine
Mus

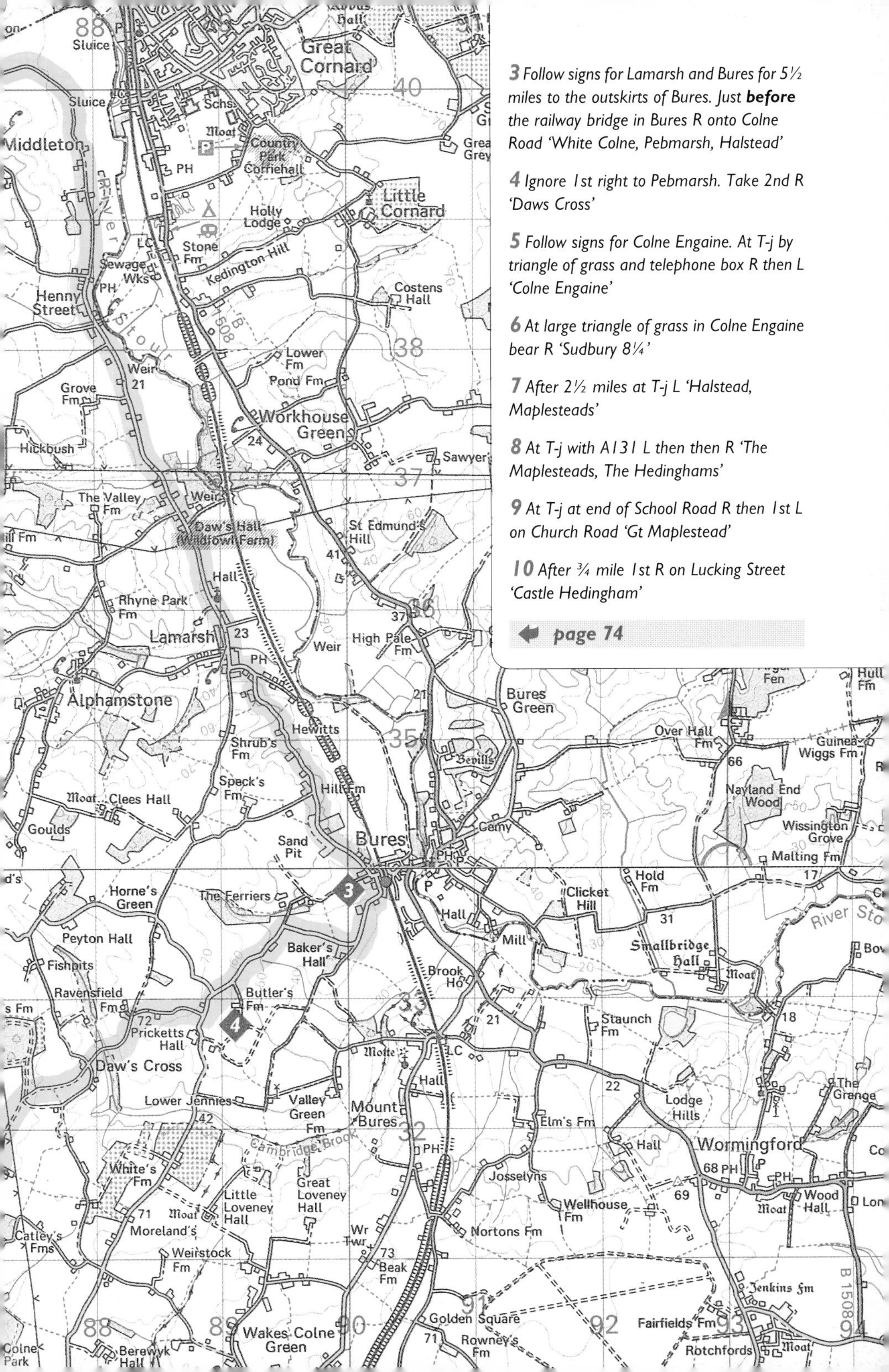

3 *Follow signs for Lamarsh and Bures for 5½ miles to the outskirts of Bures. Just* ***before*** *the railway bridge in Bures R onto Colne Road 'White Colne, Pebmarsh, Halstead'*

4 *Ignore 1st right to Pebmarsh. Take 2nd R 'Daws Cross'*

5 *Follow signs for Colne Engaine. At T-j by triangle of grass and telephone box R then L 'Colne Engaine'*

6 *At large triangle of grass in Colne Engaine bear R 'Sudbury 8¼'*

7 *After 2½ miles at T-j L 'Halstead, Maplesteads'*

8 *At T-j with A131 L then then R 'The Maplesteads, The Hedinghams'*

9 *At T-j at end of School Road R then 1st L on Church Road 'Gt Maplestead'*

10 *After ¾ mile 1st R on Lucking Street 'Castle Hedingham'*

page 74

11 South from Lavenham to Boxford, Stoke-by-Nayland and Hadleigh

This ride could easily be combined with the route starting from Hadleigh by making a link on the section between Stoke-by-Nayland and Hadleigh (via Shelley). The route takes in the lovely villages of Boxford and Stoke-by-Nayland. The stretch northeast from here to Hadleigh is remarkable in that you follow the same tiny country lane for six miles without needing to turn off to the right or left until reaching Hadleigh. The latter is an attractive town with plenty of facilities. In order to avoid the busy A1141 you have twice to climb out of the valley of the River Brett. Open cycling past the remains of two castle earthworks returns you to the delights of Lavenham.

80 81 82 83 Hadleigh

Start

The Tourist Information Centre, Lavenham, 10 miles southeast of Bury St Edmunds

P Follow signs for long stay car park just off the B1071 Sudbury road

Distance and grade

30 miles

Easy / moderate

Terrain

Gently rolling. Several 100 feet climbs. Lowest point – 50 feet (16 mts) at the River Box near Stoke-by-Nayland. Highest point – 270 feet (81 mts) betwen Kersey and Lavenham

Nearest railway

Manningtree, 10 miles southeast of Hadleigh

Lavenham Acton Great Waldingfield Edwardstone Boxford Stoke-by-Nayland

Places of interest

Boxford *7*
Thatched cottages and willows on the banks of the River Lambourn, where the magnificent watermill still turns. Medieval murals can be viewed in the church

Polstead *10*
A hall was recorded at Polstead in the Domesday Book. The present hall was built in the 18th century and the title was passed down in an unusual manner called 'Borough English' whereby the youngest son, rather than the eldest, inherited all

Stoke-by-Nayland *11*
The church is featured in several of Constable's paintings

▲ *Kersey*

Kersey *17*
Peaceful village of red-tiled houses on steep slope descending to ford and rising again to the summit of Church Hill. The wooden panels in the church are masterpieces of 15th-century craftsmanship. Afternoon teas served at the Bell Inn

Refreshments

Plenty of choice ***in Lavenham***
Fleece PH, White Hart PH, ***Boxford***
Angel Inn PH, The Crown PH,
Black Horse PH, ***Stoke-by-Nayland***
Queens Head PH, ***Lower Layham***
Plenty of choice, ***Hadleigh***

Lower Layham
Hadleigh
Kersey

1 *With back to the Tourist Information Centre L downhill. At T-j R then at next T-j L 'Long Melford 4, Sudbury 6'*

2 *½ mile after passing Lavenham's fine church, by a petrol station, R on to Melford Road 'Acton 3, Long Melford 4'*

3 *After 1 mile 1st L 'Acton 1¼' then at T-j by triangle of grass R 'Acton 1½, Sudbury 4'*

4 *At T-j at the end of Barrow Hill L (NS) through Acton*

5 *At X-roads with B1115 R 'Sudbury 2½, Newton 2', then after 400 yards 1st L on to Folly Road 'Boxford 5½, Edwardstone 3½'*

6 ***Easy to miss**. Keep following signs for Edwardstone and Boxford. After 3 miles, by a triangle of grass R 'Edwardstone 1, Boxford 3'*

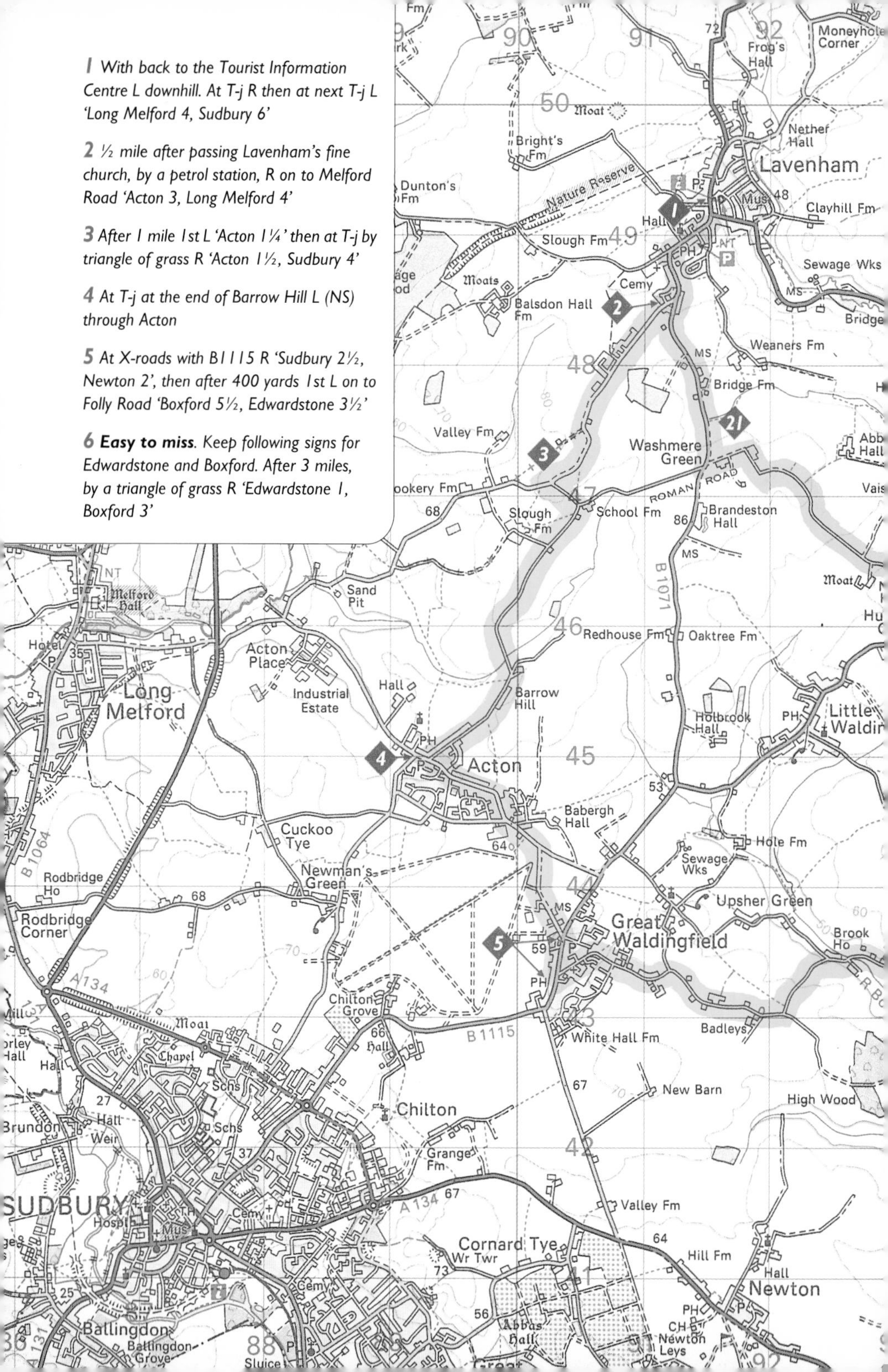

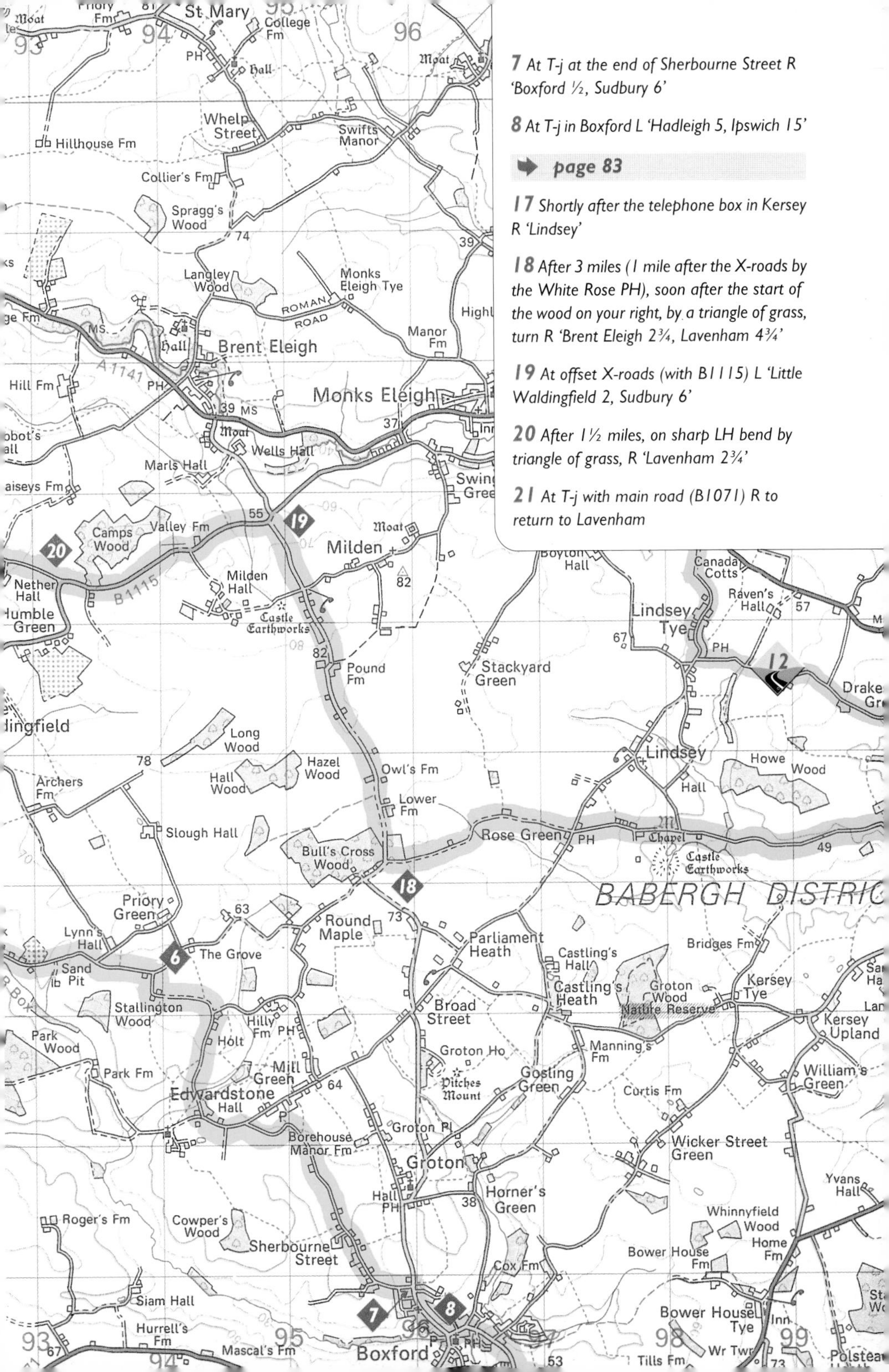

7 *At T-j at the end of Sherbourne Street R 'Boxford ½, Sudbury 6'*

8 *At T-j in Boxford L 'Hadleigh 5, Ipswich 15'*

page 83

17 *Shortly after the telephone box in Kersey R 'Lindsey'*

18 *After 3 miles (1 mile after the X-roads by the White Rose PH), soon after the start of the wood on your right, by a triangle of grass, turn R 'Brent Eleigh 2¾, Lavenham 4¾'*

19 *At offset X-roads (with B1115) L 'Little Waldingfield 2, Sudbury 6'*

20 *After 1½ miles, on sharp LH bend by triangle of grass, R 'Lavenham 2¾'*

21 *At T-j with main road (B1071) R to return to Lavenham*

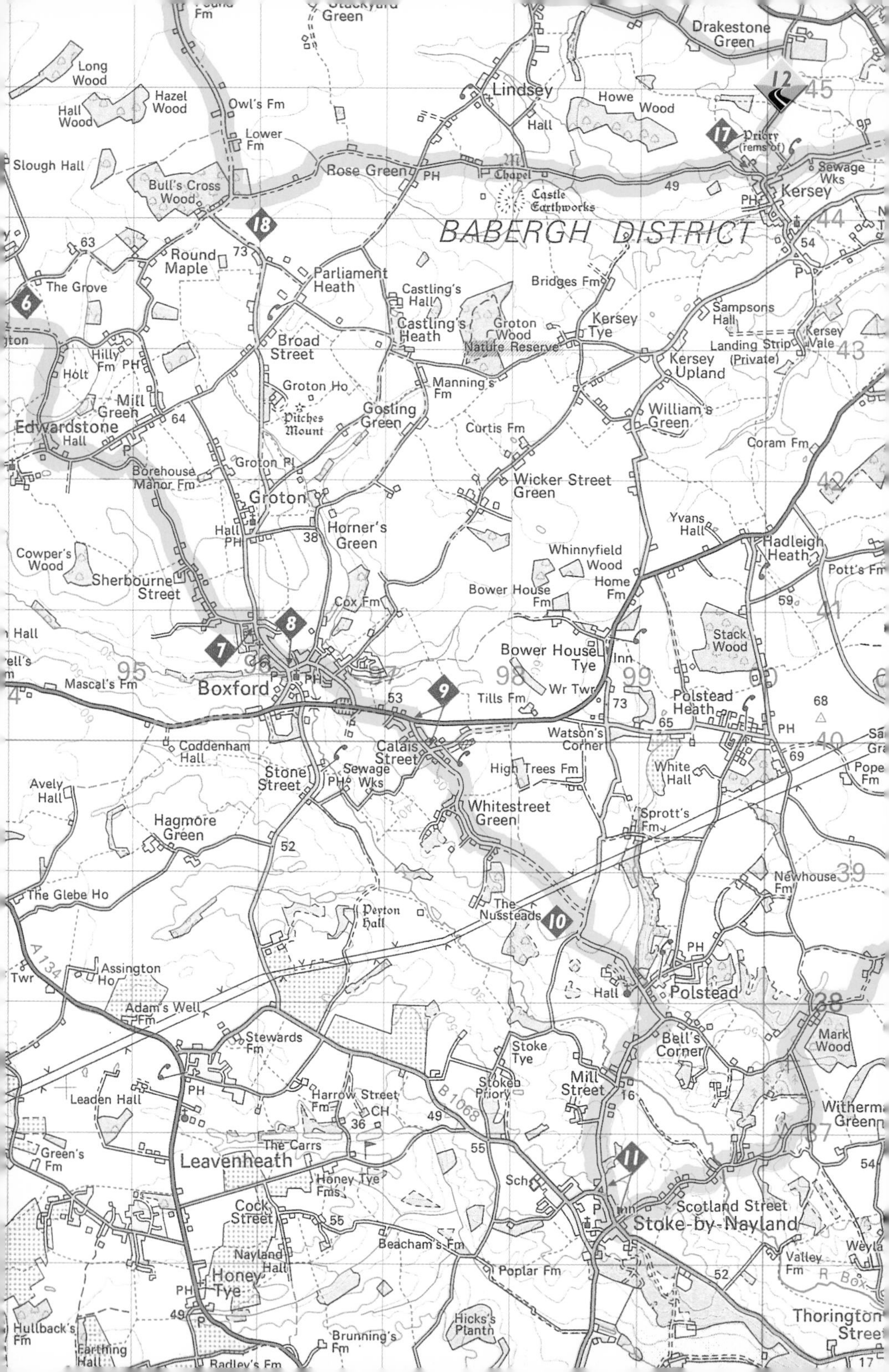

Drakestone Green
Long Wood
Hazel Wood
Hall Wood
Owl's Fm
Lindsey
Howe Wood
Hall
Lower Fm
Priory (rems of)
Slough Hall
Rose Green
PH
Chapel
Castle Earthworks
Sewage Wks
Kersey
Bull's Cross Wood
BABERGH DISTRICT
Round Maple
Parliament Heath
The Grove
Castling's Hall
Castling's Heath
Bridges Fm
Groton Wood Nature Reserve
Kersey Tye
Sampsons Hall
Broad Street
Landing Strip (Private)
Kersey Vale
Kersey Upland
Holt
Hilly Fm
Mill Green
Groton Ho
Manning's Fm
Gosling Green
Pitches Mount
William's Green
Edwardstone Hall
Curtis Fm
Coram Fm
Borehouse Manor Fm
Groton Pl
Groton
Wicker Street Green
Horner's Green
Yvans Hall
Hadleigh Heath
Cowper's Wood
Sherbourne Street
Whinnyfield Wood
Pott's Fm
Home Fm
Bower House Fm
Cox Fm
Stack Wood
Bower House Tye
Inn
Mascal's Fm
Boxford
Tills Fm
Wr Twr
Polstead Heath
Watson's Corner
Coddenham Hall
Calais Street
Stone Street
Sewage Wks
High Trees Fm
White Hall
Pope Fm
Avely Hall
Hagmore Green
Whitestreet Green
Sprott's Fm
The Glebe Ho
Newhouse Fm
The Nussteads
Peyton Hall
Assington Ho
A 134
Hall
Polstead
Adam's Well Fm
Stewards Fm
Mark Wood
Stoke Tye
Bell's Corner
Leaden Hall
Harrow Street Fm
Stoke Priory
Mill Street
Witherm Green
B 1068
The Carrs
Green's Fm
Leavenheath
Honey Tye Fms
Sch
Cock Street
Scotland Street
Stoke-by-Nayland
Beacham's Fm
Nayland Hall
Valley Fm
Poplar Fm
R Box
Honey Tye
Hullback's Fm
Hicks's Plantn
Thorington Street
Brunning's Fm
Earthing Hall
Radley's Fm

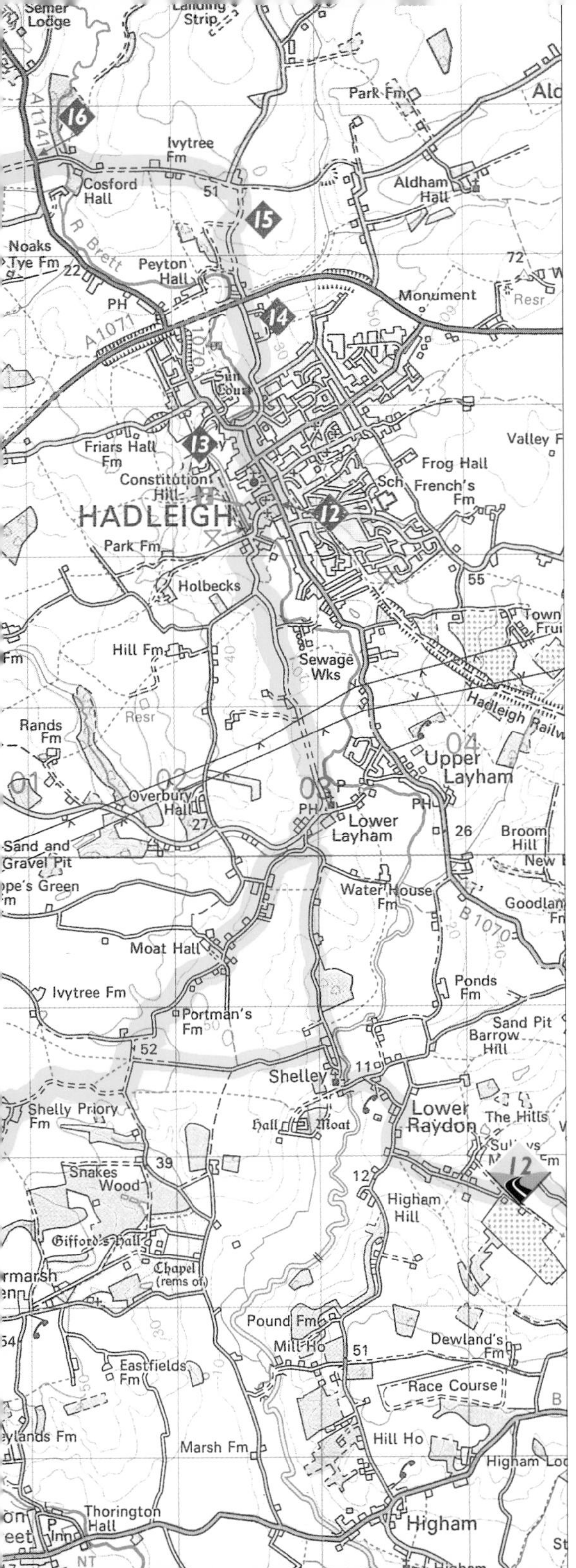

6 ***Easy to miss***. *Keep following signs for Edwardstone and Boxford. After 3 miles, by a triangle of grass R 'Edwardstone 1, Boxford 3'*

7 *At T-j at the end of Sherbourne Street R 'Boxford ½, Sudbury 6'*

8 *At T-j in Boxford L 'Hadleigh 5, Ipswich 15'*

9 *At T-j with the busy A1071 L 'Hadleigh 5, Ipswich 15' then 1st R 'Calais Street, Whitestreet Green, Polstead'. After 300 yards, on sharp LH bend R (passing to the left of Corner Cottage) 'Whitestreet Green, Polstead'*

10 *After 1 mile, at T-j R 'Stoke-by-Nayland 1¾, Colchester 9'*

11 *At T-j by large triangle of grass L 'Thorington Street 2, Higham 3¼, Ipswich 14½'. At X-roads in Stoke-by-Nayland by the Angel Inn L 'Withermarsh 1½, Layham 4, Hadleigh 5½'*

12 *Follow this lane and signs for Hadleigh for 6 miles, ignoring turns to the left and right. (**Or** for link with route 12 to form a 60 mile loop, after 3 miles keep an eye out for a right turn to Shelley and join the other route at instruction 2)*

13 *Through Hadleigh along the High Street. On sharp LH bend towards the end of the town R 'Aldham, Elmsett, Recreation Ground'*

14 *At X-roads with the A1071 SA on to Aldham Mill Hill 'Whatfield 2'*

15 *At the top of the hill, on a sharp RH bend bear L by a triangle of grass 'Kersey 2, Boxford 5'*

16 *At X-roads with the A1141 SA 'Kersey 1, Lindsey 2'*

17 *Shortly after the telephone box in Kersey R 'Lindsey'*

18 *After 3 miles (1 mile after the X-roads by the White Rose PH), soon after the start of the wood on your right, by a triangle of grass, turn R 'Brent Eleigh 2¾, Lavenham 4¾'*

page 81

12 A ring around Hadleigh returning via the attractive villages of Bildeston and Chelsworth

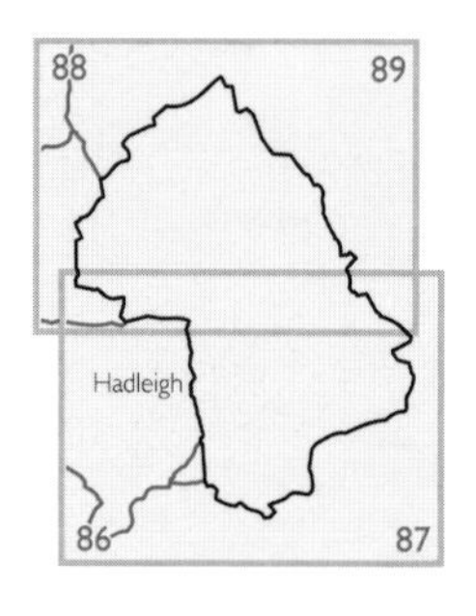

Hadleigh is an attractive, bustling town in south Suffolk. The ride starts southwards following the River Brett before cutting east and northeast on tiny lanes across open farmland towards Washbrook. The short busy section on the A1071 comes as something of a shock but you are soon back in the domain of the cyclist as attractive lanes bear you north through Flowton and Offton, around the airfield at Wattisham and back via the charms of Bildeston, Chelsworth and Kersey. This ride can easily be linked with route 11 to form a sixty-mile loop.

Start

The Kings Head PH, the High Street, Hadleigh, 10 miles west of Ipswich

P Long stay car park just off the High Street near the Kings Head PH

Distance and grade

33 miles
Easy / moderate

Terrain

Several climbs of between 50 and 100 feet. Lowest point – 36 feet (11 mts) at Shelley. Highest point – 290 feet (88 mts) at Wattisham

Nearest railway

Manningtree, 7 miles southeast of the route at Raydon or Stowmarket, 6 miles north of the route at Ringshall

Hadleigh Lower Layham Great Wenham Burstall Flowton

Places of interest

▲ Near Hadleigh

Hadleigh *1*
Town of colour-washed houses with decorative plaster work on the walls (pargeting). Fine Georgian and medieval buildings, including a 15th-century Guildhall

East Bergholt *(just off the route) 3*
In the heart of Constable country, this is still an unspoilt village. The painter was born here in 1776 in a house near the parish church. Only an outbuilding remains – since converted into a private dwelling

Bildeston *16*
Medieval wool centre with multi-coloured Tudor houses. Ghostly footsteps at The Crown, said to be a haunted pub

Chelsworth *17*
Timbered cottages, 14th-century church and 18th-century double humped bridge straddling the River Brett

Refreshments

Queens Head PH, ***Lower Layham***
Limeburners PH, ***Offton***
Red Lion PH, Kings Head PH, Crown PH ♥, ***Bildeston***
Peacock Inn PH ♥♥, ***Chelsworth***
Red Rose PH ♥, ***Lindsey Tye***
The Bell PH ♥♥, ***Kersey***

Offton
Wattisham
Chelsworth
Kersey

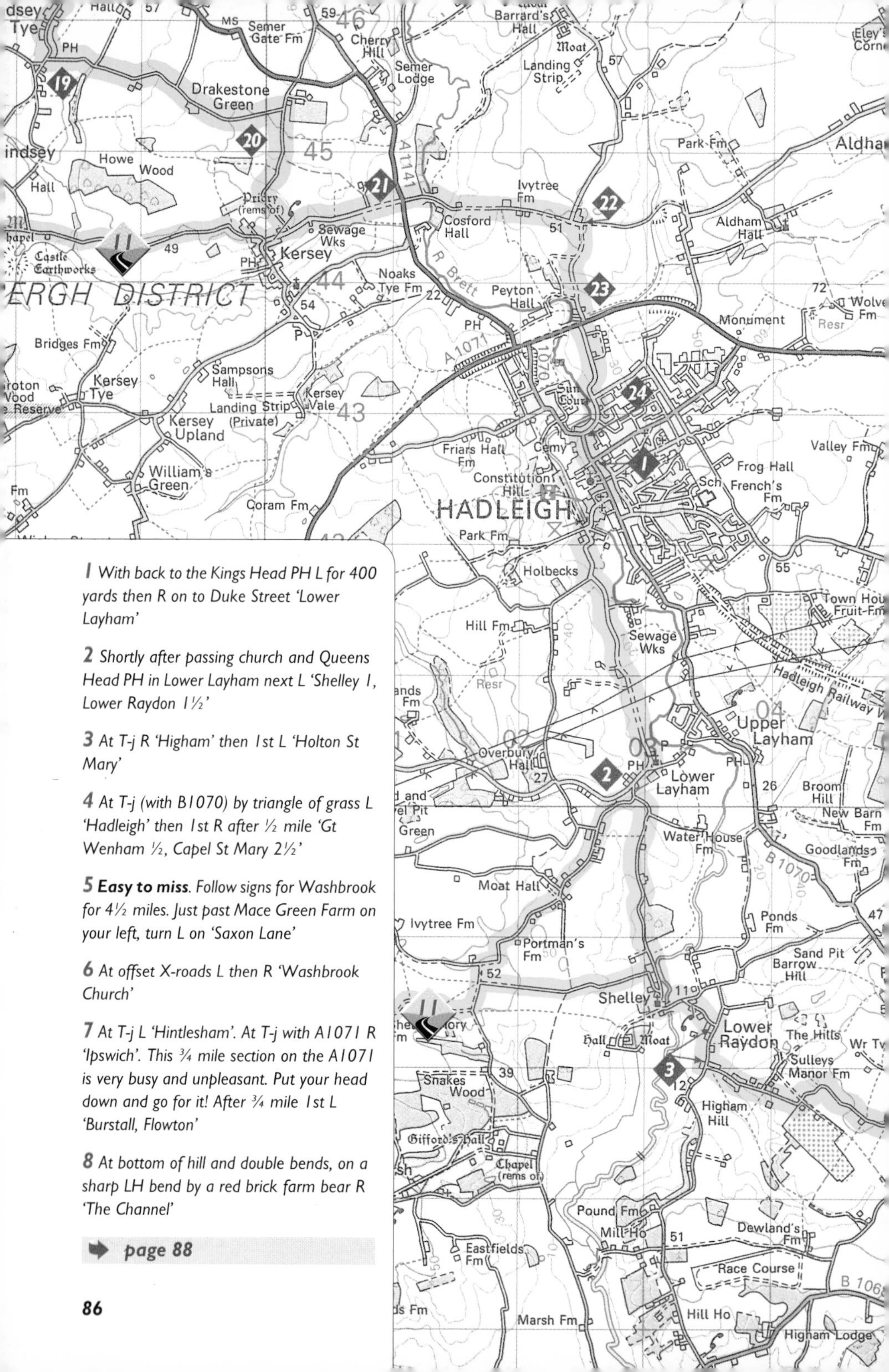

1 With back to the Kings Head PH L for 400 yards then R on to Duke Street 'Lower Layham'

2 Shortly after passing church and Queens Head PH in Lower Layham next L 'Shelley 1, Lower Raydon 1½'

3 At T-j R 'Higham' then 1st L 'Holton St Mary'

4 At T-j (with B1070) by triangle of grass L 'Hadleigh' then 1st R after ½ mile 'Gt Wenham ½, Capel St Mary 2½'

5 **Easy to miss**. *Follow signs for Washbrook for 4½ miles. Just past Mace Green Farm on your left, turn L on 'Saxon Lane'*

6 At offset X-roads L then R 'Washbrook Church'

7 At T-j L 'Hintlesham'. At T-j with A1071 R 'Ipswich'. This ¾ mile section on the A1071 is very busy and unpleasant. Put your head down and go for it! After ¾ mile 1st L 'Burstall, Flowton'

8 At bottom of hill and double bends, on a sharp LH bend by a red brick farm bear R 'The Channel'

page 88

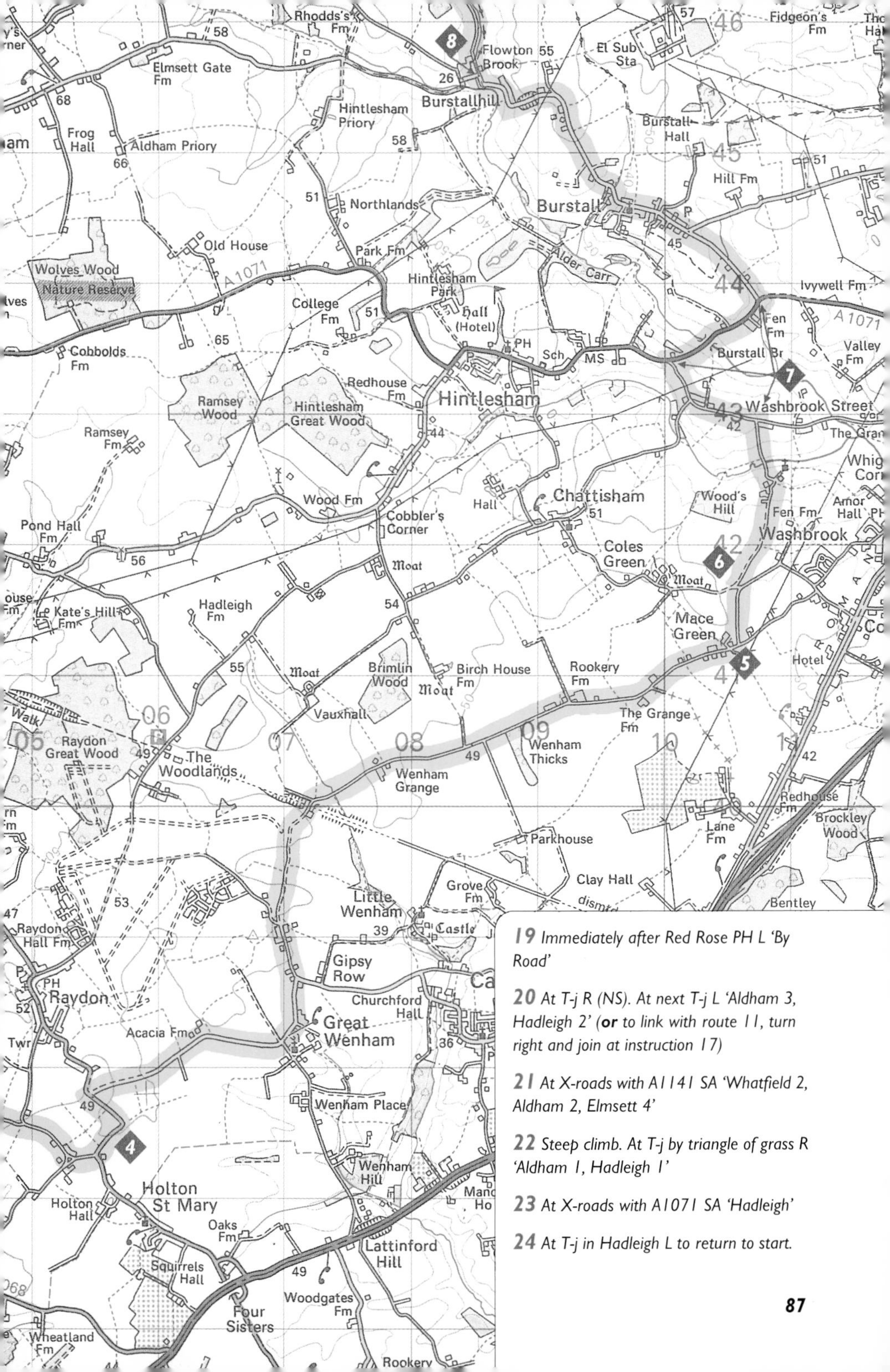

19 *Immediately after Red Rose PH L 'By Road'*

20 *At T-j R (NS). At next T-j L 'Aldham 3, Hadleigh 2' (**or** to link with route 11, turn right and join at instruction 17)*

21 *At X-roads with A1141 SA 'Whatfield 2, Aldham 2, Elmsett 4'*

22 *Steep climb. At T-j by triangle of grass R 'Aldham 1, Hadleigh 1'*

23 *At X-roads with A1071 SA 'Hadleigh'*

24 *At T-j in Hadleigh L to return to start.*

8 *At bottom of hill and double bends, on a sharp LH bend by a red brick farm bear R 'The Channel'*

9 *At T-j L 'Flowton Church ½, Somersham 2, Elmsett 2¾', then just past the church R 'Somersham 1½'*

10 *After ½ mile by small triangle of grass, L 'Elmsett'*

11 *At T-j by triangle of grass bear R 'Offton'. At next T-j L 'Offton, Needham Market'.*

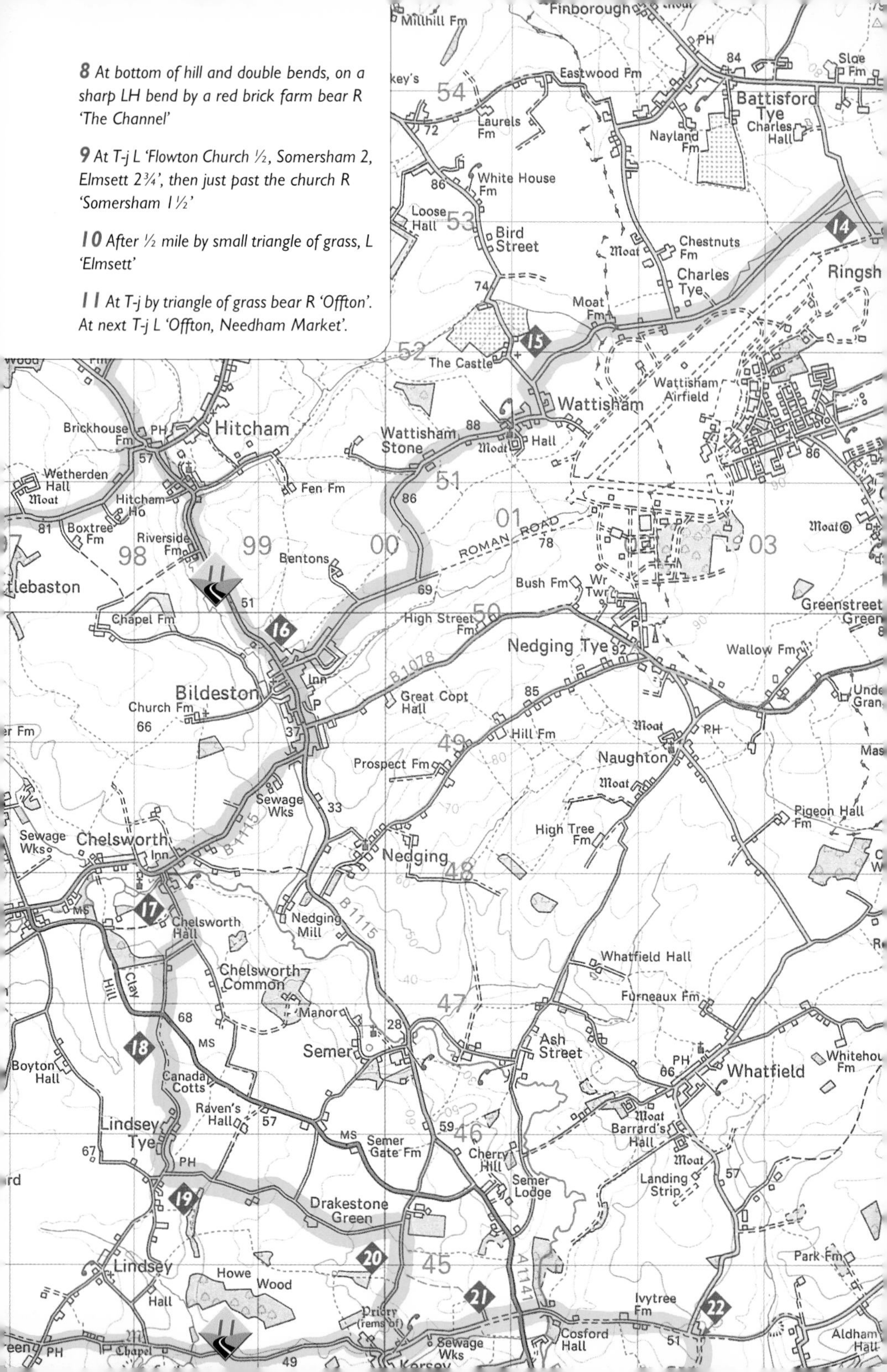

12 After Limeburners PH 1st L 'Offton ½, Bildeston 5¾'. Following white railings bear R downhill on 1st right turn

13 At X-roads with B1078 SA 'Ringstall, Battisford 2½'. At offset X-roads R then L 'Battisford, Stowmarket'

14 Shortly after passing between the landing lights either side of the road next L 'Wattisham Village 2¾, Bildeston 3¾'

15 At T-j by triangle of grass L 'Bildeston 2½'

16 At T-j with B1115 in Bildeston, L 'Hadleigh 5'. At the end of the village R on B1115 'Sudbury, Chelsworth, Monks Eleigh'

17 Opposite Peacock Inn in Chelsworth L 'Lindsey 2'

18 At X-roads with A1141 SA 'Lindsey 1, Boxford 6'

19 Immediately after Red Rose PH L 'By Road'

*20 At T-j R (NS). At next T-j L 'Aldham 3, Hadleigh 2' (**or** to link with route 11, turn right and join at instruction 17)*

21 At X-roads with A1141 SA 'Whatfield 2, Aldham 2, Elmsett 4'

22 Steep climb. At T-j by triangle of grass R 'Aldham 1, Hadleigh 1'

page 87

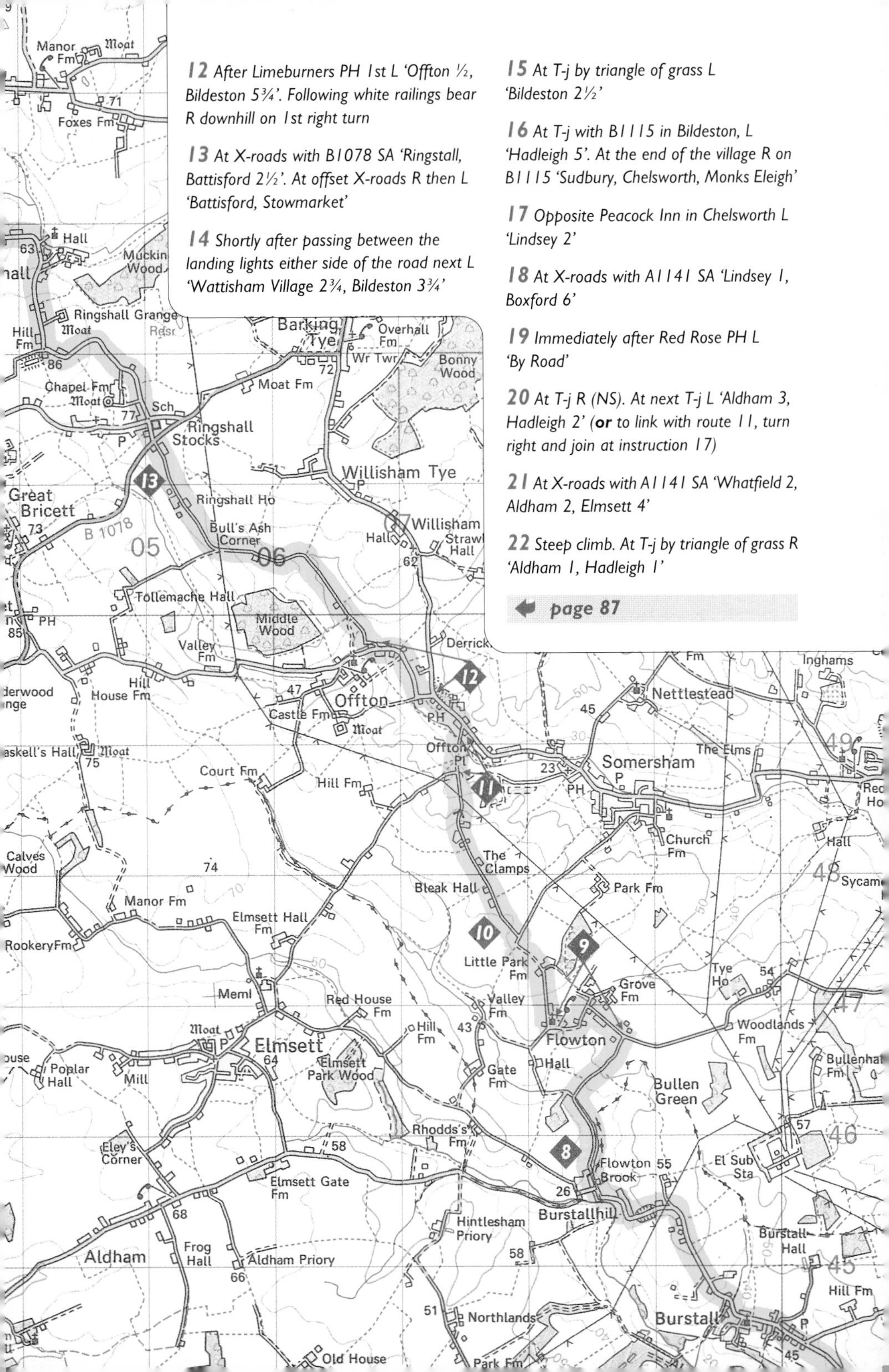

Manor Fm
Moat
71
Foxes Fm
Hall
63
Muckin Wood
Ringshall Grange
Hill Fm
Moat
Resr
86
Chapel Fm
Moat
77
Sch
P
Ringshall Stocks
Barking Tye
Overhall Fm
Wr Twr
72
Bonny Wood
Moat Fm
Willisham Tye
P
Great Bricett
73
B 1078
05
Ringshall Ho
Bull's Ash Corner
06
Willisham Hall
Strawl Hall
62
Tollemache Hall
Middle Wood
PH
85
Valley Fm
Derrick
Hill House Fm
47
Offton
Castle Fm
Moat
PH
Offton Pl
45
Nettlestead
Inghams
The Elms
49
Somersham
P
23
PH
Court Fm
Hill Fm
75
Moat
Red Ho
Church Fm
Hall
The Clamps
Calves Wood
74
Bleak Hall
Park Fm
48
Sycam
Manor Fm
Elmsett Hall Fm
Rookery Fm
Little Park Fm
Grove Fm
Tye Ho
54
Meml
Red House Fm
Valley Fm
43
Woodlands Fm
47
Moat
P
Elmsett
64
Hill Fm
Flowton
Poplar Hall
Mill
Elmsett Park Wood
Gate Fm
Hall
Bullen Green
Bullenhall Fm
57
46
Eley's Corner
58
Rhodds's Fm
Flowton Brook
55
El Sub Sta
Elmsett Gate Fm
26
68
Burstallhill
Hintlesham Priory
Burstall Hall
45
Aldham
Frog Hall
Aldham Priory
66
58
Hill Fm
51
Northlands
Burstall
P
Old House
Park Fm
45

13 West from Framlingham via quiet Suffolk lanes to the attractive village of Debenham

One of two rides from Framlingham, deep in the heart of Suffolk. The route takes you past many attractive thatched cottages and pretty villages, almost all of which boast flint-built churches and an ornate village sign which depicts one of the most salient characteristics of the locale. The countryside is gently undulating with many wild flowers growing in the verges besides the road. The antique centre in Debenham is a fine, ornate building and the village has other attractive half-timbered and thatched properties. One of the best attractions of the ride is at the end – the working windmill at Saxtead Green.

Start

The Square, Framlingham, 15 miles northeast of Ipswich

P Follow signs for long stay car park on Albert Road, just off the B1116 road to Wickham Market

Distance and grade

29 miles
Easy

Terrain

No major hills. Lowest point – 80 feet (25 mts) in Framlingham. Highest point – 210 feet (63 mts) near to Worlingworth

Nearest railway

Wickham Market, 6 miles southeast of Framlingham

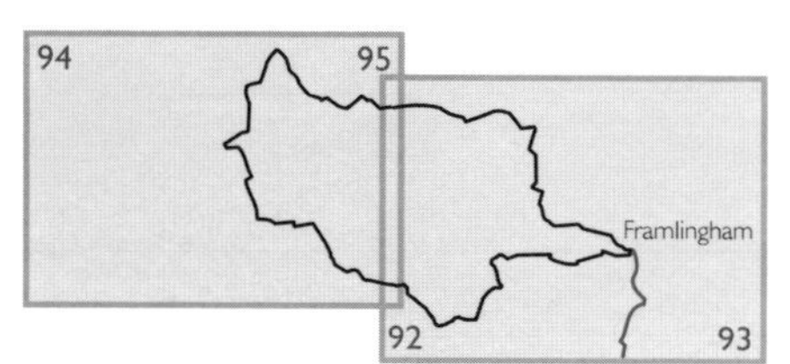

Framlingham   Earl Soham   Broad Green

▼ *Morris dancers at Saxtead Green*

Places of interest

Framlingham *1*
Market town with a patchwork of architectural periods dating from the 12th century. The castle, dating from 1100, was largely rebuilt in the 16th century and has a walk linking nine of the towers, two ditches and the lower court beside the artificial lake. The church contains splendid 16th-century Howard monuments

Earl Soham *2*
The church contains some superb woodwork: a double hammerbeam roof spans the nave, and the bench-ends are carved with a rich variety of birds, beasts, angels and men. The nearby rectory dates from Tudor times

Saxtead Green *15*
Superb example of an 18th-century Suffolk post mill in full working order, with three-storey roundhouse, sails and fantail

Otley Hall *(just off the route) 16*
Fine panelling and Jacobean wall decorations are outstanding features of this 16th-century house. Magnificent gardens

Helmingham Hall *(just off the route) 16*
Tudor house with moated gardens, herbaceous borders and rare roses

Refreshments

Plenty of choice ***in Framlingham***
Victoria PH, Falcon PH, ***Earl Soham***
The Bell PH, ***Cretingham*** *(just off the route)*
Cherry Tree PH, Red Lion PH, The Angel PH, ***Debenham***
Black Horse PH, ***Thorndon*** *(just off the route)*
Beaconsfield Arms PH, ***Occold***
Plough Inn PH, ***Southolt*** *The Swan PH,* ***Worlingworth***

Thorndon
Bedingfield
Worlingworth
Tannington
Saxtead Green

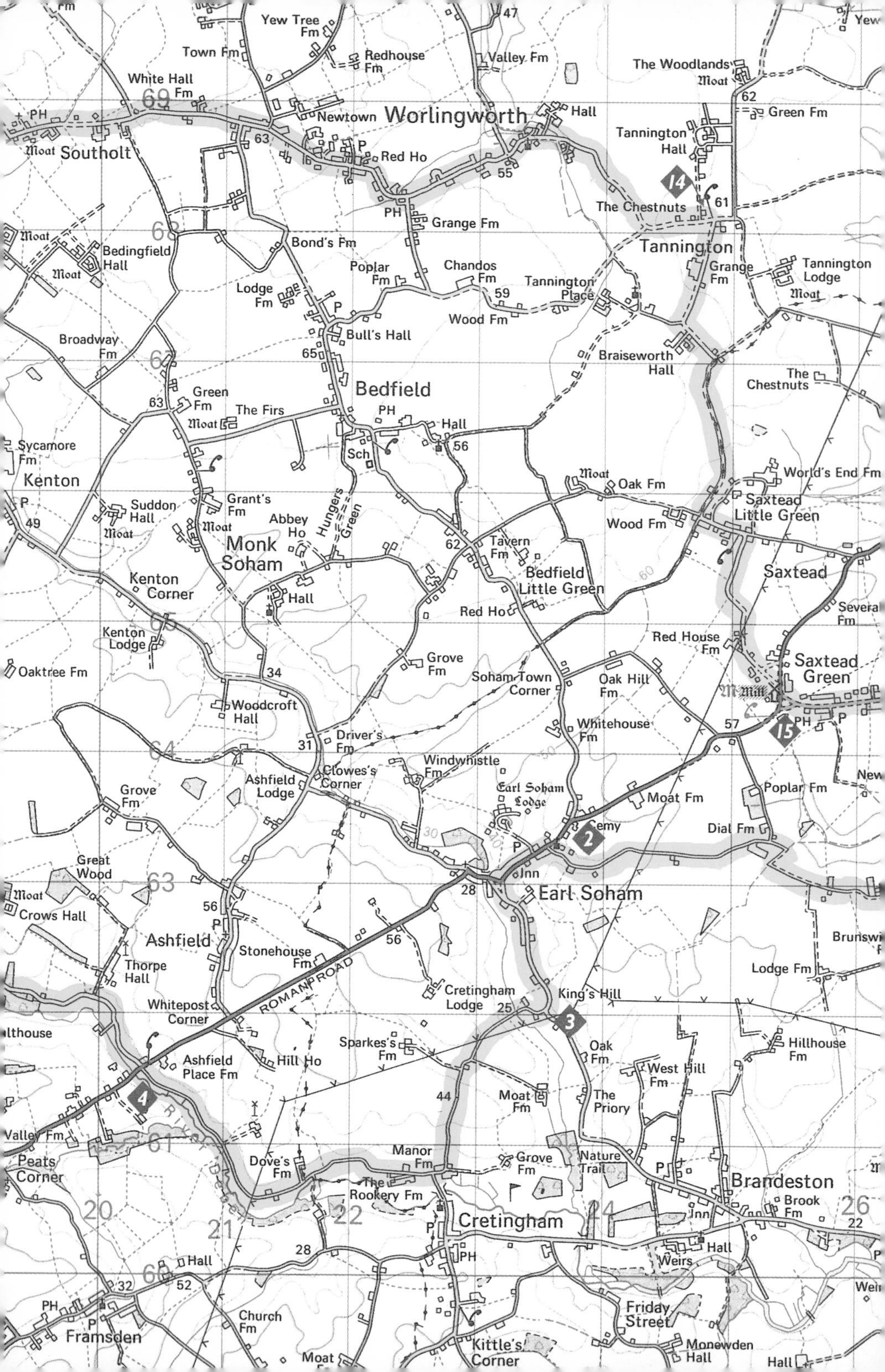

Worlingworth
Southolt
Bedfield
Tannington
Kenton
Monk Soham
Saxtead
Saxtead Little Green
Saxtead Green
Bedfield Little Green
Earl Soham
Ashfield
Cretingham
Brandeston
Framsden
Yew Tree Fm
Town Fm
Redhouse Fm
White Hall Fm
Valley Fm
The Woodlands
Moat
Newtown
Hall
Green Fm
Red Ho
Tannington Hall
The Chestnuts
Grange Fm
Bedingfield Hall
Bond's Fm
Poplar Fm
Chandos Fm
Tannington Place
Tannington Lodge
Lodge Fm
Wood Fm
Bull's Hall
Braiseworth Hall
Broadway Fm
Green Fm
The Firs
Sycamore Fm
Sch
Oak Fm
World's End Fm
Grant's Fm
Suddon Hall
Abbey Ho
Hungers Green
Tavern Fm
Kenton Corner
Kenton Lodge
Oaktree Fm
Grove Fm
Soham Town Corner
Red House Fm
Oak Hill Fm
Mill
Woodcroft Hall
Driver's Fm
Whitehouse Fm
Several Fm
Windwhistle Fm
Clowes's Corner
Ashfield Lodge
Earl Soham Lodge
Moat Fm
Poplar Fm
New
Cemy
Dial Fm
Great Wood
Crows Hall
Inn
Stonehouse Fm
Brunswick
Thorpe Hall
Lodge Fm
ROMAN ROAD
Cretingham Lodge
King's Hill
Whitepost Corner
Althouse
Sparkes's Fm
Hillhouse Fm
Ashfield Place Fm
Hill Ho
West Hill Fm
The Priory
Valley Fm
RIVER DEBEN
Peats Corner
Dove's Fm
Manor Fm
Grove Fm
Nature Trail
The Rookery Fm
Brook Fm
Weirs
Church Fm
Friday Street
Kittle's Corner
Monewden Hall
PH
P
2
3
4
14
15

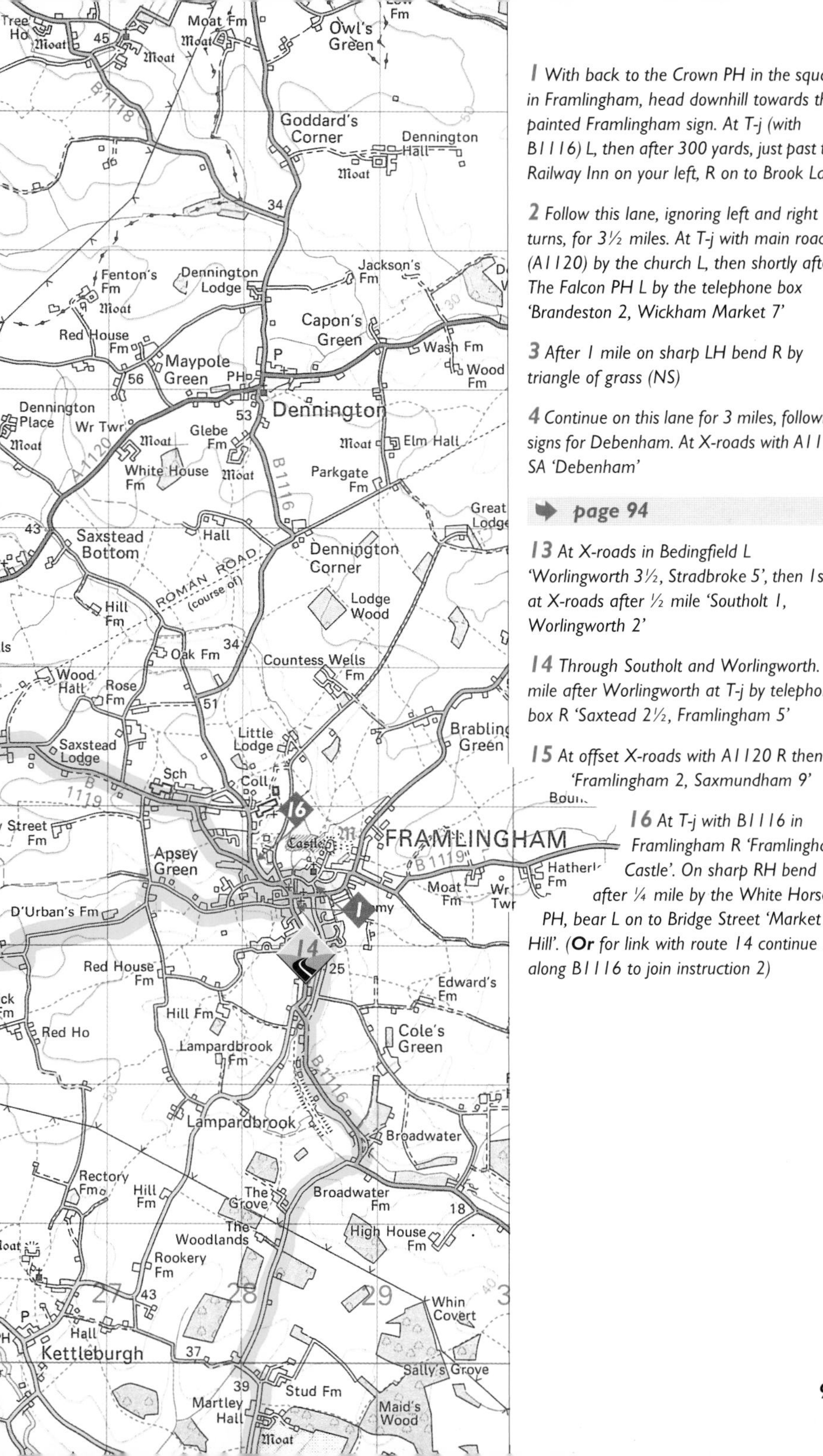

1 With back to the Crown PH in the square in Framlingham, head downhill towards the painted Framlingham sign. At T-j (with B1116) L, then after 300 yards, just past the Railway Inn on your left, R on to Brook Lane

2 Follow this lane, ignoring left and right turns, for 3½ miles. At T-j with main road (A1120) by the church L, then shortly after The Falcon PH L by the telephone box 'Brandeston 2, Wickham Market 7'

3 After 1 mile on sharp LH bend R by triangle of grass (NS)

4 Continue on this lane for 3 miles, following signs for Debenham. At X-roads with A1120 SA 'Debenham'

page 94

13 At X-roads in Bedingfield L 'Worlingworth 3½, Stradbroke 5', then 1st R at X-roads after ½ mile 'Southolt 1, Worlingworth 2'

14 Through Southolt and Worlingworth. 1 mile after Worlingworth at T-j by telephone box R 'Saxtead 2½, Framlingham 5'

15 At offset X-roads with A1120 R then L 'Framlingham 2, Saxmundham 9'

*16 At T-j with B1116 in Framlingham R 'Framlingham Castle'. On sharp RH bend after ¼ mile by the White Horse PH, bear L on to Bridge Street 'Market Hill'. (**Or** for link with route 14 continue SA along B1116 to join instruction 2)*

5 At T-j (with B1077) after 2 miles R 'Aspall 2, Eye 8'

6 Just past the Red Lion PH in Debenham L, then bear R 'Unsuitable for HGV'. Ignore left and right turns, continue SA on to Little London Hill 'Wetheringsett 3, Mendlesham 6'

7 After 2 miles, on sharp LH bend with a pink house ahead, R by triangle of grass 'Thorndon 4, Eye 8'

8 After 3 miles at slightly offset X-roads by a triangle of grass R (signs for every other direction except this one!)

9 At T-j by church in Thorndon R 'Debenham 5, Framlingham 13' (or left for the Black Horse PH)

10 At T-j with B1077 L 'Eye 3, Norwich 26, Occold 1'

11 After 1 mile on sharp LH bend 2nd R 'Occold, Bedingfield 2'

12 After 2 miles, just after a sharp RH bend, 1st L 'Bedingfield 1, Monk Soham 4'

page 93

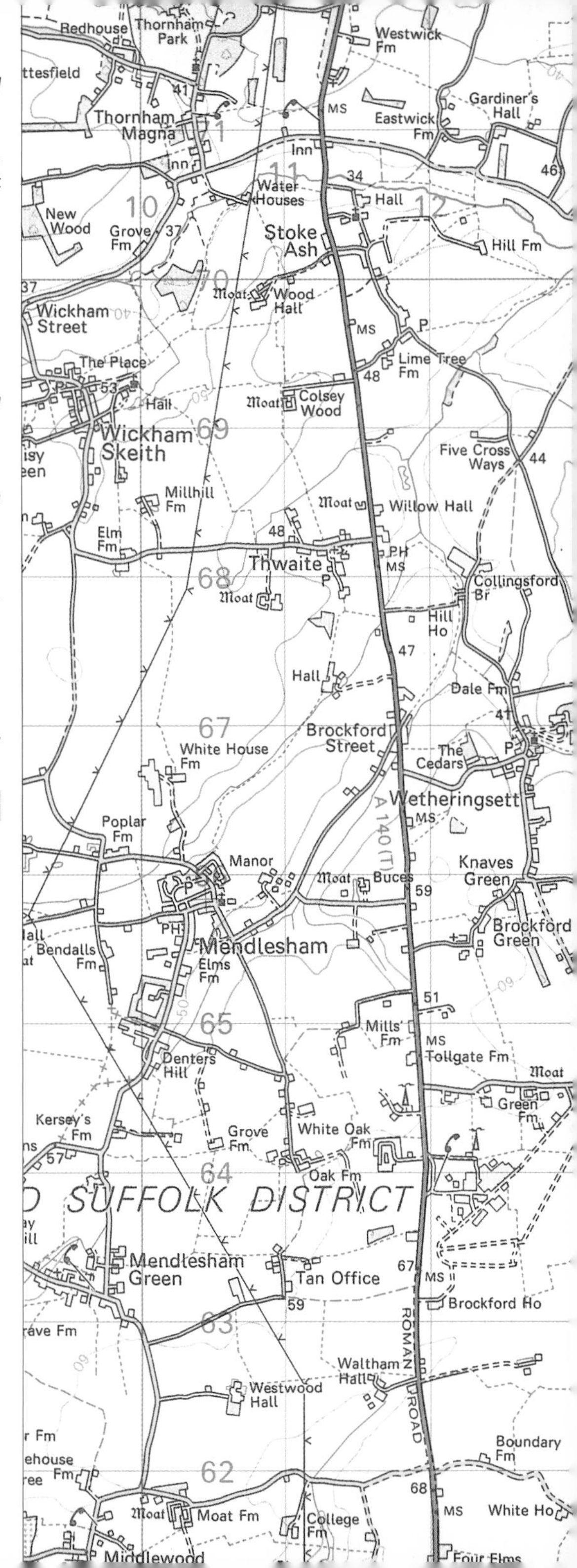

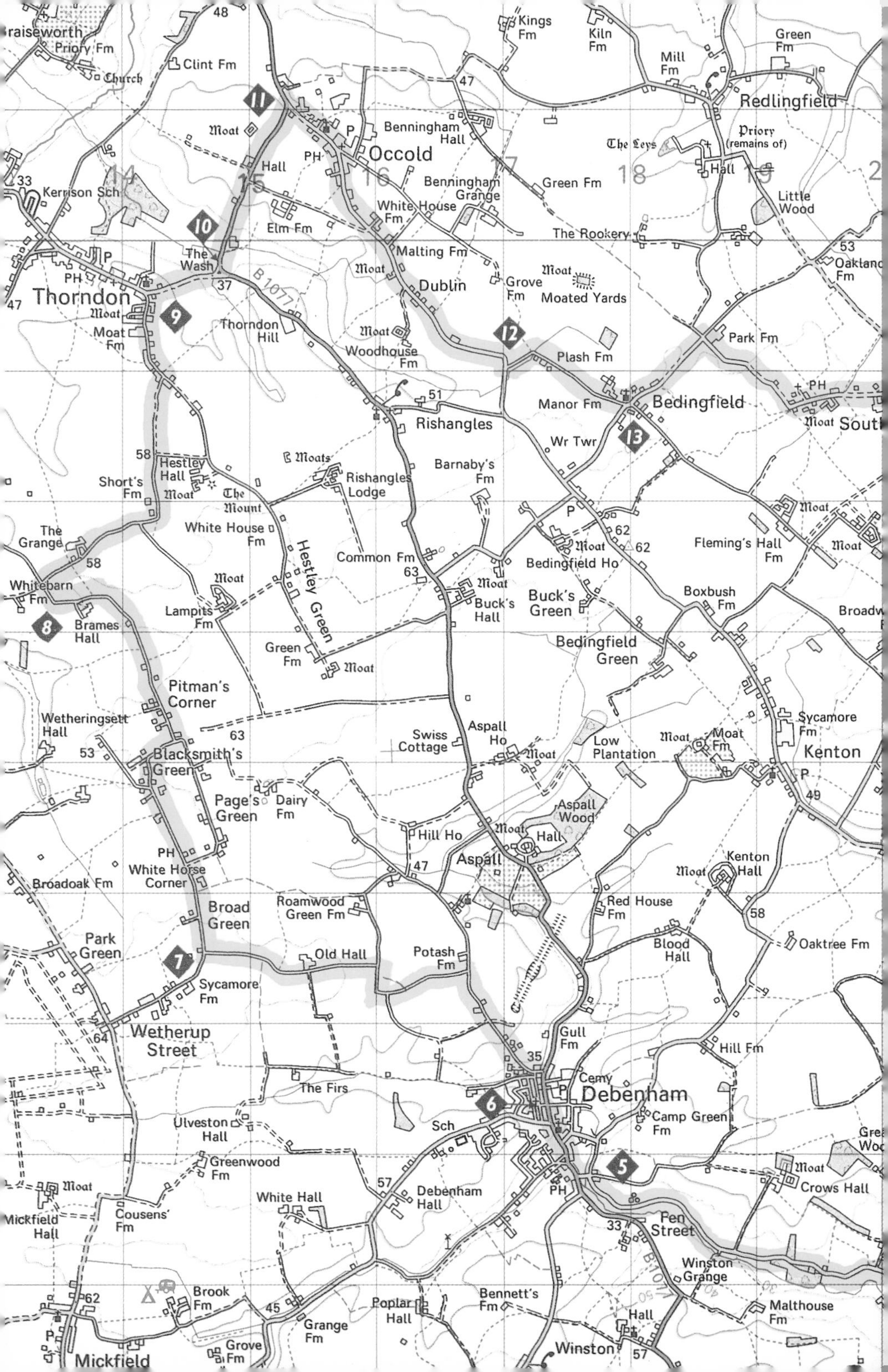

Braiseworth
Priory Fm
Church
Clint Fm
Kings Fm
Kiln Fm
Mill Fm
Green Fm
Redlingfield
Priory (remains of)
The Leys
Hall
Little Wood
Moat
Occold
Benningham Hall
Benningham Grange
Green Fm
White House Fm
Elm Fm
Malting Fm
The Rookery
Oakland Fm
Kerrison Sch
The Wash
Thorndon
Moat Fm
Thorndon Hill
Dublin
Grove Fm
Moated Yards
Woodhouse Fm
Park Fm
Plash Fm
Manor Fm
Bedingfield
Rishangles
Wr Twr
Barnaby's Fm
Hestley Hall
Short's Fm
The Mount
Rishangles Lodge
White House Fm
The Grange
Common Fm
Bedingfield Ho
Fleming's Hall Fm
Whitebarn Fm
Brames Hall
Lampits Fm
Hestley Green
Buck's Hall
Buck's Green
Boxbush Fm
Green Fm
Bedingfield Green
Pitman's Corner
Wetheringsett Hall
Swiss Cottage
Aspall Ho
Low Plantation
Moat Fm
Sycamore Fm
Kenton
Blacksmith's Green
Page's Green
Dairy Fm
Aspall Wood
Hill Ho
Aspall
Hall
Kenton Hall
White Horse Corner
Broadoak Fm
Roamwood Green Fm
Red House Fm
Broad Green
Park Green
Old Hall
Potash Fm
Blood Hall
Oaktree Fm
Sycamore Fm
Wetherup Street
Gull Fm
Hill Fm
The Firs
Cemy
Debenham
Camp Green Fm
Sch
Ulveston Hall
Greenwood Fm
Crows Hall
White Hall
Debenham Hall
Mickfield Hall
Cousens' Fm
Fen Street
Winston Grange
Brook Fm
Poplar Hall
Bennett's Fm
Malthouse Fm
Grange Fm
Hall
Mickfield
Grove Fm
Winston
B 1077

14 East from Framlingham to the Maltings at Snape and the Minsmere Levels

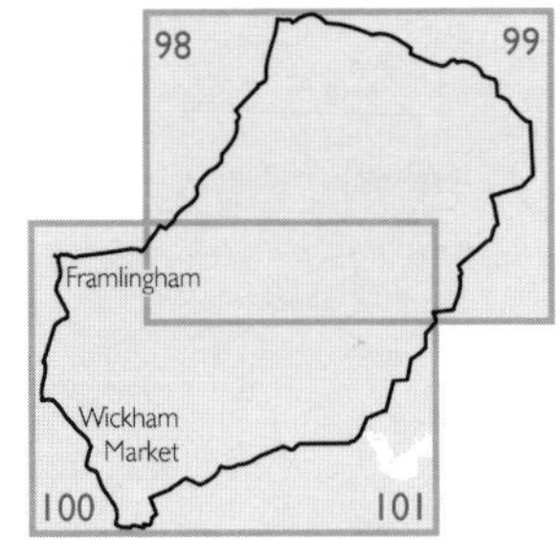
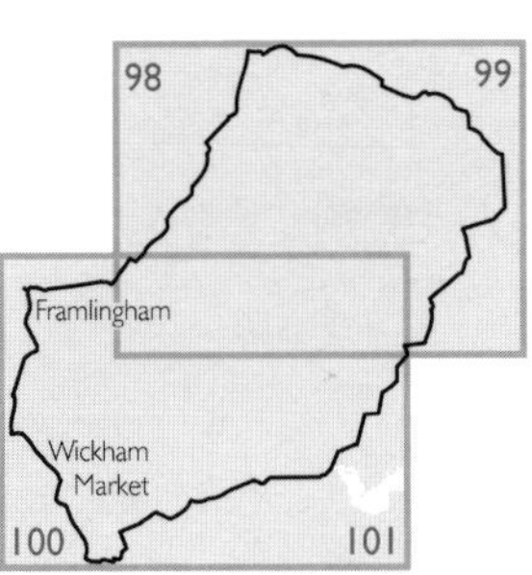

The Maltings at Snape are internationally famous for their staging of major musical events. This ride follows quiet lanes through Easton, Wickham Market and Blaxhall to arrive at Snape with its picturesque setting by the river and a fine choice of refreshment stops. Heading north and parallel to the coast, you will experience a short section of off-road north from Eastbridge to Westleton on a good track running through gorse bushes. Westleton is another attractive village with good pubs. The ride now heads west and south through Sibton and Bruisyard to return to the start.

Start

The Crown PH, The Square, Framlingham, 15 miles northeast of Ipswich

P Follow long stay car park signs on to Albert road, just off the B1116 towards Wickham Market

Distance and grade

37 miles

Easy

Terrain

No major hills. Lowest point – sea level at Minsmere Level. Highest point – 170 feet (51 mts) near to Bruisyard

Nearest railway

Darsham Station, less than a mile from the route near Darsham

Refreshments

Plenty of choice ***in Framlingham***
White Horse PH, ***Easton***
The Ship PH, ***Blaxhall***
Plough and Sail PH, The Maltings, ***Snape***
Granary Tea Shop, ***Snape***

Framlingham
Wickham Market
Campsey Ash
Blaxhall
Friston

Places of interest

For ***Snape*** see off-road route 10

Aldeburgh *(just off the route) 13*

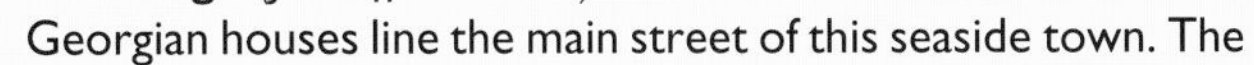

Georgian houses line the main street of this seaside town. The half-timbered 16th-century Moot Hall, now a museum, fronts the shingle beach

▼ *Framlingham town sign*

Minsmere *21*

Major bird reserve; nesting places for over 100 species. Breeding birds include avocets, bitterns, nightjars and nightingales

Heveningham Hall *(just off the route) 23*

Georgian mansion built in 1780 as the Vannek family home. Grounds by Capability Brown

Peasenhall *25*

The church has an unusual welcome above the porch; a carved dragon and a woodwose, a mythical half-human woodland creature whose origins remain a mystery

Bruisyard Vineyard *26*

10-acre vineyard, winery, herb centre and gardens, picnic and play areas and a restaurant

Theberton

Westleton

Sibton Green

Peasenhall

Bruisyard

Little Lodge
Brabling Green
Sweffling Hall
Boundary Fm
Fiddler's Hall
FRAMLINGHAM
Castle
B1119
Hatherleigh Fm
West Fm
Hill Fm
Moat Fm
Wr Twr
Rookery Fm
Hall Fm
Cemy
63
Oak Fm
Pound Fm
25
Edward's Fm
High Grove
Stone Fm
Cole's Green
North Green
The Grove
Street Fm
B1116
Parham Ho
62
Paul's Grove Fm
Great Glemham
PH
P
Broadwater
Parham Wood
Park Fm
Red House Fm
The Grove
Broadwater Fm
Mill Green
18
High House Fm
Whitehouse Fm
24
Parham
Great Glemham Wood
Grove Fm
28
29
Whin Covert
30
31
Silverlace Green
33
34
PH
Hall
39
Sally's Grove
Parham Old Hall
60
Great Wood
39
Stud Fm
Moat Hall Farm
Common Fm
Maid's Wood
The Willows
Moat
Easton Park
Hacheston
Hall Fm
Blomvyle Hall
P
Glemham Hall
PH
Moat
Bentries Fm
Abbey Fm
59
27
MP
Cemy
36
Kennels
Easton
Sch
Hall
Moat Fm
Moat
P
Poplar Fm
Marlesford
PH
Little Glemham
Great Wood
The Rookery
Old Hall
58
MP
Hill Ho
Glevering Ho
PH
River Deben
Glevering Hall
LC
Alder Carr
SUFFOLK COASTAL
Glevering Hall Fm
Lower Hacheston
B 1078
Valley Fm
Moat
Mill
Red Fm
16
11
LC
Jolly's Fm
16
Gelham Hall
Ash Corner
Campsey Ash
Sch
56
P
PH
Church Fm
Long Grove
32
WICKHAM MARKET STA
Whitehouse Fm
WICKHAM MARKET
B 1438
Quill Fm
Chantry Fm
Shrubbery Fm
Cemy
California
17
Grove Fm
29
Ashgreen Fm
55
Home Fm
Copperas Wood
Moat Fm
Wr Twr
MS
PH
Pettistree
Priory (remains of)
Park Fm
Mill
Ash Abbey
Rendlesham Hall

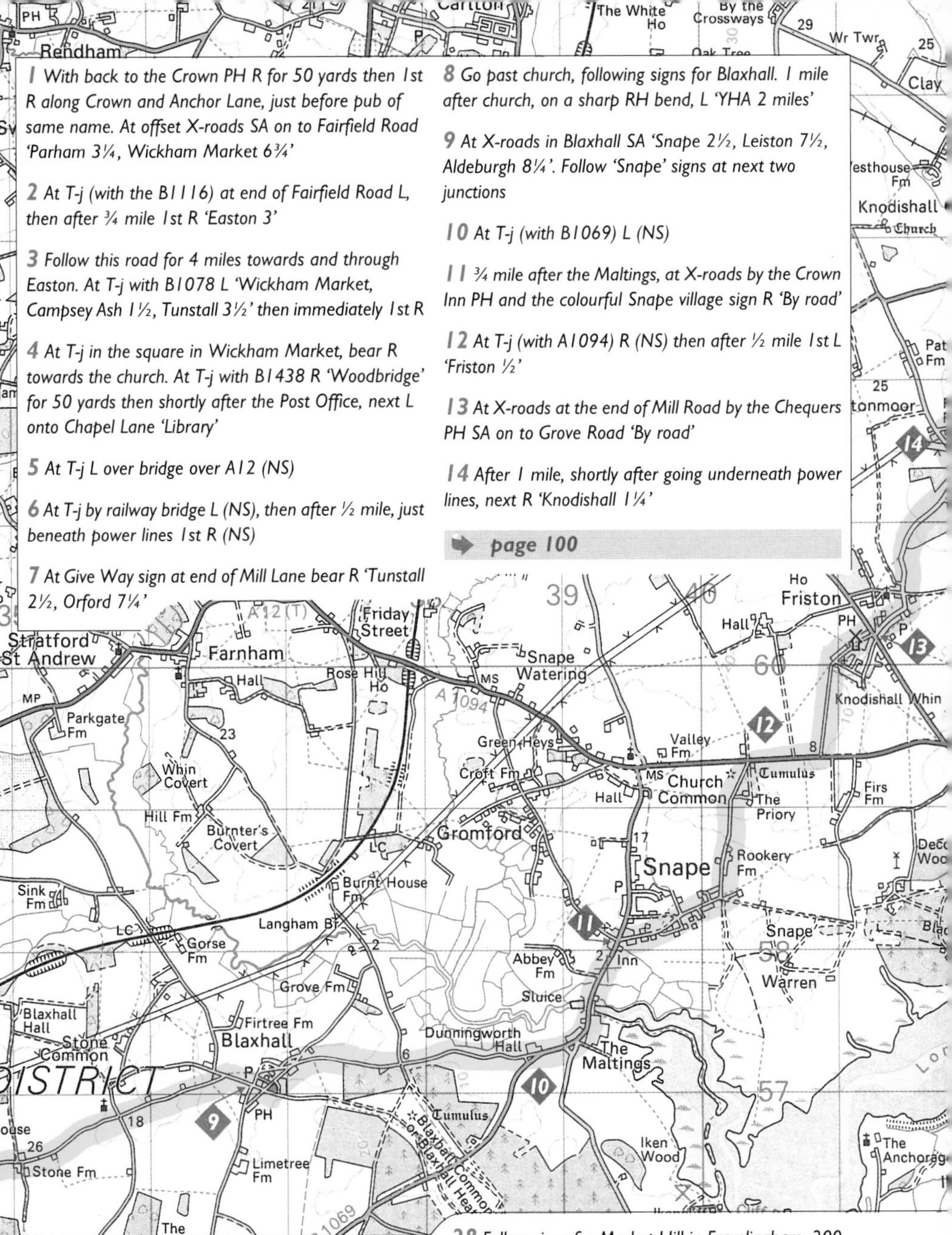

1 With back to the Crown PH R for 50 yards then 1st R along Crown and Anchor Lane, just before pub of same name. At offset X-roads SA on to Fairfield Road 'Parham 3¼, Wickham Market 6¾'

2 At T-j (with the B1116) at end of Fairfield Road L, then after ¾ mile 1st R 'Easton 3'

3 Follow this road for 4 miles towards and through Easton. At T-j with B1078 L 'Wickham Market, Campsey Ash 1½, Tunstall 3½' then immediately 1st R

4 At T-j in the square in Wickham Market, bear R towards the church. At T-j with B1438 R 'Woodbridge' for 50 yards then shortly after the Post Office, next L onto Chapel Lane 'Library'

5 At T-j L over bridge over A12 (NS)

6 At T-j by railway bridge L (NS), then after ½ mile, just beneath power lines 1st R (NS)

7 At Give Way sign at end of Mill Lane bear R 'Tunstall 2½, Orford 7¼'

8 Go past church, following signs for Blaxhall. 1 mile after church, on a sharp RH bend, L 'YHA 2 miles'

9 At X-roads in Blaxhall SA 'Snape 2½, Leiston 7½, Aldeburgh 8¼'. Follow 'Snape' signs at next two junctions

10 At T-j (with B1069) L (NS)

11 ¾ mile after the Maltings, at X-roads by the Crown Inn PH and the colourful Snape village sign R 'By road'

12 At T-j (with A1094) R (NS) then after ½ mile 1st L 'Friston ½'

13 At X-roads at the end of Mill Road by the Chequers PH SA on to Grove Road 'By road'

14 After 1 mile, shortly after going underneath power lines, next R 'Knodishall 1¼'

➡ page 100

26 Keep following signs for Cransford and Framlingham through Bruisyard. At T-j R 'Framlingham 3, Wickham Market 6¼' then 1st L 'Framlingham 2½, Parham 3'

27 At T-j (with B1119) R

28 Follow signs for Market Hill in Framlingham. 200 yards after a petrol station on your left, turn R 'No access except loading'. At T-j in the centre of Framlingham L. Push your bike along this one way street for 50 yards back to the start. (**Or** for link with route 13 continue SA to join at instruction 1)

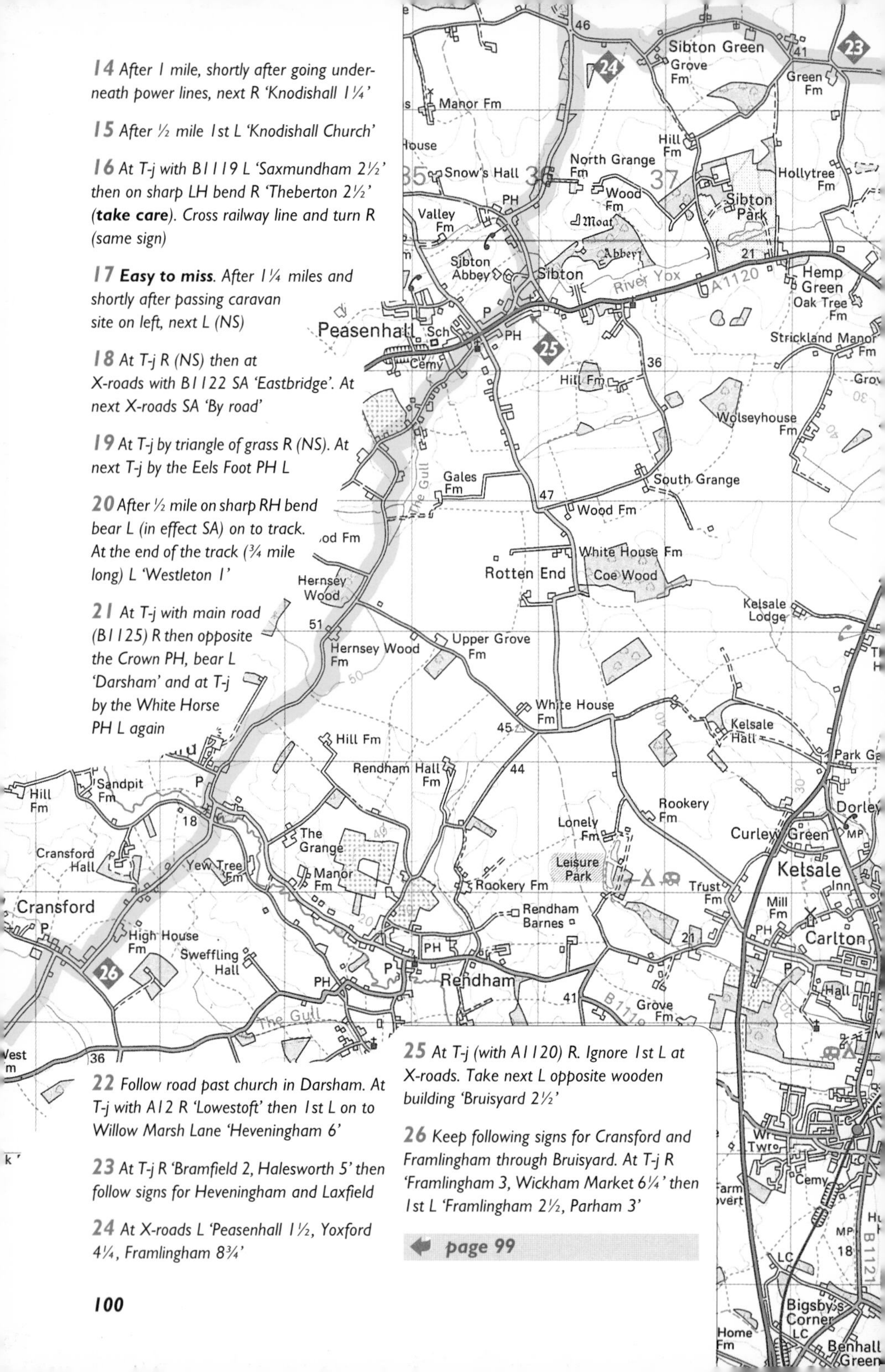

14 After 1 mile, shortly after going underneath power lines, next R 'Knodishall 1¼'

15 After ½ mile 1st L 'Knodishall Church'

16 At T-j with B1119 L 'Saxmundham 2½' then on sharp LH bend R 'Theberton 2½' (**take care**). Cross railway line and turn R (same sign)

17 **Easy to miss**. After 1¼ miles and shortly after passing caravan site on left, next L (NS)

18 At T-j R (NS) then at X-roads with B1122 SA 'Eastbridge'. At next X-roads SA 'By road'

19 At T-j by triangle of grass R (NS). At next T-j by the Eels Foot PH L

20 After ½ mile on sharp RH bend bear L (in effect SA) on to track. At the end of the track (¾ mile long) L 'Westleton 1'

21 At T-j with main road (B1125) R then opposite the Crown PH, bear L 'Darsham' and at T-j by the White Horse PH L again

22 Follow road past church in Darsham. At T-j with A12 R 'Lowestoft' then 1st L on to Willow Marsh Lane 'Heveningham 6'

23 At T-j R 'Bramfield 2, Halesworth 5' then follow signs for Heveningham and Laxfield

24 At X-roads L 'Peasenhall 1½, Yoxford 4¼, Framlingham 8¾'

25 At T-j (with A1120) R. Ignore 1st L at X-roads. Take next L opposite wooden building 'Bruisyard 2½'

26 Keep following signs for Cransford and Framlingham through Bruisyard. At T-j R 'Framlingham 3, Wickham Market 6¼' then 1st L 'Framlingham 2½, Parham 3'

page 99

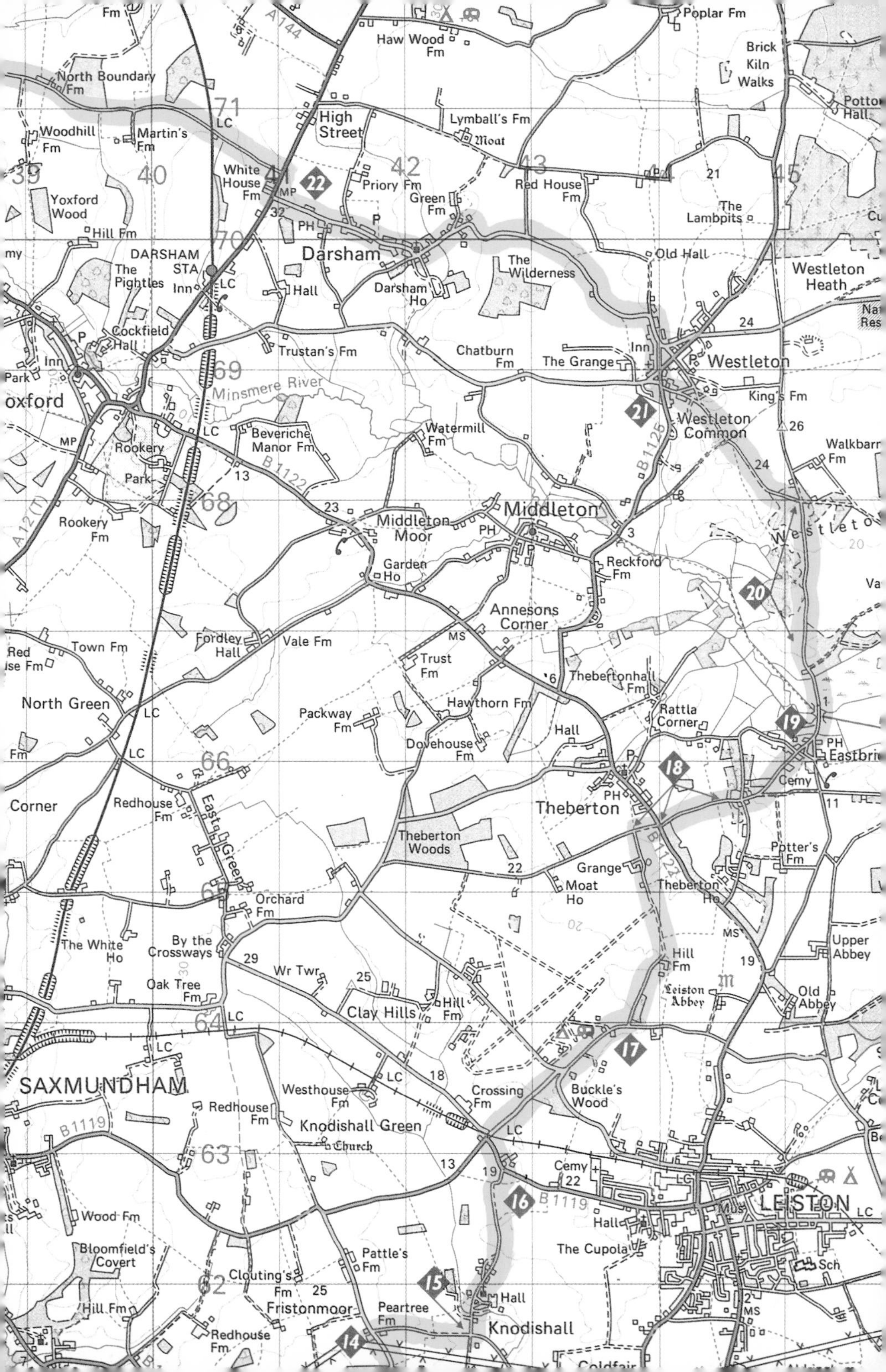
Fm
A144
Poplar Fm
Haw Wood
Fm
Brick
Kiln
Walks
North Boundary
Fm
Potton
Hall
71
LC
High
Street
Lymball's Fm
Moat
Woodhill
Fm
Martin's
Fm
39
40
White
House
Fm
41
MP
22
42
Priory Fm
43
Red House
Fm
21
45
Green
Fm
The
Lambpits
Yoxford
Wood
32
PH
P
Hill Fm
70
DARSHAM
STA
Inn
LC
Darsham
Old Hall
The
Pightles
Hall
Darsham
Ho
The
Wilderness
Westleton
Heath
Cockfield
Hall
24
P
Inn
Trustan's Fm
Chatburn
Fm
The Grange
Inn
Westleton
Park
69
Minsmere River
oxford
King's Fm
21
Westleton
Common
B1125
26
MP
Beveriche
Manor Fm
Watermill
Fm
Walkbarn
Fm
Rookery
Park
13
B1122
24
A12(T)
68
Middleton
Rookery
Fm
23
Middleton
Moor
PH
3
Westleton
20
Garden
Ho
Reckford
Fm
20
Annesons
Corner
MS
Town Fm
Fordley
Hall
Vale Fm
Red
use Fm
Trust
Fm
6
Thebertonhall
Fm
North Green
LC
Packway
Fm
Hawthorn Fm
Rattla
Corner
19
LC
Hall
Dovehouse
Fm
PH
Eastbridge
66
P
18
Cemy
Corner
Redhouse
Fm
East
Green
PH
Theberton
11
Theberton
Woods
B1124
Potter's
Fm
22
Grange
Moat
Ho
Theberton
Ho
65
Orchard
Fm
The White
Ho
By the
Crossways
20
MS
Upper
Abbey
29
Hill
Fm
19
Wr Twr
25
Oak Tree
Fm
Leiston
Abbey
Old
Abbey
30
Clay Hills
Hill
Fm
64
LC
17
LC
SAXMUNDHAM
Westhouse
Fm
LC
18
Crossing
Fm
Buckle's
Wood
Redhouse
Fm
B1119
Knodishall Green
Church
LC
63
13
19
Cemy
22
16
B1119
LC
Mus
LEISTON
LC
Wood Fm
Hall
The Cupola
Bloomfield's
Covert
Pattle's
Fm
Sch
62
Clouting's
Fm
25
15
Hall
Hill Fm
Fristonmoor
Peartree
Fm
2
MS
Knodishall
Redhouse
Fm
14
Coldfair

From Aldbury, along the Icknield Way and back through the woodland of Berkhamsted Common

The ride starts from the pretty village of Aldbury and lets you warm up with three miles on road into Ivinghoe. The condition of the Icknield Way at this point is variable and may have been damaged by horses riding through in wet conditions. The church at Edlesborough, set dramatically on a small hill, represents the end of this section. A steep climb to Whipsnade follows. You have the alternative of cycling on the road or pushing/ cycling off-road to reach the village of Whipsnade. Beyond Whipsnade you once again face the choice of a rough three miles off-road or a road alternative that may at times be busy. This is known as Hobson's choice! Beyond Hudnall things improve with a combination of disused county roads (including an extraordinary section beyond the church in Nettleden between high flint walls and beneath a bridge). The ride soon reaches Berkhamsted Common and follows lovely woodland trails for almost five miles back to Aldbury.

Start

The Greyhound PH, Aldbury, 3 miles east of Tring, 10 miles east of Aylesbury

P Some parking by the Greyhound PH close to the X-roads in Aldbury. Otherwise park with consideration

Distance and grade

20 miles

Moderate / strenuous according to conditions underfoot

Terrain

335 feet climb from the Icknield Way to Whipsnade (one short but very steep off-road push to avoid the busy B4540). 200 feet climb from the A4146 up to Hudnall. The steepest rideable climb is south from the church at

Aldbury
Ivinghoe
Edlesborough

Refreshments

The Valiant Soldier PH, The Greyhound PH, ***Aldbury***
Rose and Crown PH, ***Ivinghoe*** *The Bell PH,* ***Edlesborough***
The Plough PH, ***at X-roads with B489***
Chequers Inn PH, ***Whipsnade***
The Bell PH, Red Lion PH, ***Studham***
(just off the route)
Alford Arms PH, ***Frithsden***

Nettleden between amazing flint walls. Lowest point – 330 feet (100 mts) on Icknield Way near to Edlesborough. Highest point – 700 feet (210 mts) at Whipsnade

Nearest railway

Tring Station, 1 mile west of Aldbury

Places of interest

Ivinghoe Beacon *4*
One of several beacon points established during the reign of Elizabeth I to summon men in case of Spanish invasion

Whipsnade Zoo *11*
Open air zoo on Dunstable Downs where 200 animals roam in the 500-acre park. Rarities include a herd of white rhinoceroses

Ashridge Park *23*
The 108-feet tall Bridgewater Monument was erected in 1831 in memory of the canal pioneer, the 3rd Duke of Bridgwater. On the eastern side of the park is the Gothic revival Ashridge House (now a college) set in gardens landscaped by Capability Brown

▲ *The Icknield Way near the church at Edlesborough*

Studham

Great Gaddesden

Frithsden

1 With back to the Greyhound PH L out of Aldbury on the road towards Ivinghoe

2 After 2½ miles at T-j with B488 bear R downhill 'Ivinghoe ½, Dunstable 6, Leighton Buzzard 7'

3 Ignore the B488 to Dunstable. Take the next R in Ivinghoe onto Vicarage Lane then 1st R by the Rose and Crown PH on to Wellcroft

4 Follow this in the same direction as it becomes track, at times muddy and pocked with horse hoofmarks. Join tarmac lane and continue in same direction

5 At X-roads with lane SA on to track towards church on hill

6 At X-roads by the church and the Bell PH in Edlesborough SA 'Village Centre' then 2nd R on to Pebblemoor by the Village Hall

7 At the end of the village on a sharp RH bend L onto lane (NS). 1st road R (NS). At T-j R (NS)

8 At roundabout (with B489) by the Plough PH SA 'Dagnall B4506, Whipsnade (B4540)' then 1st L onto B4540 'Whipsnade 1¼, The Zoo 1'

9 Shortly after a prominent Footpath sign on the left, turn L onto Bridleway. (This starts as a very steep push but avoids the busy road. If you wish to continue on the road, go SA as far as the Chequers PH and rejoin at 2nd part of instruction 11)

10 Shortly after passing a sign on your left to Dunstable Downs, at a X-roads with a broader track SA uphill. At the next track junction bear R then once in the field bear L following 'Icknield Way' sign

11 The track joins tarmac by a wooden gate. Follow to the road, turn L for 400 yards then 1st R by triangle of grass towards the Chequers PH

12 Follow this lane along the edge of the fence around Whipsnade. After ½ mile turn R onto bridleway following the fence on your right

13 At end of wood carry SA along LH field edge. Go into wood and bear L onto superb, improved surface. It doesn't last long! At end of wood SA on to rougher track

14 At tarmac R then at T-j by letter box in brick pillar, R onto Valley Road. At T-j by triangle of grass R onto Common Road then after 300 yards L onto track by 'Home Reddings' 'Bridleway'

15 Rough field edge. Descend on bumpy track to road. At road SA along field edge (check to see whether the track is better on the RH or LH side of the hedgerow. If you take the RH track you will need to cross back through the hedge via a gate after 400 yards). The bridleway swings uphill and left beneath the edge of the wood. Follow the track into the wood with a property to your right

16 At tarmac bear L. At X-roads with road by Little Gaddesden sign SA on to No Through Road

17 Tarmac turns to track then back to tarmac. At T-j sharply R steeply uphill

18 Fast descent. At T-j by church R then L 'Unsuitable for motor vehicles'. High brick and flint walls either side of the steep track

19 At T-j by the Alford Arms PH L. At T-j after 150 yards R 'Potten End, Berkhamsted'

20 Steady climb. After ¾ mile, and 30 yards after passing the first road turning to the left to Potten End, turn R onto Public Bridleway and take the RH fork

21 Follow this along the edge of the wood past the golf course. At road SA and continue in the same direction through woodland with the fairway on your left. The route is not always clear but as long as you avoid going onto the golf course and stay just on the border of the wood you should be on target

22 Go past Brick Kiln Cottage and continue in the same direction. At X-roads with a broad well-made track by a brick barn to the left SA

23 At X-roads with main road (B4506) R for ¼ mile then L onto Bridleway opposite a small parking area in the woodland. (**Or** for link to route 2 SA and 1st L to join instruction 9)

24 Continue in same direction until reaching property with National Trust sign. Carry SA for 400 yards. With the slope dropping away steeply ahead, bear R on broad track as it swings round contouring through the woodland. (**Or** for link to route 2 L along track to join instruction 7)

25 ***Easy to miss***. *After almost ½ mile, watch out for a broad track descending steeply to your left. At T-j with road R to return to the start*

2 *Through woods and hills between Tring and Berkhamsted*

Although Tring and Berkhamsted may seem two somewhat improbable centres for off-road cycling in Hertfordshire, there are many fine bridleways through the woods above the two towns and if all else fails the Grand Union Canal with its generally well-maintained towpath runs between them. The ride leaves Tring to the east, crosses the canal and soon joins an excellent stretch of improved bridleway. If only it were all of this quality! You climb up on to Aldbury Common and around the edge of Northchurch Common. There is an abrupt change of scenery as you pass from wooded bridleway straight into the centre of Berkhamsted. You soon climb out of the town, under the new bypass and head off-road to the ruins of Marlin Chapel. A lovely disused county road through woodland drops you on the road that runs through Cholesbury. From here you climb to the highest point of the ride at Hastoe and the best descent of the day back to Tring.

Start

The car park in the centre of Tring, on the High Street. (Alternatively, the Sports Centre in Berkhamsted)

P As above

Distance and grade

17 miles

Moderate / strenuous according to the conditions underfoot

Terrain

Two major climbs out of the valley through which the Grand Union Canal passes. The first of 260 feet from Tring Station to Aldbury Common, the second of 400 feet steeply at first then more gradually from Berkhamsted to Hastoe on the edge of the escarpment above Tring. Lowest point – 360 feet (110 mts) in Berkhamsted. Highest point – 780 feet (234 mts) at Hastoe

Nearest railway

Tring or Berkhamsted

Tring

Aldbury

Berkhamsted

Places of interest

Tring *1*
Small market town with Zoological Museum crammed with hundreds of stuffed species. Tring Reservoirs National Reserve is home to many water birds including the great crested grebe, heron and pochard

Berkhamsted *12*
Country town on the Grand Union Canal where William the Conqueror accepted the English throne in 1066. The Norman Castle was a favourite royal residence until the time of Elizabeth I – it is now in ruins

Hertfordshire mud is renowned for its sticky, cement-like quality. Although every attempt has been made to use tracks that are passable for a large part of the year, you are likely to encounter mud at various points and this will be much worse from late autumn to late spring and after any particularly wet periods. Wear appropriate footwear and hose your bike down after use. Should you wish to cycle away from traffic on easier tracks, try the Grand Union Canal towpath or the dismantled railways listed in the introduction

Refreshments

Plenty of choice ***in Tring and Berkhamsted***
The Valiant Soldier PH, The Greyhound PH,
Aldbury *(just off the route)*
The Full Moon PH, ***Cholesbury***

▼ *The windmill at Cholesbury*

1 *Turn L out of the car park. At the roundabout SA then 1st L on to Station Road 'Tring Station'.*

2 *After ½ mile, shortly after X-roads sign, L on to Grove Road. After ½ mile 1st road R onto Marshcroft Road 'No Through Road'*

3 *Tarmac becomes track. At T-j with road R then after 200 yards L onto Bridleway between the fence and the hedge. At offset X-roads with track, R then L along lower edge of wood (ie keep wood to your left)*

4 *Carry on in same direction as track improves just inside the woodland. At X-roads of bridleways SA. At road bear L*

5 *After 400 yards, on sharp LH bend, bear R onto track. At T-j with road R (ignore tempting track ahead: it soon deteriorates into a steep muddy push)*

6 *After ¾ mile L onto a good track towards barn with corrugated roof 'Bridleway'. Past barn, through gate into field then diagonally L across field towards signpost and into the wood via a wooden gate 'Bridleway'*

7 *Continue in same direction through several gates and through farm. Track improves. At T-j with road on steep bend R uphill. (**Or** for link to route 1 SA to join instruction 24)*

8 ***Easy to miss**. Ignore 1st muddy bridleway on right after ¼ mile. After further ½ mile, just past the timber building of 'Chiltern Base Camp' and a clearing on your left, and 300 yards before the road junction, turn R through a rough car park*

9 *You will eventually exit the wood and arrive at the edge of Northchurch Common. Turn R along the track which borders the wood, keeping the wood on your right as the track swings round to the left*

10 *Emerge at road opposite Hill Farm. Turn R for 200 yards then L onto Bridleway. Take the track which leads away from the road bearing L and slightly uphill. At the T-j with driveway leading to Northchurch Farm L then R just before farm. At better track by Long Acre bear R*

11 *At T-j with tarmac lane by triangle of grass SA onto track in woodland 'Bridleway'. The track runs along parallel with the houses to your right. Emerge in a housing estate and go SA downhill on road called 'Bridleway'*

12 *At T-j with Bridgwater Road R then L down Billet Lane. At traffic lights at the end of Billet Lane, cross the main road and go SA between railings towards the Sports Centre*

13 *At T-j just past Sports Centre at the end of Douglas Gardens L then at X-roads by 'Stop' sign at the end of Shrublands Road R uphill on to Cross Oak Road*

14 *Steep climb. At X-roads at the end of Cross Oak Road SA on to Denny Lane. 200 yards after passing underneath bridge R through wooden gates on to concrete track*

15 *At end of concrete track L on to stone track. 50 yards short of the chapel ruins bear L 'Public Bridleway'. Cross new plantation of trees diagonally L to the far corner. Muddy patch near gate. Turn L onto track. (**Or** for link to route 3 turn immediately R to join instruction 25)*

16 At road R. At T-j at end of Hog Lane, R then L 'Unsuitable for Motor Vehicles'

17 At T-j with track bear R. At T-j with road by black wooden house R 'Cholesbury'. At T-j with more major road R

18 400 yards after the Full Moon PH in Cholesbury next R 'Wigginton 2, Tring 3'. Ignore 1st L on Shire Lane. Take next L onto Kiln Road 'Tring 2½'

19 After 400 yards on sharp RH bend bear L (in effect SA) through field gate 'Bridleway' 'No vehicles except access'

20 Fine track. At road L then R by triangle of grass 'Bridleway'. At the end of the track pass to the right of the house and SA downhill 'Hastoe Lane 1, Park Road, Tring 1'

21 At road R under bridge. At T-j at end of Duckmore Lane R. Follow signs for 'Town Centre' to return to the start

3 Woodland tracks and the Grand Union Canal in southwest Hertfordshire

For an area so close to the large centres of population of Hemel Hempstead, Rickmansworth and Amersham this ride has a very rural, wooded feel to it. From the centre of Bovingdon you soon leave tarmac for a woodland track that runs past a golf course and before long drops down onto the towpath of the Grand Union Canal through Kings Langley. You pass underneath the M25 on the towpath then over it as you climb from Hunton Bridge up towards Commonwood. The avenue of trees as soon as you cross the motorway and go off-road seems to welcome you to a different world from the traffic mayhem you have just passed over. Permissive bridleways, tiny lanes and unclassified roads take you down into the valley of the River Chess near Chenies. A two mile stretch through woodland is followed by a complete contrast: two busy road miles. Push hard for ten minutes and you are back off-road again, climbing towards Ley Hill along Broomstick Lane. A last off-road section, which may at times be rough takes you to within a mile of Bovingdon and the start.

1 Take the minor road between the Bull PH and the half-timbered house away from the centre of Bovingdon. After ¼ mile opposite the corner of the cemetery, R onto track 'Unsuitable for motors'

*2 **Easy to miss.** After 1 mile (track has become tarmac), just after sharp LH bend and a sign for Shothanger Way, leave the road and turn R uphill onto track by sign for Berry Wood, taking the LH fork after 10 yards*

page 113

14 At T-j by triangle of grass L 'Chenies' then 1st track R 'Bridleway'. After 400 yards at T-j of tracks L

15 At X-roads of tracks SA downhill onto narrower track. At 2nd X-roads of tracks SA downhill ('No Horses' signs to right and left). Maybe muddy

16 At bottom of hill L through gate (blue arrow) onto better track alongside the stream. Follow through farm. At T-j with road R. At T-j with more major road by large triangle of grass L

17 1st road R by large triangle of grass. At T-j R 'Amersham 4½' then after 50 yards on sharp LH bend R 'Great House Farm access. Bridleway'

18 After 100 yards at T-j R, then after 100 yards L through black metal gate opposite concrete drive

19 Superb track. At road R, then L onto upper, narrower track 'Sporting rights reserved'

20 State of track is variable. At road with 'Forest Cottages' ahead R. At T-j at bottom of Bell Lane L 'Chesham 3'

*21 **Easy to miss.** After 2 miles on this busy road, past the sign at start of Chesham, and 200 yards past car showroom on your right, R onto Hill Farm Road 'Bridleway to Botley'. As road swings sharp right bear L steeply uphill onto tarmac track 'Bridleway to Botley'*

Bovingdon Felden Rucklers Lane Kings Langley Belsi

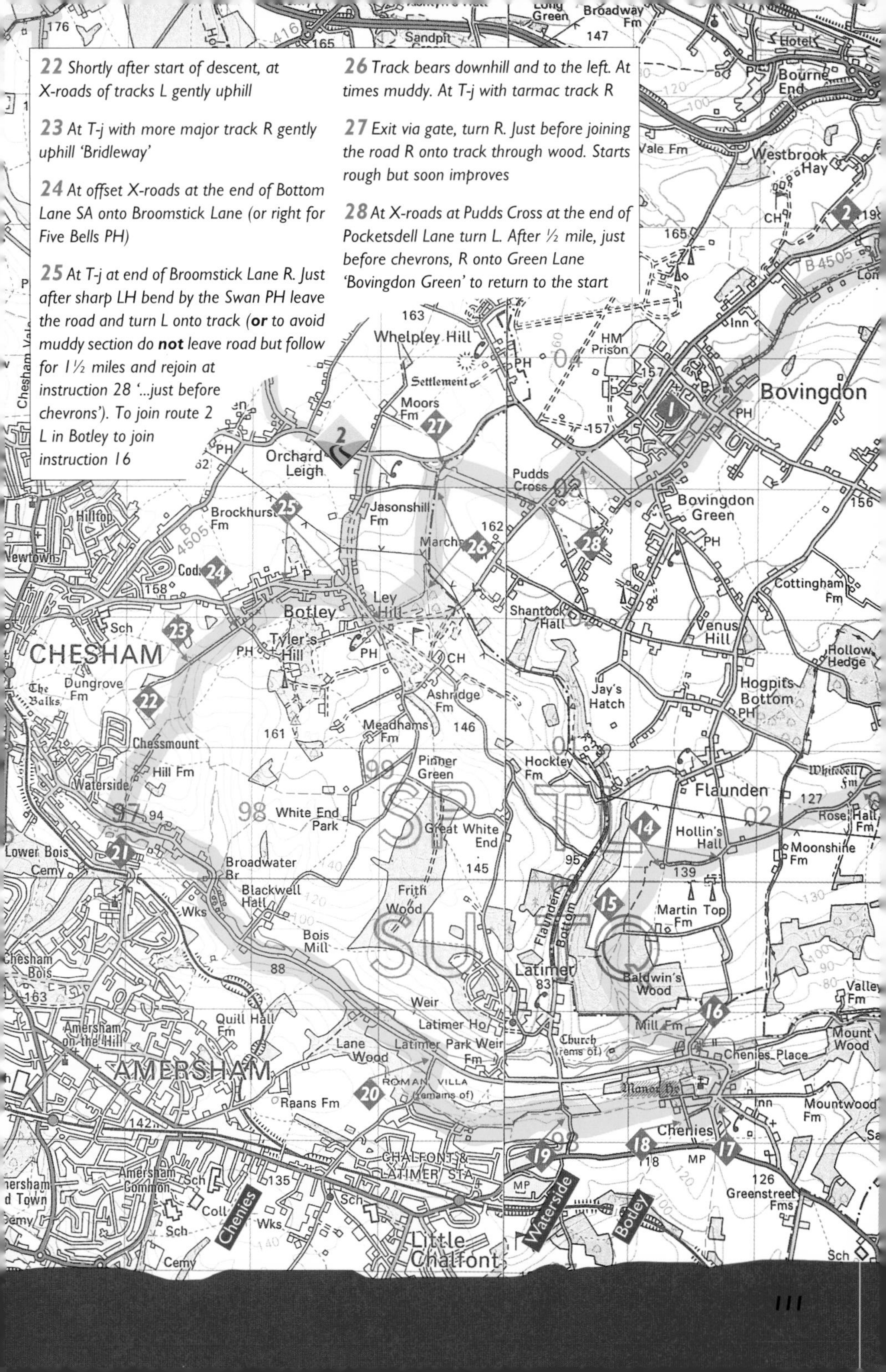

22 Shortly after start of descent, at X-roads of tracks L gently uphill

23 At T-j with more major track R gently uphill 'Bridleway'

24 At offset X-roads at the end of Bottom Lane SA onto Broomstick Lane (or right for Five Bells PH)

25 At T-j at end of Broomstick Lane R. Just after sharp LH bend by the Swan PH leave the road and turn L onto track (**or** to avoid muddy section do **not** leave road but follow for 1½ miles and rejoin at instruction 28 '...just before chevrons'). To join route 2 L in Botley to join instruction 16

26 Track bears downhill and to the left. At times muddy. At T-j with tarmac track R

27 Exit via gate, turn R. Just before joining the road R onto track through wood. Starts rough but soon improves

28 At X-roads at Pudds Cross at the end of Pocketsdell Lane turn L. After ½ mile, just before chevrons, R onto Green Lane 'Bovingdon Green' to return to the start

Boxmoor
Bourne End
Hotel
Weir
Sch
Ski Centre
Bennetts End
Schs
Bunkers Fm
Well Fm
Highwood Hall Fm
136
ROMAN VILLA (site of)
Two Waters
Roughdown Common
Felden
Sheethanger Common
Twr
B 4505
Longcroft Fm
155
153
Apsley
Mills
Apsley Manor Fm
81
Nash Mills
73
Abbot's Hill (Sch)
Hyde Fm
Shendish
Rucklers Lane
Grand Union Canal
Bovingdon
Barnes Lodge
106
Barnes Fm
129
Nuffield Fm
121
Scatterdells Wood
Sch
Numbers Fm
156
Bulstrode
134
Balls Pond Fm
Palace (site of)
Tower Hill
Cottingham Fm
Chipperfield Ho
Whippendell Bottom
Kings Langley
A 4251
A 41(T)
Mill
Chipperfield
133
Hollow Hedge
Clapgate Fm
Woodmans Fm
Inn
Manor Ho
121
Langley Lodge Fm
Tumuli
Chipperfield Common
Penman's Green
Callipers Hall
Berrybushes Wood
River Gade
Whitedell Fm
106
Belsize
Enclosure
113
126
Hunton Bridge
127
Rose Hall Fm
PH
Commonwood
06
Model Fm
07
04
05
Moonshine Fm
Great Sarratt Hall
116
Bucks Hill
Sch
Langleybury
63
96
108
Great Westwood
105
Sarratt
Newhall Fm
Buck's Hill Bottom
M 25
Heath Wood
Valley Fm
111
105
The Grove
Mount Wood
Sarratt Bottom
White Ho
Yew Court Fm
The Grove Mill
Weir
PH
116
Micklefield Green
84
86
Church End
Goldingtons
Mountwood Fm
Chandler's Cross
Lees Wood
Sarratt Mill Ho
65
Harrocks Wood
Whippendell Wood
115
Redhall
84
Jacotts Hill
Micklefield Hall
86
Redheath
Sch
63
Beechengrove Wood
Chorleywood Ho
Cemy
Waterdell Ho
84
56
109
Loudwater
87
Thurlwood Ho
Schs
CHORLEYWOOD
18
R Chess
79
CH
Chorleywood
Croxley
20
19
2
3
4
5
6
7
8
9
10
11
12
13

2 ***Easy to miss.*** *After 1 mile (track has become tarmac), just after sharp LH bend and a sign for Shothanger Way, leave the road and turn R uphill onto track by sign for Berry Wood, taking the LH fork after 10 yards*

3 *At 1st X-roads of tracks SA. At 2nd X-roads / T-j (with tyres on ropes ahead) L downhill on broad track then just beyond white fence by Gosnells turn R 'Bridleway'*

4 *Follow this track alongside the golf fairway. At X-roads with the road through the golf course SA 'Bridleway'. At T-j with road R*

5 *At X-roads at the end of Felden Lane L onto Featherbed Lane 'Apsley 1'. After ¾ mile, just before crossing bridge over A41, R onto track 'Bridleway'. At times muddy*

6 *At T-j with road L*

7 *At traffic lights at the end of Rucklers Lane by the railway bridge L then R. Cross the bridge over the canal and turn R onto towpath*

8 *Follow towpath for 2½ miles. It changes sides and goes beneath the M25. At the round-arched brick bridge no. 162, with a sign for the Dog and Partridge PH, leave the towpath and turn R onto the road. At X-roads with the A41 SA onto Langleybury Lane*

9 *After ½ mile, shortly after passing a turning on the left to Langleybury School, next R onto tarmac lane and bridge over M25 'Public Footpath'*

10 *At black and white timber farm building leave tarmac on a sharp RH bend and bear L (in effect SA) on to track*

11 *Fine track turns to tarmac. At T-j with road L then R onto Quickmoor Lane. After ½ mile on sharp LH bend by Cart and Horses PH R onto No Through Road 'Penman's Green'*

12 *After ¾ mile, as road swings sharp left to Hillmeads Farm, SA onto track 'Permissive Bridleway'*

13 *Follow in same direction as it improves near to houses and becomes concrete track. At T-j with road near the Plough PH L onto the major road 'Dunny Lane. Poles Hill' then after 300 yards sharply R onto Bragmans Lane. At T-j L (NS)*

 **page 110**

Start

The Bull PH, Bovingdon, 3 miles southwest of Hemel Hempstead

P No specific car park. Please park with consideration

Distance and grade

22 miles

Moderate

Terrain

200 feet climb from the Grand Union Canal at Hunton Bridge to Commonwood.
260 feet climb from Latimer to Ley Hill.
Lowest point – 210 feet (63 mts) Grand Union Canal at Hunton Bridge.
Highest point – 530 feet (160 mts) at Pudds Cross near Bovingdon

Nearest railway

Kings Langley (on the route), Little Chalfont (just south of the route near Latimer)

Refreshments

Bull PH, Bell PH, ***Bovingdon*** *Rose and Crown PH,* ***Kings Langley*** *Cart and Horses PH,* ***Commonwood*** *The Plough PH,* ***Belsize*** *Bricklayers Arms PH,* ***Hogpits Bottom, Flaunden*** *(just off the route) Red Lion PH,* ***Chenies*** *Five Bells PH,* ***Cowcroft*** *The Swan PH, The Crown PH,* ***Ley Hill***

4 From Great Offley along the Icknield Way Path

Although it may seem a slightly unlikely centre, the village of Great Offley not only boasts four pubs and a restaurant but has within a five mile radius of the village dozens of miles of good quality tracks ideal for off-road cycling, whether these be bridleways, byways or old, unclassified county roads that have fallen into a state of benign neglect. Most famous of these is the Icknield Way which runs from the end of the Ridgeway and connects with the Peddars Way making it part of a track that used to run from Dorset to the Wash. The highest point of the ride is reached on the Icknield Way at the top of Telegraph Hill which is followed by an enjoyable, gentle descent to the road. Hitchin is skirted on three sides before the lanes link up with an old county road that climbs over 300 feet back to Great Offley.

Refreshments

Green Man PH, Bull PH, Red Lion PH, Prince Henry PH, ***Great Offley***
Lilley Arms PH, ***Lilley***
Cat and Fiddle PH, Motte and Bailey PH, Fox PH, ***Pirton***
Bird in Hand PH, Bull PH, ***Gosmore***

Start

The Bull PH, Great Offley, just off the A505 between Luton and Hitchin

P Visitors car park - with back to the Bull PH turn R for 300 yards then 1st R onto Gosling Road, 1st L onto Clarion Close and 1st L again (alternatively, park in High Street, showing consideration)

Distance and grade

20 miles (Short route - 10 miles)
Moderate
(Short route - easy)

Terrain

210 feet climb from Lilley Bottom to Telegraph Hill. 330 feet climb (100 mts) from St Ippollitts back to Great Offley. Lowest point – 165 feet (50 mts) at Ickleford. Highest point – 610 feet (183 mts) on Telegraph Hill (Icknield Way)

Nearest railway

Hitchin, 1 mile from the route at the A505 between Hitchin and Letchworth

Places of interest

Icknield Way *5*
Stretching from the Thames at Goring where it joins the Ridgeway, northeast to Thetford, where it joins the Peddars Way, the Icknield Way is part of a prehistoric trading route that ran from the Dorset Coast to the Wash

Lilley *3*
Home of the 19th-century eccentric, Captain Dimpers, who claimed to be the last descendant of the medieval alchemists and to possess the secret of turning base metal into gold. The family crest of the Salusburys, local landowners, is carved on many of the cottages

Pirton *8*
This was once a fortified village owing allegiance to a Norman knight named Stefan d'Arquelle who built a timber castle here, quite possibly on the site of prehistoric ramparts. The Motte and Bailey pub owes its name to the remnants of the Norman fortifications. The ghost of a headless horseman, a Cavalier named Simon Crossley, is said to ride around Midsummer's Day from the Elizabethan manor of High Down to Hitchin. During the Civil War he hid at High Down but he was caught and beheaded by the Roundheads

▼ *East of Great Offley*

Ickleford

Hitchin

Gossmore

1 With back to the Bull PH L. At X-roads at the end of High Street L 'Lilley'. 200 yards after Prince Henry PH, on RH bend 1st L

2 At T-j with Lilley Bottom R 'Lilley, Hexton'

3 Just after church in Lilley, 1st L onto West Street

4 Tarmac becomes track. At X-roads of tracks SA. Just past start of golf course to your left, at major X-roads with better track, R (Icknield Way)

5 At T-j with road by Mortgrove Farm bear L (in effect SA). After ¼ mile on sharp LH bend bear R into Treasures Grove Picnic Area 'Icknield Way'

*6 Steady climb then fine gentle descent. At T-j with road R for 200 yards (very busy – **take care**) then 1st track L along line of telegraph poles 'Bridleway' (**or** for short route, turn R here onto broad track. At T-j of tracks R to return to Great Offley)*

7 At T-j of tracks at end of field R 'Bridleway. Icknield Way' (maybe muddy)

8 At junction with road SA '30 MPH'. At T-j with the Fox PH ahead R. At X-roads SA onto Hambridge Way

*9 **Easy to miss**. Follow for 2 miles (rough in parts). At junction of bridleways SA. 100 yards before telegraph poles on the path (where the lines cross the track) R 'Bridleway. Icknield Way'*

10 At road L 'Icknield Way'. At roundabout with A600 SA onto Turnpike Lane 'Ickleford, Arlesey'

*11 Just past the church in Ickleford R onto track 'Icknield Way'. Cross the railway with **extreme care** (you will need to lift your bike over the gates)*

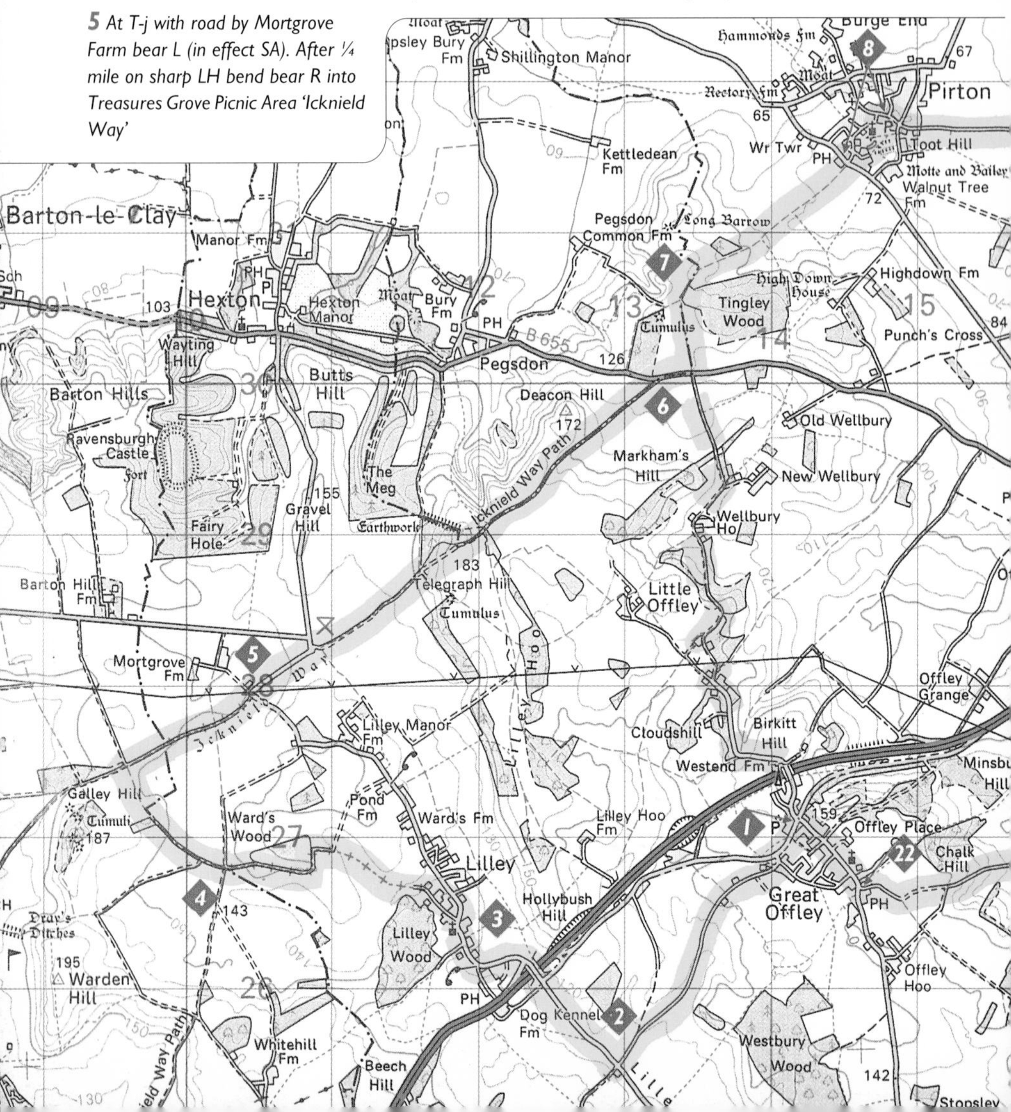

12 *At T-j with road R*

13 *At roundabout SA onto Queenswood Drive. At X-roads SA onto Kingswood Avenue*

14 *At bottom of hill on sharp RH bend bear L (in effect SA) on to track*

15 *At X-roads with road SA 'Bridleway. Little Wymondley 1'*

16 *At T-j with road R. At roundabout R then L just before bus shelter onto track 'Bridleway'*

17 *Go under road bridge.* ***Easy to miss****. At the far end of field, just before going under power lines, as the track swings right, turn L over small bridge*

18 *At T-j with lane R. Just past church, by triangle of grass, L 'Gosmore, Preston'*

19 *At X-roads with B656 SA onto Waterdell Lane 'Gosmore'*

20 *At X-roads by the Bull PH SA onto Maydencroft Lane 'Unsuitable for HGV'*

21 *At T-j L. After ¼ mile on sharp LH bend bear R (in effect SA) onto No Through Road 'Unsuitable for motors'*

22 *Follow in same direction, at times climbing steeply, to Great Offley. At T-j with road near the Red Lion PH R to return to the start*

5 Woods, lanes, streams and fords southeast of Stevenage

Southeast of Stevenage is a bewildering network of lanes and tracks. Many of the lanes are explored in road route 3 starting from Codicote. By contrast, this ride links together a dozen off-road stretches with quiet lanes meandering in a lazy circle from Watton at Stone through the estates at Sacombe and Youngsbury to the first ford at the River Rib near to Cold Christmas. Fords can be very useful to the off-road cyclist to clean the bike of accumulated mud as well as providing some adventure in the crossing! The route follows the valley of the River Rib north towards Standon before turning west through High Trees Farm and Green End to the attractive village of Benington. A fine byway and a fast descent on a tiny lane bring you back to the start.

Start

The George and Dragon PH, Watton at Stone just off the A602 between Stevenage and Hertford

P Small car park near playing fields. Follow sign 'toilets' from opposite the Bull PH in Watton at Stone. Otherwise near railway station or park in the main street showing consideration

Distance and grade

24 miles

 Moderate

Terrain

220 feet climb from Stapleford to Sacombe Green. 200 feet climb from the River Rib near to Latchford up to Levens Green. Lowest point – 160 feet (48 mts) at Stapleford. Highest point – 400 feet (120 mts) near Levens Green

Nearest railway

Watton at Stone

Watton at Stone

Stapleford

Sacombe Green

High Cross

Cold Christmas

Places of interest

Watton at Stone *1*
The elegant, canopied, cast-iron pump dates back to the early 19th century

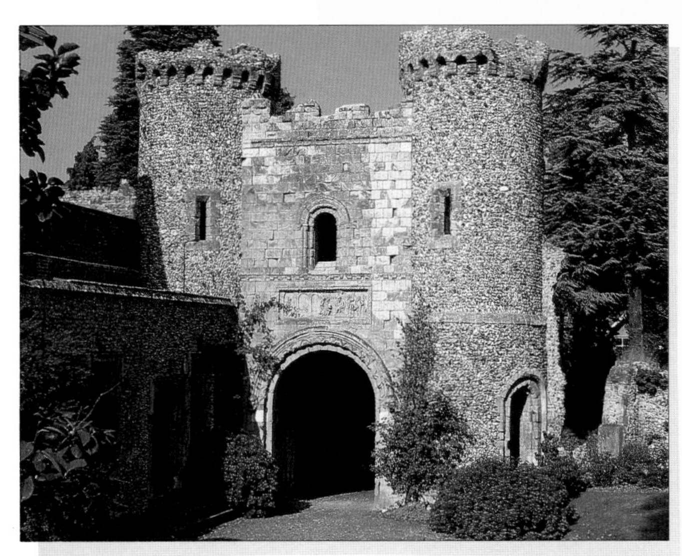

▲ *The neo-Norman gatehouse at Benington Lordship Gardens*

Much Hadham *(just off the route) 13*
Showpiece village, for centuries the country seat of the Bishops of London. Their palace, near the 12th-century church, is mainly Jacobean. The main street has many Elizabethan cottages and Regency houses

Benington Lordship Gardens *26*
Hill-top gardens designed around an 18th-century manor house with Norman keep which includes a rock, water and walled kitchen garden and magnificent display of roses. The village of Benington is one of the prettiest in Hertfordshire with all the right ingredients – church, folly, stately home, pub, timbered cottages, village green and duck-pond

Refreshments

George and Dragon PH, The Bull PH, Waggon and Horses PH, ***Watton at Stone***
Woodhall Arms PH, ***Stapleford***
Three Harts PH, ***Stonyhills***
White Horse PH, ***High Cross***
Ye Olde College Tavern PH, ***Old Hall Green***
The Bell PH, ***Benington***

Barwick
Latchford
Benington

1 With back to the George and Dragon PH L then after 300 yards 1st L onto Station Road 'Watton Station, Datchworth'

2 Immediately after crossing railway bridge L then at T-j R onto No Through Road 'Bridleway'

3 At T-j with farm and barns ahead L then after 100 yards, just beyond gate bear L

4 At T-j L then after 200 yards just before farm R onto track 'Bridleway. Stapleford 1½, Bramfield 1¾'

5 At T-j with road L. At T-j with A119 R 'Hertford' then 1st L 300 yards after Woodhall Arms PH onto Church Lane 'Stonyhills 1'

6 At T-j with red-brick house ahead L

7 After 1 mile, on LH bend bear R 'Ware'. At X-roads (with A602) SA on to tarmac drive 'Bridleway'. At farm leave tarmac, turn L over cattle grid between lodge and farm then 1st R

8 At fork of tracks just after big house L. At next fork by two ordinary houses L

9 At road R then R again 'High Cross'

10 After 2 miles at T-j with A10 L then R onto North Drive 'Thundridge 1½, Wadesmill 1½, Ware 3½'

11 As lane swings right bear L through white gate onto track

12 At T-j with road L

13 After 2 miles, at T-j L 'Barwick'

14 **Easy to miss.** After ¾ mile, towards the bottom of the hill, 100 yards before the ford, sharply R uphill onto track 'Bridleway'. After ¼ mile as main track swings right uphill bear L (in effect SA) onto narrower track in wood

15 At T-j with lane R. Ignore 1st left over bridge. As road turns right uphill bear L downhill between hedges

16 Tarmac becomes track. Take the middle track passing just to the R of round roofed low barn. Up and down hill. At X-roads of tracks with field gate and bridle gate ahead, turn L

17 Exit field onto track by wooden barn. Bear L uphill. At X-roads with lane SA onto track 'Bridleway'

18 At T-j with road L. At T-j with A10 R (**take care** – busy road) then 1st L 'Old Hall Green'

19 At T-j by Ye Olde College Tavern PH L 'Levens Green. Dane End'. After ¾ mile 1st L onto No Through Road 'Beggarmans Lane. Dane End 1¾'

20 Through High Trees Farm. At T-j with road L. At T-j with more major road L 'Dane End' then 1st R 'Haultwick, Green End'

21 After 100 yards L 'Green End. Hotel' then 1st R at triangle of grass by church 'Green End ½. Hotel'

22 Go past hotel. 50 yards after passing pond on your right, as road swings left downhill, bear R onto track by triangle of grass 'Bridleway'

23 After 300 yards leave main track and bear R onto rougher track. Fine descent. At bottom cross bridge, turn L through metal gate then R along field edge

24 Exit at end of long field via bridle gate, turn L over small bridge then R along field edge. Track improves

25 Go through farm and past houses. At road R. In Benington, 200 yards past the Bell PH L 'Aston, Stevenage'

26 After ½ mile, at bottom of hill L onto track 'Bridleway'

27 At T-j with road R then at T-j at bottom of hill L 'Watton'

28 At T-j at end of Walkern Road by the Waggon and Horses PH L to return to the start

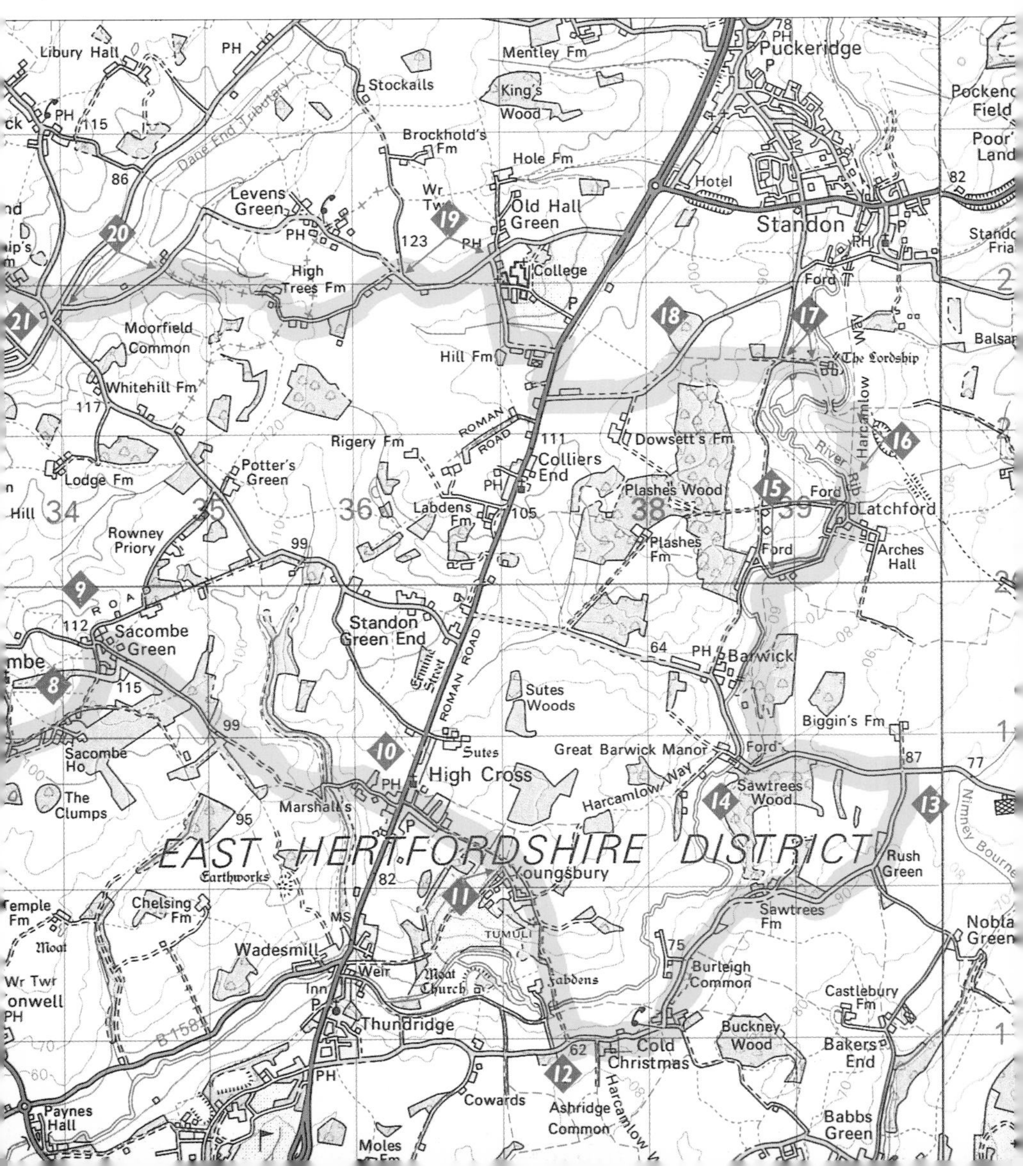

6 Woodland tracks and a dismantled railway path southwest from Hertford

Encircled by built-up areas running alongside the A1 and A10 and bounded to the north by the A414 and the south by the M25 there is a patch of countryside that offers many miles of fine off-road riding along broad gravel tracks through woodland. This short ride links together lanes and byways from the southwestern corner of Hertford through Brickendon to Newgate Street. The middle section runs along predominantly quiet lanes, including one which appears to have an identity crisis – it is signed 'Berkhamsted' on one side of the road and 'Berkhampstead' on the other! Just before Cole Green you find yourself at the start of the Cole Greenway, a magnificent conversion of an old dismantled railway line for recreational use which drops you right back at the start.

Start

The car park next to Hertford Town Football Club, West Street, Hertford (just off the A414 Hatfield road past Hartwells car showroom)

P As above. Follow West Street for 400 yards. Shortly after the end of the houses on the left, turn R, on a LH bend, down a tarmac lane

Distance and grade

14 miles

Easy

Terrain

200 feet climb from the start to Brickendon. Lowest point – 140 feet (42 mts) at the start. Highest point – 420 feet (126 mts) at the start of Cucumber Lane

Nearest railway

Hertford

Hertford

Brickendon

Newgate Street

Places of interest

***Hertford** 1*
An attractive county town with many fine buildings faced with decorative plasterwork. Some of the most interesting are in Salisbury and Parliament Squares. The present castle is the 15th-century gatehouse to the now demolished Norman castle. The timber-framed Old Verger's House dates from 1450

Hatfield House *(5 miles west of the route) 8*
Superb red-brick Jacobean mansion built by Robert Cecil, 1st Earl of Salisbury, between 1607 and 1611 which boasts a Marble Hall, Grand Staircase and Long Gallery. The West Gardens have been re-created in 17th-century formal style

Refreshments

Plenty of choice in ***Hertford***
Farmers Boy PH, ***Brickendon***
Coach and Horses PH, Crown PH,
Newgate Street
Cowpers Arms PH, ***Cole Green***

Hatfield House:
◀ the knot garden ▼ part of the old Palace of Hatfield

WELWYN GARDEN CITY
Birchall
Cole Green
Birch Green
Staines Green
Hertingfordbury
Hotel
Convent (Sch)
Settlement (site of)
Letty Green
East End Green
Woolmer's Park
Roxford
Moat
Gravel Pit
Water Hall Fm
Holwell Court
Burnside
Essendonbury Fm
Howe Green
Kennel Hall Fm
Broadgreen Wood
Bayfordbury Park Fm
Bayfordbury (Coll)
Clements Fm
Bayford Hall
Warren Ho
Culverwood Ho
Bayford
Bayford Wood
Bayford Ho
Essendon
West End
Bedwellpark Fm
Little Berkhamsted
Twr
Essendon Place
Bedwell Park
Fanshaws
Brickendon
Brickendon Grange
Blackfan Wood
Bush Fm
Bucks Fm
Bedwell Lodge Fm
Cucumber Hall Fm
Woodcock Lodge
Epping Ho
Epping Green
Ashendene Fm
Old Claypits Fm
Broxbourne Wood
Camfield Pl
Warrenwood Park
Woodcock Lodge Fm
Tylers Causeway
Wormley Wood
Woodfield Fm
Coldharbour Fm
Barbers Lodge Fm
Hotel
Ponsbourne Park
Ponsbourne Tunnel
Derry's Wood
Beaumont Manor
New Park Fm
Newgate Street
St Lawrence Fm
Tanfield Stud Fm
Justice Hill
Great Wood (Country Park)
Grimes Brook
Burleigh Fm
Hammond Street
Tolmers
Home Wood
Cheshunt Common
Woodlands
The Ridgeway
Well Wood
Cuffley
Lucas End
Goffs Oak
Nyn Park
Hartham
Weir
River Mimram
Sch
Hospl
Co Hall
Morgan's Walk
Edwa Fm
Bencroft Wood
B 1000
A 414
B 158
B 1455
B 157

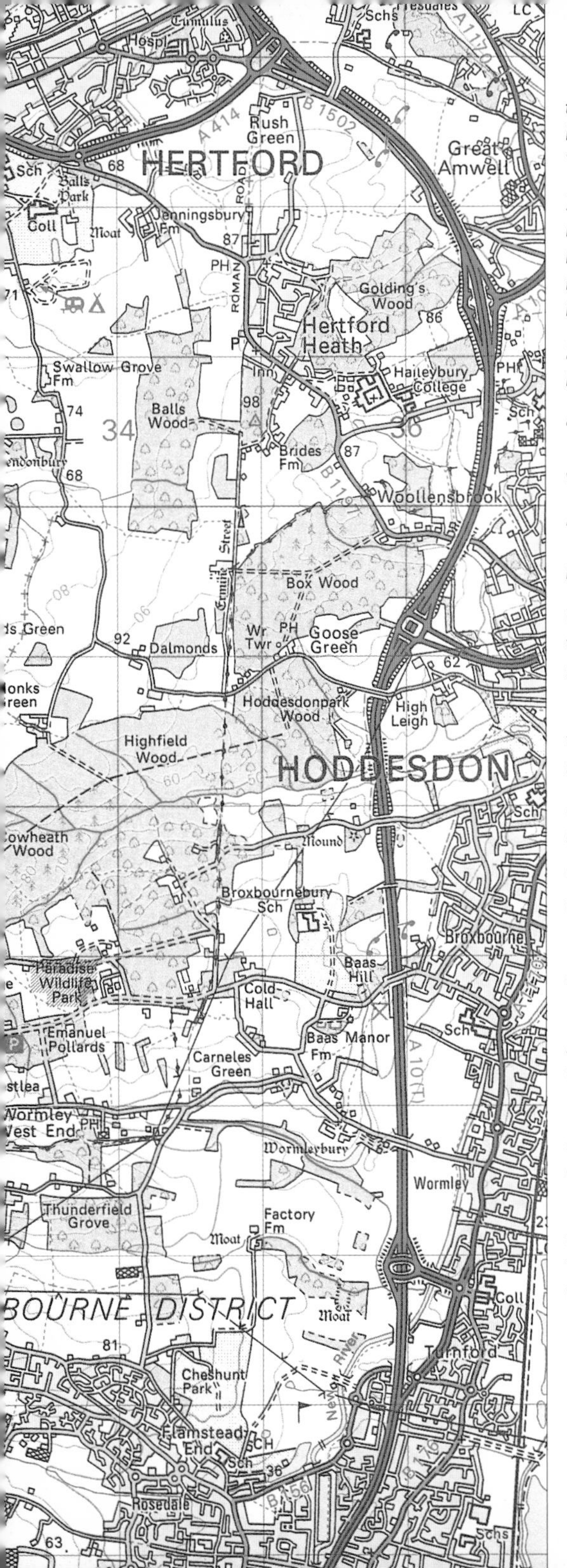

1 From the car park return to the road and turn R. At the roundabout SA onto Horns Mill Road then 2nd L onto Brickendon Lane 'Brickendonbury 1, Brickendon 2½'

2 **Easy to miss**. After almost 2 miles, after reaching the top of the hill, on a LH bend bear R by a large red brick house onto a broad gravel track. Shortly, at fork of tracks, bear L

3 At T-j at the end of Fanshaw's Lane by the Farmer's Boy PH turn R

4 Shortly after crossing bridge over railway 1st L onto track 'Bridleway'. At black and white timber house bear R

5 At T-j with road by garden centre L then 1st R onto broad gravel track by red brick lodge house

6 Track becomes tarmac. At T-j with road R then at roundabout SA. 1st L onto New Park Road 'No Through Road'

7 Follow as it turns to track and back to tarmac. At road L then 1st R onto Cucumber Lane 'Essendon'

8 After 1¼ miles 1st R onto Berkhamsted Lane 'Little Berkhamsted'

9 Go down then uphill. Turn L onto track by white gates and lodge house 'Bridleway'

10 At bottom of hill L over stream then R onto broad gravel track

11 Continue SA through bridle gate. At X-roads at end of Bedwell Avenue SA 'Letty Green, Cole Green'

12 Just after passing beneath railway bridge and before Cowpers Arms PH turn R through car park and onto dismantled railway track

13 After 2½ miles at 1st proper fork of tracks bear R (blue arrow on white circle) then L to go under railway viaduct and return to the start

7 *Tracks, lanes and the Icknield Way through undulating countryside southeast of Royston*

This ride has a greater proportion of road than is usual for an off-road route but the lanes are quiet and scenic and the best section is left till last – a five mile length of the Icknield Way. The route leaves the southwest of Royston and climbs 300 feet to the mast on the A10 near to Reed. A bridleway east from Reed brings you to the most attractive village of Barkway with several old thatched buildings. Next, you pass through the estate of Cokenach with its fine house. A steady climb brings you past the squat square tower of Little Chishill church and onto the middle off-road section through woodland. Through Chrishall and just before Chrishall Grange, the route turns west along the Icknield Way for five miles back to Royston.

Start

The Priory Church of St John Baptist, Royston, 12 miles southwest of Cambridge

P Follow Melbourn Road (A10 towards Cambridge). At roundabout L onto King James Way and long stay car park

Distance and grade

22 miles

Easy / moderate

Terrain

300 feet climb from the start to crossing the A10 near Reed.
200 feet climb to Little Chishill. 170 feet climb on the last stretch of the Icknield Way just before Royston.
Lowest point – 160 feet (52 mts) on Icknield Way just to west of B1368. Highest point – 520 feet (173 mts) on the A10 near to Reed

Nearest railway

Royston

Royston

Therfield

Reed

Barkway

Shaftenhoe End

Places of interest

Royston Cave *1*
A unique bell-shaped chamber cut from the chalk beneath Melbourn Street, of unknown origin but the carvings are clearly medieval and most have religious and historical significance. It is believed to have been used by the Knights Templar before their proscription by the Pope in the 14th century (open in the afternoon on summer weekends)

▲ *A carving in Royston Cave showing Saint Catherine*

Barkway *8*
Attractive village of thatched cottages dating back to the 17th century. Jacobean Manor Farm near to the 13th-century church. The village grew and prospered as a handy stopping place between Ware and Cambridge

Great Chishill *(just off the route) 14*
The showpiece of the village is the lofty 18th-century postmill, with white-painted timbers and a graceful fantail that turns the mill so that the sails always face into the wind

Refreshments

Plenty of choice in ***Royston***
Fox and Duck PH, ***Therfield***
Cabinet PH♣*,* ***Reed***
Tally Ho PH, Chaise and Pair PH, ***Barkway***
Red Cow PH, ***Chrishall***

Building End
Chrishall
Chrishall Grange

1 With back to the Priory Church L on the road towards Baldock. At traffic lights SA. Shortly after filling station on left L onto Briary Lane

2 Tarmac turns to track. Just past Lee Valley Water Works SA downhill onto rougher track

3 Track turns sharp R then sharp L. Follow blue arrows and signs for 'Icknield Way'. Ignore a stone track which crosses the grassy track and continue in the same direction

4 At top of steep hill bear R following blue arrows. Track becomes tarmac. At offset X-roads at the end of Mill Lane L 'Reed 2, Buckland 3¼'

5 At T-j with A10 R 'London' then 1st L onto Blacksmith's Lane 'Reed ½'. 1st R by telephone box onto Church Lane then 1st L onto Driftway

6 After ¼ mile on sharp LH bend R onto tarmac track 'Public path to Barkway 1¼'. After 100 yards 1st track L alongside hedgerow / trees

7 At T-j of tracks at the end of the field R and follow the main track as it turns L then R then L again to continue in the same eastwards direction. Rough middle section

8 Track improves. At T-j turn L downhill on good track which turns to tarmac. Go past church. At the end of Church Lane L

9 After ¾ mile as the road starts to descend, 1st R onto lane / tarmac drive between brick-walled entrance to 'Cokenach'

10 Shortly after passing house and immediately after last of round green silos L onto track into wood

11 At the end of the wood leave concrete track and turn L onto earth track

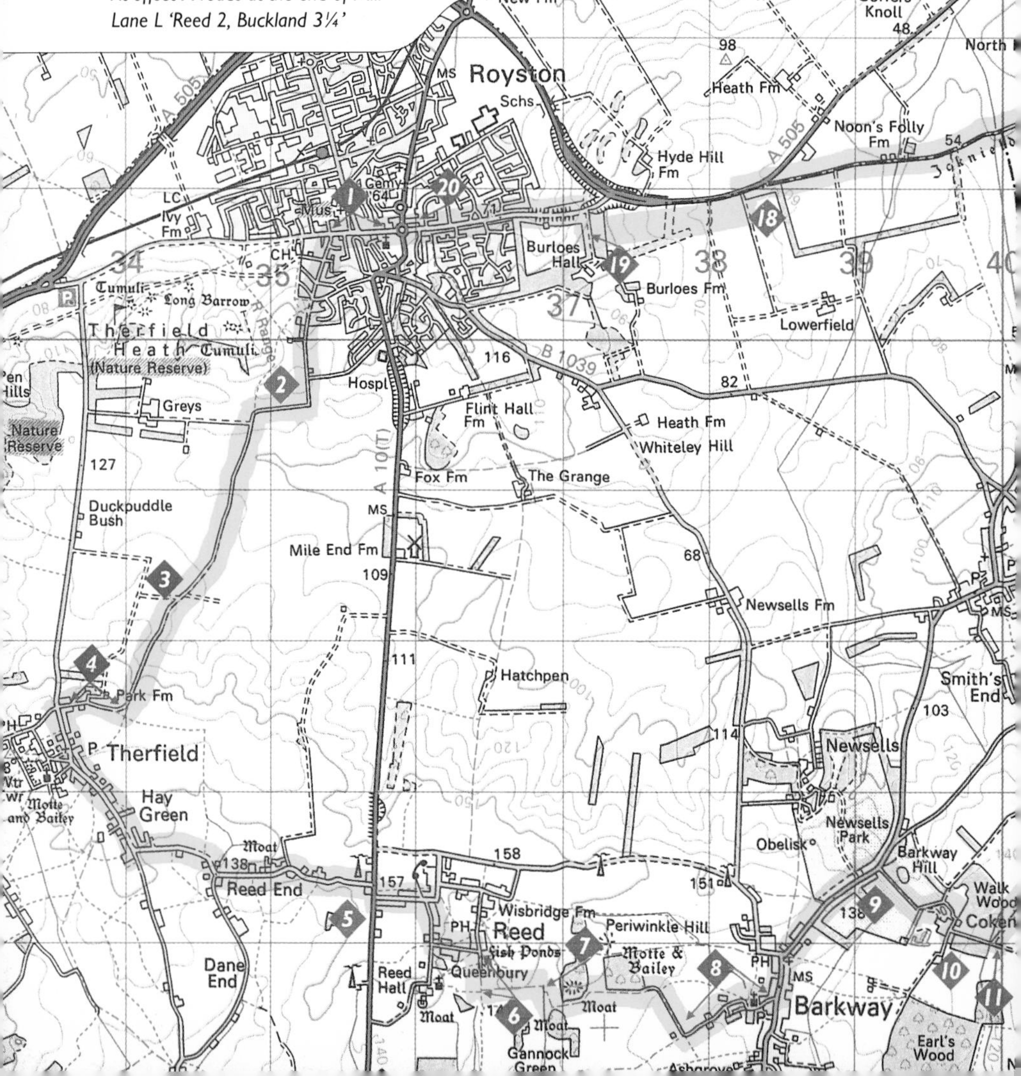

12 At T-j with road L

13 At T-j with Putty Hall Cottages ahead R 'Little & Great Chishill, Barley'

14 After ½ mile at bottom of hill 1st road R 'Little Chishill ½, Langley 3'

15 Climb past church and spread-out barns of Gypsy Corner Farm. On sharp RH bend by beige brick house L 'Byway'

16 Short muddy section at far end of the wood. At road L. At T-j with B1039 R 'Audley End, Saffron Walden' then 1st L 'Chrishall ½, Chrishall Grange 3½'

17 **Easy to miss**. 2 miles after Chrishall, opposite a road turning to the right and just before a 'Chrishall Grange' sign, turn L onto track 'Bridleway. Royston 4¾. Icknield Way'

18 Follow this track in the same direction for 3½ miles over three X-roads with tarmac roads. 100 yards before joining the noisy and busy A505 turn L through wooden barrier 'Icknield Way'

19 This is variable in quality as it follows the field edge but passes through a lovely wooded section at the end. At T-j with tarmac drive R then after 20 yards at T-j L

20 At 1st roundabout SA (**or** R onto King James Way for car park). At 2nd roundabout R to return to the start

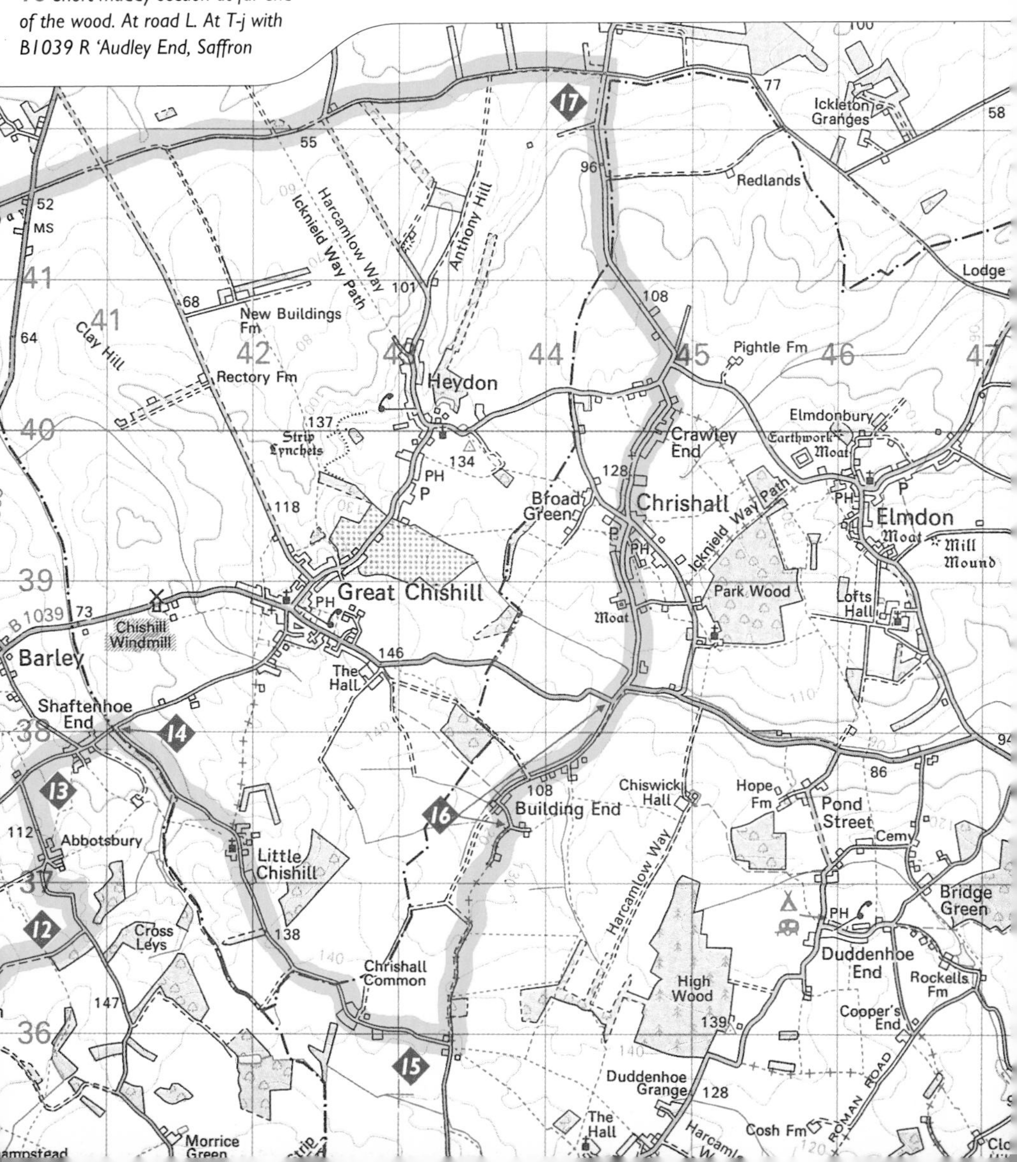

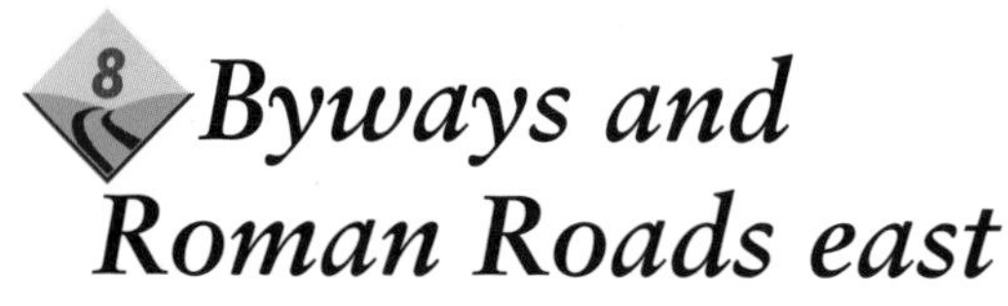

Byways and Roman Roads east from Fulbourn near Cambridge

The best is left till last in this ride with a seven mile section on the Roman Road of Worstead Street which constitutes one of the finest stretches of off-road cycling in the whole of East Anglia: the track rises and falls on gently undulating country through a canopy of trees and among a carpet of wildflowers. The surface is excellent and it seems that the local authority has taken a real pride in maintaining this length to an exceptionally high standard. The ride starts from the bustling village of Fulbourn and heads northeast then east along quiet lanes and byways to cross the A11 and the railway line. There is a remarkable sense of remoteness about parts of this ride given its proximity to Cambridge. Turning south the ride follows further byways through Balsham. At the second crossing of the B1052 you are faced with a decision – tea at the Chilford Hall Vineyard or straight ahead onto the Roman Road back to Fulbourn? With luck you should have time for both

Start

The Church, Fulbourn, 4 miles east of Cambridge

P Large car park at Fulbourn recreation ground behind the scout hut. From the Post Office go SA onto Manor Walk towards Balsham. Go past the Townley Memorial Hall and take the next L 'Fulbourn Institute'

Distance and grade

23 miles

Easy

Terrain

270 feet climb from the start to Hungry Hill. Lowest point – 30 feet (10 mts) just north of Fulbourn. Highest point 365 feet (110 mts) just south of Balsham

Nearest railway

Dullingham 2 miles north of the route at Underwood Hall

Fulbourn

Cambridge Hill

Places of interest

***Fulbourn** 1*

Reed-thatched houses line the streets of the village. The 13th-century church is only one of two in England dedicated to St Vigor. To the east of the village is Fleam Dyke, a massive 7th-century earthwork built to defend East Anglia against the Mercians

***Great Wilbraham** 2*

In the 7th century King Penda successfully marched against East Anglia and named this area after his daughter 'Wilburgh'

***Swaffham Bulbeck** (north of the route at Great Wilbraham) 2*

A Dutch-style Merchant's House, granary and malt house remain from its 17th century past as an inland port. The Italian portable altar in the 13th-century church is 500 years old. The pew-ends have 15th-century carvings of fabulous beasts

Refreshments

*Six Bells PH, White Hart PH, **Fulbourn***
*Carpenters Arms PH, **Great Wilbraham***
*Black Bull PH, The Bell PH, **Balsham***
*Teashop at **Chilford Hall Vineyard** (just off the route between Balsham and Linton)*

***Chilford Hall Vineyard** 15*

18-acre vineyard with tours, wine tastings and a tea shop

***Worsted Street (Roman Road)** 17*

A Roman link between the trading town of Cambridge and the major Roman Road from London (now the A11)

***Wandlebury** (just off the route southwest of Fulbourn) 18*

The Gog Magog hills are crowned by an Iron Age fort whose ramparts enclose 15 acres. The hills take their name from a Romano-British giant who appears in legend, sometimes as one person, Gogmagog, sometimes as two, Gog and Magog. The nearby building is a stable block of the now-demolished mansion. The famous Arab stallion Elpappo was buried beneath the central arch in 1753

Balsham

Worsted Lodge

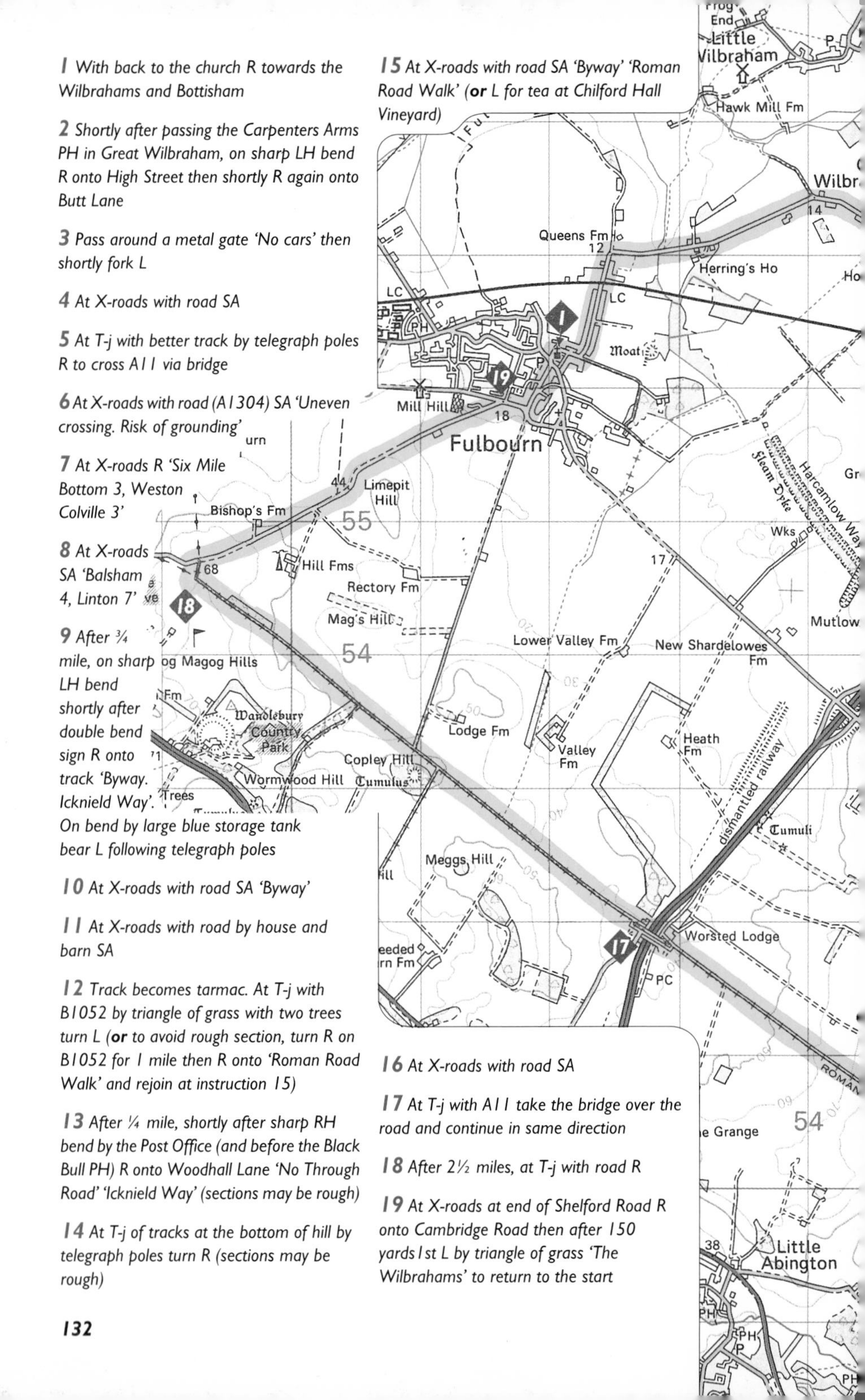

1 With back to the church R towards the Wilbrahams and Bottisham

2 Shortly after passing the Carpenters Arms PH in Great Wilbraham, on sharp LH bend R onto High Street then shortly R again onto Butt Lane

3 Pass around a metal gate 'No cars' then shortly fork L

4 At X-roads with road SA

5 At T-j with better track by telegraph poles R to cross A11 via bridge

6 At X-roads with road (A1304) SA 'Uneven crossing. Risk of grounding'

7 At X-roads R 'Six Mile Bottom 3, Weston Colville 3'

8 At X-roads SA 'Balsham 4, Linton 7'

9 After ¾ mile, on sharp LH bend shortly after double bend sign R onto track 'Byway. Icknield Way'. On bend by large blue storage tank bear L following telegraph poles

10 At X-roads with road SA 'Byway'

11 At X-roads with road by house and barn SA

12 Track becomes tarmac. At T-j with B1052 by triangle of grass with two trees turn L (**or** to avoid rough section, turn R on B1052 for 1 mile then R onto 'Roman Road Walk' and rejoin at instruction 15)

13 After ¼ mile, shortly after sharp RH bend by the Post Office (and before the Black Bull PH) R onto Woodhall Lane 'No Through Road' 'Icknield Way' (sections may be rough)

14 At T-j of tracks at the bottom of hill by telegraph poles turn R (sections may be rough)

15 At X-roads with road SA 'Byway' 'Roman Road Walk' (**or** L for tea at Chilford Hall Vineyard)

16 At X-roads with road SA

17 At T-j with A11 take the bridge over the road and continue in same direction

18 After 2½ miles, at T-j with road R

19 At X-roads at end of Shelford Road R onto Cambridge Road then after 150 yards 1st L by triangle of grass 'The Wilbrahams' to return to the start

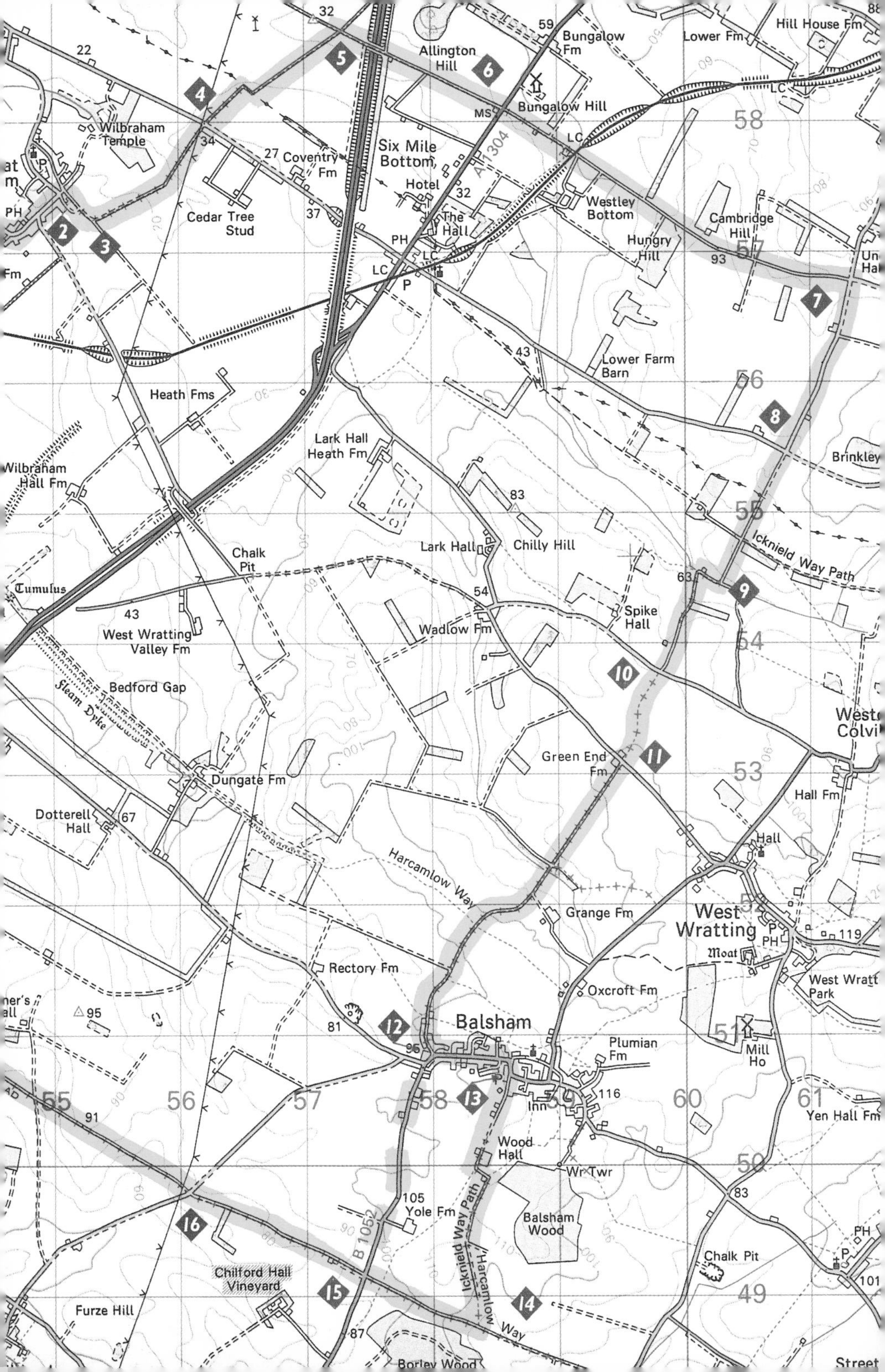

Wilbraham Temple
Cedar Tree Stud
Coventry Fm
Six Mile Bottom
Hotel
The Hall
Allington Hill
Bungalow Fm
Bungalow Hill
Lower Fm
Hill House Fm
Westley Bottom
Hungry Hill
Cambridge Hill
Heath Fms
Lower Farm Barn
Wilbraham Hall Fm
Lark Hall Heath Fm
Lark Hall
Chilly Hill
Brinkley
Icknield Way Path
Chalk Pit
Tumulus
West Wratting Valley Fm
Wadlow Fm
Spike Hall
Bedford Gap
Fleam Dyke
Dungate Fm
Green End Fm
Dotterell Hall
Hall Fm
Harcamlow Way
Grange Fm
West Wratting
Moat
Rectory Fm
Oxcroft Fm
West Wratt Park
Balsham
Plumian Fm
Mill Ho
Inn
Wood Hall
Wr Twr
Yen Hall Fm
Yole Fm
Balsham Wood
Chilford Hall Vineyard
Furze Hill
Chalk Pit
Icknield Way Path
Harcamlow Way
Borley Wood
A1304
B 1052

9 A figure of eight loop on the Suffolk Coast heathland east of Westleton

As with the ride starting from Snape (to which this could easily be linked) the terrain consists of predominantly well-drained sandy soils so mud does not present a problem. Westleton is an attractive village with fine pubs and should you be worried about filling your stomach, there is a large café and another pub at Dunwich, where you have the chance of dipping your toes into the waters of the North Sea. The ride heads south past the Nature Reserve at Minsmere and the curiously named Eels Foot pub at Eastbridge. The vast structures of Sizewell soon loom on the horizon. A loop is drawn around the golf course near Thorpeness before returning north back to Westleton.

Start

The Post Office, Westleton, 25 miles northeast of Ipswich, on the road between Aldeburgh and Southwold

P No specific car park. Show consideration

Distance and grade

18 miles
Easy

Terrain

No hills!

Nearest railway

Darsham, 3 miles to the west of Westleton

Refreshments

The Crown PH, The White Horse PH, **Westleton** *Ship Inn PH, Café on the beach,* **Dunwich**
Eels Foot PH, **Eastbridge**
Vulcan Arms PH, **Sizewell**

Westleton
Dunwich
Eastbridge
Leiston Common

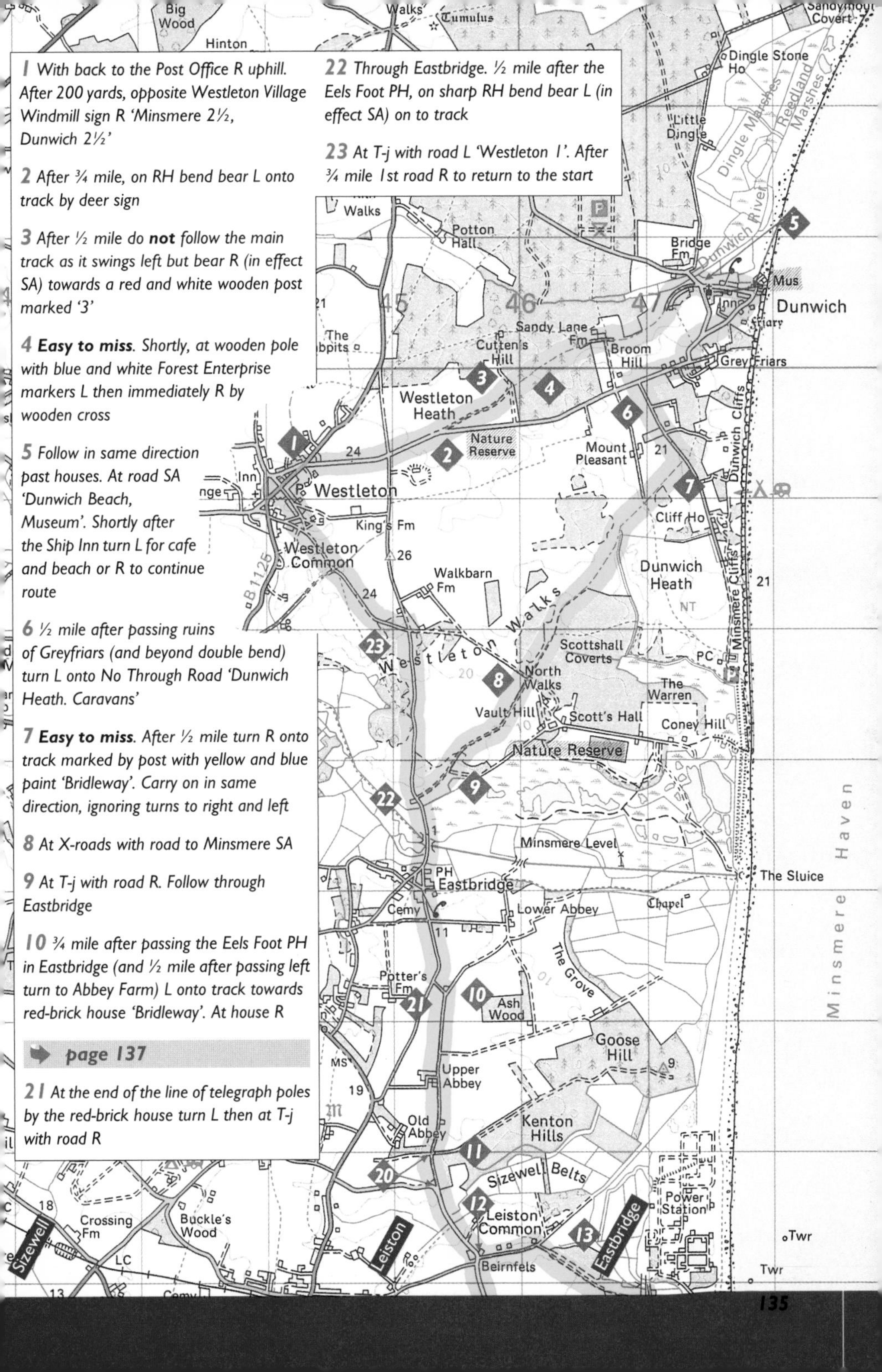

1 With back to the Post Office R uphill. After 200 yards, opposite Westleton Village Windmill sign R 'Minsmere 2½, Dunwich 2½'

2 After ¾ mile, on RH bend bear L onto track by deer sign

3 After ½ mile do **not** follow the main track as it swings left but bear R (in effect SA) towards a red and white wooden post marked '3'

4 **Easy to miss**. Shortly, at wooden pole with blue and white Forest Enterprise markers L then immediately R by wooden cross

5 Follow in same direction past houses. At road SA 'Dunwich Beach, Museum'. Shortly after the Ship Inn turn L for cafe and beach or R to continue route

6 ½ mile after passing ruins of Greyfriars (and beyond double bend) turn L onto No Through Road 'Dunwich Heath. Caravans'

7 **Easy to miss**. After ½ mile turn R onto track marked by post with yellow and blue paint 'Bridleway'. Carry on in same direction, ignoring turns to right and left

8 At X-roads with road to Minsmere SA

9 At T-j with road R. Follow through Eastbridge

10 ¾ mile after passing the Eels Foot PH in Eastbridge (and ½ mile after passing left turn to Abbey Farm) L onto track towards red-brick house 'Bridleway'. At house R

page 137

21 At the end of the line of telegraph poles by the red-brick house turn L then at T-j with road R

22 Through Eastbridge. ½ mile after the Eels Foot PH, on sharp RH bend bear L (in effect SA) on to track

23 At T-j with road L 'Westleton 1'. After ¾ mile 1st road R to return to the start

Theberton
Theberton Woods
Grange
Moat Ho
Theberton Ho
Potter's Fm
Ash Wood
The Grove
Goose Hill
Upper Abbey
Hill Fm
Leiston Abbey
Old Abbey
Kenton Hills
Sizewell Belts
Power Station
Hills
Hill Fm
Crossing Fm
Buckle's Wood
Leiston Common
Beirnfels
Green
Cemy
LEISTON
Crown Fm
B 1119
Hall
The Cupola
Sch
Halfway Cottages
Sizewell
Hall
Peartree Fm
Knodishall
Coldfair Green
Aldringham Ho
The Walks
Aldringham
B 1353
Manor Fm
Grove Wood
Ness Ho
Knodishall Common
Tumuli
Tumulus
Thorpe Ness
Bull's Hall
Billeaford Hall
Hundred River
Partables Fm
Church Fm
Wks
B 1353
Inn
Thorpeness
The Fens
The Meare
B 1069
Park Fm
Great Wood
Nature Reserve
Rushmere Lodge Fm
North Warren
Hazlewood Hall
Grange Fm
Haven Ho
The Haven
dismtd rly
Hazelwood Common
South Warren
Heath Wood
Black Heath
A 1094
Red Ho
Cliff Plantation
Ham Creek
Round Hill
Reach
Barber's Point
Cob Island
LB Sta
ALDEBURGH
Marshes
Fort Green
Aldeburgh Marshes
Yarn Hill
Redlands Covert
Short Reach
Hill Fm
Poplar
Slaughden
BAY
Minsme
Twr

10 *¾ mile after passing the Eels Foot PH in Eastbridge (and ½ mile after passing left turn to Abbey Farm) L onto track towards red-brick house 'Bridleway'. At house R*

11 *At T-j with more major track bear R then at T-j with road L*

12 *At top of short hill, just before X-roads sign, bear L then after 50 yards turn L onto broad gravel track 'Bridleway'*

13 *After ¼ mile leave broad gravel track by triangle of grass and bear R onto sandy track 'Bridleway'*

14 *At T-j immediately after going beneath power lines R. At T-j with road L then R 'Sizewell Hall'*

15 *Tarmac turns to track. After ½ mile fork R 'Byway'. Continue on main track in same direction. At T-j with road R*

16 *After ½ mile, just after the telephone lines cross from the road from one side to the other R onto broad track. Take the middle of the three tracks*

17 *Follow the broad track as it swings right by the remarkable red-brick Providence Baptist Church then L alongside golf course*

18 *At the end of a row of houses bear L onto narrow grassy track. Go beneath power lines At T-j with major track R and follow this past Crownlands Cottage as it swings left to the road*

19 *At road junction bear L 'Yoxford, Saxmundham (A12)'*

20 *After 1 mile, at top of short hill on LH bend by mast, turn R onto broad gravel track. Shortly after car park bear L (in effect SA) off the main track*

21 *At the end of the line of telegraph poles by the red-brick house turn L then at T-j with road R*

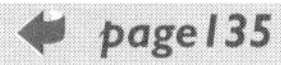
page 135

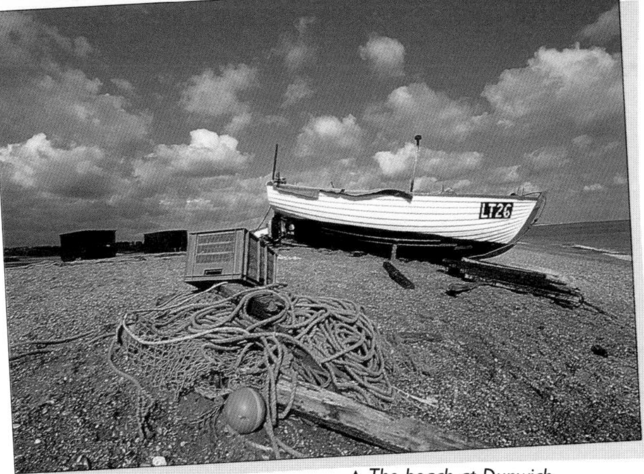

▲ *The beach at Dunwich*

Places of interest

Westleton Heath *2*
Sandy heaths, woodland, heather and bracken with bird life including stone curlews, nightjars, red-backed shrikes and woodlarks

Dunwich *5*
The relentless erosion of wind and tide caused this town to be lost beneath the waves after a huge storm in 1326. Only a small village, the ruins of a leper chapel and a medieval friary remain of what was once the capital of the Saxon Kingdom of East Anglia. It is said that submerged bells ring out a storm warning. There is an excellent museum on the town's history

Minsmere *9*
A major bird reserve with nesting places for over 100 species. Breeding birds include avocets, bitterns, nightjars and nightingales

Thorpeness *(just off the route) 15*
Eccentric holiday village, planned before World War I, surrounding a specially created 65-acre lake called the Meare. One of the town's most distinctive buildings is the extraordinary House in the Clouds. It looks like a mock-Tudor building but beneath the facade is a water tower on stilts

10 South from the Maltings at Snape along a section of the Three Forest Trail

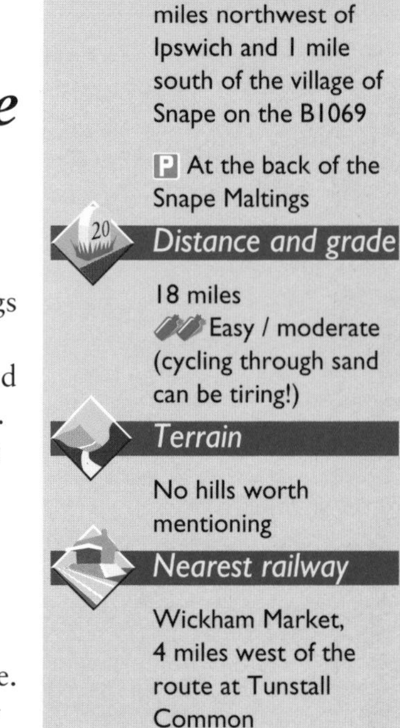

Start

The Maltings, Snape, 18 miles northwest of Ipswich and 1 mile south of the village of Snape on the B1069

P At the back of the Snape Maltings

Distance and grade

18 miles

Easy / moderate (cycling through sand can be tiring!)

Terrain

No hills worth mentioning

Nearest railway

Wickham Market, 4 miles west of the route at Tunstall Common

Snape is internationally renowned for the musical festivals held in the famous Maltings Concert Hall. This ride starts here with its fine tea shop and nearby pubs (both here and in the village of Snape, a mile to the north). There are no real hills and this an excellent choice for a social, conversational ride as most of the time is spent on broad, well-drained forest tracks where you could ride two or three abreast. The ride follows the course of the Three Forest Cycle Trail, designed by the local Forest Enterprise office. The bicycle signs should show you the way but at times certain junctions are unsigned so it is advisable to refer to the instructions as well. Indeed, a compass might be useful as a back-up should forestry operations render any of the instructions obsolete. The soil is sandy, a striking change from the clay of the rides further west which when soft, can be fairly tough cycling. At the southern end of the ride you will pass two buildings of note: the Priory at Butley Abbey and the thatched church just south of the village of Butley.

The Maltings

Wantisden Corner

Places of interest

Snape *1*
Unique among villages as an international centre of music. The composer Benjamin Britten and tenor Peter Pears founded the annual Aldeburgh Festival in 1948 which moved here in 1967 when a superb concert hall complex was created within a former malt house. The creeper-covered 19th-century brick maltings buildings were originally used to prepare fine Suffolk barley for brewing, the malt produced being shipped out via the River Alde. The combination of farming and shipping gave the nearby Plough and Sail pub its name

▼ *The Maltings, Snape*

Orford *(just off the route) 15*
Quiet village of brick-and-timber buildings with magnificent 12th-century castle built by Henry II

Butley Priory *13*
A medieval gatehouse with heraldic decoration incorporating the arms of 12th-century England and France. The gateway was once part of an 1171 Augustinian priory

Refreshments

Plough and Sail PH, The Maltings, Snape
Granary Tea Shop, ***Snape***
The Crown PH, The Golden Key PH,
Snape Village *(just off the route)*
Oyster Inn PH, ***Butley***
Tea shop at ***the pottery in Butley***

Capel Green

Chillesford

1 Out of the car park, turn L then L again 'Iken 2, Orford 5¼'

*2 After 2 miles (and 1¼ miles after X-roads) turn R onto track into forest by a red and white painted post marked '13' (**NB** this is the **second** painted post you will see by the side of the road)*

3 Follow bike signs along broad, gravel-based track

4 After 1 mile at X-roads with road (B1078) SA

5 After almost 1 mile at a major T-j of tracks at the edge of the wood with red and white posts nos. 11 and 18, turn L (remember this point for the return route)

6 Go past the church (this section may be sandy and tough going). At road R

7 After 1 mile, shortly after start of Butley village, on a sharp LH bend turn R 'Tunstall 3¼, Snape 4' then after 100 yards by triangle of grass L onto No Through Road 'Caravans'

8 Pass between strips of woodland meeting the road to the right and left. At the start of a fenced off area ahead turn L onto track lined with concrete lumps 'Bridleway'

9 Follow bike signs, turning L onto broad track by red and white post no. 13 towards a metal barrier with yellow strips

10 At X-roads with road SA. The track swings left past a cluster of shipping containers

11 Join a better, broader track. At T-j with road by red and white posts nos. 2 and 5 turn R for 300 yards then at the end of the wire compound to your right (airfield runway) and opposite house, turn L

12 At T-j with road L (there is a red-brick house 100 yards to your right). Shortly at next T-j R 'Butley Low Corner, Butley High Corner'

13 At X-roads L 'Butley 1, Snape 5¼'. (Keep an eye out for the lovely Priory to your right then the thatched church, also on the right)

14 At T-j with the B1084 by the Oyster Inn R then 1st R 'Village Hall, Mill Lane'

15 After 1½ miles at T-j by Post Office R then L onto track just beyond telephone box

16 At T-j with better track with a laid concrete area ahead turn R to rejoin outward route. Shortly, at red and white posts nos. 11 and 18 turn R, then after ½ mile at major X-roads of tracks turn L and follow bike signs

17 At road R then L between telegraph poles onto track. Follow bike signs, taking the second major track to the L

18 At T-j with road R. At X-roads L 'Snape'. At T-j with B1069 R to return to the start

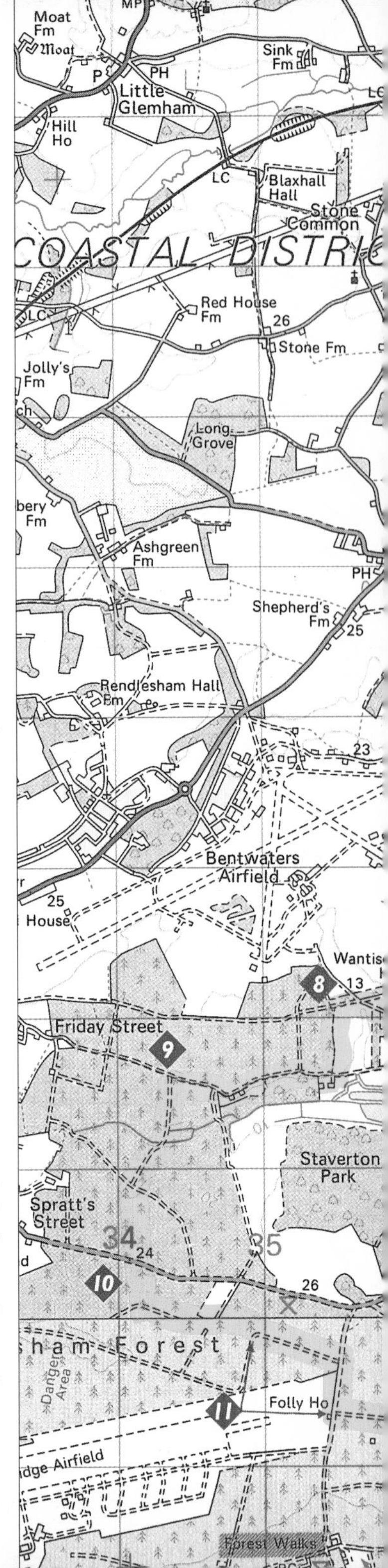

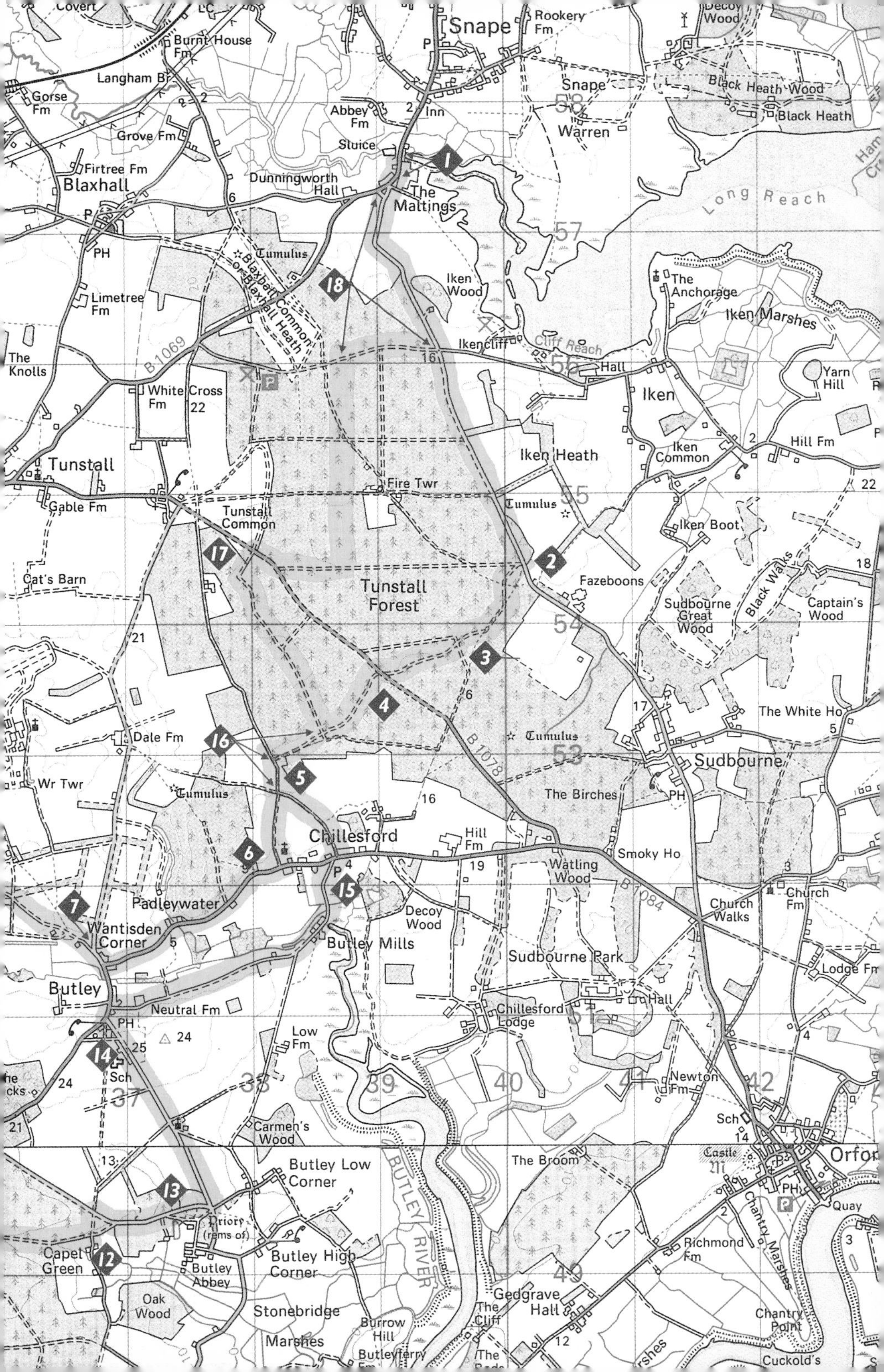
Snape
Rookery Fm
Decoy Wood
Burnt House Fm
Langham Br
Gorse Fm
Snape Warren
Black Heath Wood
Black Heath
Abbey Fm
Inn
Grove Fm
Sluice
Firtree Fm
Blaxhall
Dunningworth Hall
The Maltings
Long Reach
PH
Tumulus
Blaxhall Common or Blaxhall Heath
Iken Wood
The Anchorage
Iken Marshes
Limetree Fm
The Knolls
B 1069
Ikencliff
Cliff Reach
Hall
Yarn Hill
White Cross Fm
Iken
Iken Heath
Iken Common
Hill Fm
Tunstall
Fire Twr
Gable Fm
Tunstall Common
Iken Boot
Cat's Barn
Tunstall Forest
Fazeboons
Sudbourne Great Wood
Black Walks
Captain's Wood
The White Ho
Dale Fm
B 1078
Sudbourne
Wr Twr
The Birches
Chillesford
Hill Fm
Smoky Ho
Watling Wood
B 1084
Church Fm
Padleywater
Decoy Wood
Church Walks
Wantisden Corner
Butley Mills
Sudbourne Park
Lodge Fm
Butley
Neutral Fm
Hall
Chillesford Lodge
Low Fm
Sch
Newton Fm
Carmen's Wood
Castle
Orford
The Broom
Butley Low Corner
BUTLEY RIVER
Priory (rems of)
Quay
Chantry Marshes
Capel Green
Butley Abbey
Butley High Corner
Richmond Fm
Oak Wood
Stonebridge Marshes
Gedgrave Hall
The Cliff
Burrow Hill
Chantry Point
Butleyferry
Cuckold's